PENGUIN BOOKS

CHILDREN OF FAST-TRACK PARENTS

Andrée Aelion Brooks is a noted journalist and lecturer who specializes in family issues. She was a member of the team that wrote the "Relationships" column that ran in *The New York Times* from 1981 to 1987, and she still writes regular columns for that newspaper. Her articles have also appeared in such publications as *McCall's*, *Advertising Age*, *Woman's Day*, and *The New York Times Magazine*. She has won many awards for her writing, among them the Outstanding Achievement Award from the National Federation of Press Women.

Andrée Aelion Brooks

# CHILDREN OF FAST-TRACK PARENTS

Raising Self-sufficient
and Confident Children in an
Achievement-Oriented World

PENGUIN BOOKS

PENGUIN BOOKS
Published by the Penguin Group
Viking Penguin, a division of Penguin Books USA Inc.,
40 West 23rd Street, New York, New York 10010, U.S.A.
Penguin Books Ltd, 27 Wrights Lane, London W8 5TZ, England
Penguin Books Australia Ltd, Ringwood, Victoria, Australia
Penguin Books Canada Ltd, 2801 John Street,
Markham, Ontario, Canada L3R 1B4
Penguin Books (N.Z.) Ltd, 182–190 Wairau Road,
Auckland 10, New Zealand

Penguin Books Ltd, Registered Offices:
Harmondsworth, Middlesex, England

First published in the United States of America by
Viking Penguin, a division of Penguin Books USA Inc., 1989
Published in Penguin Books 1990

10   9   8   7   6   5   4   3   2   1

Grateful acknowledgment is made for permission to reprint excerpts from
the following copyrighted works:
*Gates of Repentance* by the Central Conference of American Rabbis. © Union
of Liberal and Progressive Synagogues 1973. © Central Conference of American
Rabbis and Union of Liberal and Progressive Synagogues 1978.
"Cat's in the Cradle" by Harry Chapin. © 1974 Story Songs Ltd.

LIBRARY OF CONGRESS CATALOGING IN PUBLICATION DATA
Brooks, Andrée Aelion.
Children of fast-track parents: raising self-sufficient and
confident children in an achievement-oriented world/Andrée Aelion Brooks.
p.   cm.
Reprint. Originally published: New York: Viking, 1989.
ISBN 0 14 01.1800 4
1. Child rearing—United States.   2. Children of the rich—United
States—Psychology.   3. Success—United States—Psychological
aspects.   4. Dual-career families—United States.   I. Title.
HQ769.B6815   1990
649'.1—dc20      89–29929

Printed in the United States of America
Set in ITC Garamond Light
Designed by Ann Gold

*Each generation has its path;*
*each a vision of its own.*
    —a prayer for the Jewish High Holy Days

# Contents

Preface     ix

I.   THE RISE OF A NEW KIND OF CHILDHOOD     1
   1.   Life in a Fast-Track Household     3
   2.   The Making of a Fast-Track Parent     10
   3.   Children of the Rich or Famous     18
   4.   Parenting Is Succeeding in a Different Way     28
   5.   The Challenges     35

II.   THE EARLY YEARS     39
   6.   Caregivers     41
   7.   As Baby Starts to Grow     53

III.   THE MIDDLE YEARS     61
   8.   Telling It Like They See It     63
   9.   Building Family Life     67
   10.   Thriving Through Those Golden Rule Days     80

IV.   THE TEEN YEARS     95
   11.   Adolescence in the Fast Track     97
   12.   Teens Talk About Parents: What Helps and
      What Hurts     108
   13.   Dollars and Sense: Money Issues     112
   14.   Derailed: Causes, Conditions, and Solutions     121
   15.   Harvard or Bust     132
   16.   A Word on Teenagers     143

V. YOUNG ADULTS 145

    17. Growing Up May Take a Little Longer 147

    18. Careers: Redefining Success 149

    19. Handling Inherited Wealth and Financial
        Support 161

    20. Private Lives 175

    21. Returning Home 179

VI. SPECIAL SITUATIONS 187

    22. High-Achieving Families with Differences 189

    23. When the Children Have Learning Disabilities 191

    24. Bulimia and Anorexia 198

    25. The Single Parent on the Fast Track 200

    26. When Mother Stays Home 210

    27. Minority Parents on the Fast Track 215

VII. FOR CHILDREN ONLY: AN OPEN LETTER 225

VIII. CONCLUSIONS 231

Acknowledgments 246

Appendix: The Fast-Track Parents' Media Shelf 248

Index 253

# Preface

It was on a bitterly cold and snowy night in February 1987 that I first became acquainted with the topic for this book. As a journalist who regularly covers family issues, I had been invited to a workshop in the shore-front town of Westport, which lies in the heart of Fairfield County, Connecticut—one of the most sophisticated and affluent suburban regions in the United States. It also happened to be the town where I had raised my own family.

The workshop had been called at the behest of a number of concerned community leaders in the area. The aim was to explore the thorny problem of what happens to children who grow up "with everything"—the best education, clothes, activities, toys, neighborhood—that money can buy, children born to success-oriented parents concerned about setting those children on a path where they will continue to "have everything" throughout their lives.

Such parents, dubbed by various newspapers and magazines interchangeably as "super-achievers," "high-achievers," and "outstanding achievers," were not only stockbrokers, lawyers, noted physicians, real estate moguls, or senior corporate executives who had already reached the top. Many were young parents still in their thirties, only part of the way up the ladder of success. Some were busy building professional practices. Others were entrepreneurs with small but lucrative businesses in retailing, technology, or property rehabilitation. Many had dual incomes. In some, the wife had temporarily chosen to stay home until the children were old enough to attend school. Not all were making six-figure incomes—yet. But all shared a zealous determination to live exceptionally well, make a lot of money, and reach the top of their chosen field in the not-too-distant future.

Were their youngsters truly as lucky as it would seem at first glance? Or were a whole new set of problems and pressures being created by the lofty expectations their parents had for them and by the exalted levels of the parents' own professional and financial goals, coupled with the unprecedented affluence enjoyed by so many of these households? Moreover, by giving these youngsters the best of everything were the parents really giving them everything that was best for them?

Called "Where Do We Go from the Garden of Eden?" that initial Westport gathering brought together about a dozen people including clergy, substance-abuse counselors, school administrators, and psychologists, many of whom were parents themselves. It took place in an exquisite setting—the antique-filled parlor of a picture-perfect New England inn. Delicate snacks and bonbons were served from silver trays, after which we all settled back into chintz-covered armchairs which had been drawn up in a circle around a blazing log fire. It was just the sort of ambience that suggested everything was right with the world.

But as the evening wore on it was clear that there was trouble and confusion looming in paradise—not just in an idyllic spot like Fairfield County, Connecticut, where we all happened to be that night, but in similar upscale enclaves around the country, places like the North Shore of Chicago; suburban Boston; Memorial in Houston; Fairfax County, Virginia; Marin County and the La Jolla area in California; and the Upper East Side of Manhattan.

While the participants at the workshop noted that the TV programs and magazines of the day dwelt heavily upon the way in which it was possible for bright and talented adults to have it all and juggle it all with equal aplomb, few people at that time thought it necessary to step back for a moment and look at the way the parents' personal ambitions and lifestyle—which exacted a fearful toll on them, in terms of time, attention, and energy—might be affecting the lives and behavior of their children despite all the material advantages. Moreover, many of these children would be the leaders of the next generation, shaping our ideas, values, and policies in government, business, and the arts. So it was important to learn what was influencing their behavior and personality development.

Thus I decided it was clearly time to take a comprehensive look, particularly as the statistics suggested that a privileged upbringing coupled with high expectations was no longer confined to a tiny, patrician class. The explosive amount of new wealth created during the early part of the 1980s (which economists said had not been equaled since the late nineteenth century) and the growing senior career opportunities for women was spreading the monied life among hundreds upon hundreds of households. By the mid-1980s the Federal Reserve was reporting that 1.3 million families had a net worth of over a million dollars. In 1986 some 57,000 taxpayers were filing tax returns for adjusted gross incomes in excess of $500,000. And 3.1 million families had $75,000 or more coming in each year—sufficient in many places for two cars, a good home, private schools, live-in help, and country club membership.

A measure of that growth and interest in the topic was immediately apparent from the response to my article about the workshop which appeared in *The New York Times* on March 16, 1987. Readers wrote in, and other publications and TV stations solicited interviews with the participants. More, much more clearly needed to be known about the children of this new haute bourgeoisie.

But how to go about the research? Children of high-achieving parents had not yet become a category defined by academics or mental health professionals as requiring special attention. Rather, bits and pieces of information available about them lay scattered all over the place with few having yet thought it worthwhile to gather it all for analysis. This I decided to do while at the same time developing some sound coping strategies. That was indeed what I was best qualified to do as a seasoned journalist. And certainly the intended audience for such information, can-do sorts of people, were not interested in findings for their own sake unless some guidance was provided on how to act once a particular issue or problem had been identified.

I therefore took a wide-angle lens to the subject. I delved into the lay and professional literature from a historical perspective—stories of children of parents who had amassed wealth and status a generation or so ago, learning what had happened to them. I spoke to teachers in public and private schools where such families were predominant. I interviewed psychiatrists, psychologists, authors, and guidance and educational counselors, speaking to some eighty of these professionals whose combined experience with these youngsters and their parents represented what was known about thousands of such families. In addition I talked to some sixty parents, in groups and individually, and nearly 100 youngsters, in both focus groups and one-on-one encounters.

Virtually no geographical differences could be perceived among these families in the effect their affluent lifestyle had on their children, whether they lived on the West or East coasts, in the South or the

Northeast. Many were peripatetic, anyway, being born here and then moving there (with a vacation home in yet another area), then again somewhere else as opportunity knocked. Visually there was even a physical resemblance to the communities they tended to select. Mill Valley, just north of San Francisco, for example, looks eerily similar to New Canaan, Connecticut. So no separation has been made in the text for regional differences.

What did seem to separate them as parents, however, were the different issues they faced depending upon the age of the child. That is why I have structured the book primarily according to age groups, with appropriate topics apportioned to each one. Certainly, there were some issues that overlapped, pertinent to several sections. So the reader should be alert for a possible crossover. For instance, what I found out about tutors may be as applicable to an eight-year-old as to a teenager, but to go over the same ground would have been simply repetitive.

In certain places I have made a few broad generalizations about the personality traits I found in many of the children. These assumptions are not intended to suggest any statistical sampling. Rather they are based upon the consensus of the dozens of youngsters I met, their comments about their peers, their parents' views, and the opinion of professionals working with them, such as counselors, therapists, and teachers. Obviously there are exceptions, but again it seemed pointless to keep repeating that fact.

Interestingly, as I went about my research for the book, traveling around the country and speaking to professionals, parents, and the youngsters themselves, I would find individuals so eager to unburden themselves about the unexpected problems these seemingly heaven-blessed children were facing that they would beg me to stay long after our scheduled time together. Some of my best material and insights were garnered during these informal talks. Parents would pepper me with questions about what I had already learned, as though desperate for news from the front. Many of the youngsters would also ask for more time during these sessions, as if for the first time someone was willing to acknowledge (as they intuitively knew) that privilege does not automatically protect: it just creates different problems. Along with the blessings come burdens.

It also seemed to be one of the first chances many of these people had to bring what appeared to be a closet subject out in the open. The idea that highly successful adults were not always able (despite good intentions) to provide a perfect environment for their children, or perfect children, was not something that apparently anyone felt comfortable about discussing in public. It was understandable. There was something not quite proper about complaining of difficulty amid good fortune. Thus it was hardly surprising that many of these parents and children did not want their identities disclosed. I respected that wish. As a result I have not used real names in certain instances.

By contrast (as expected), parents whose children had become super-achievers as well as super people were naturally overjoyed to share the secrets of their parenting success. It was heartening to meet these families and learn from them, too.

I also became personally intrigued because, in all candor, I too had probably been guilty—as a mother of two—of some of the misguided excesses I was hearing about in others. Listening to the psychologists was like being in Psychology 101: I recognized a number of the same tendencies in myself as a parent. By the time I attended that workshop my children were already grown. But I could still identify with the anxieties expressed by the parents and empathize with the concerns that lead them to do the kind of things that we now know to be counterproductive and even soul-destroying for many young people in their formative years.

For the sake of our children and the self-respect of so many of these parents—all of whom are clearly trying to do the best job they know how—I dedicate this book. Welcome, now, to the world of the children of fast-track parents.

# I

# The Rise of
# a New Kind of
# Childhood

# 1.

# Life in a Fast-Track Household

It is only ten weeks since Stacy Holland O'Donnell, a tall and slender forty-two-year-old executive recruiter, gave birth to her third child. But she is already back in her spacious, elegantly furnished office in a downtown San Francisco skyscraper. She looks so spectacular she might have stepped right out of the pages of *Vogue* magazine. Her blond hair is swept back from her face in a neat but stylish cut. She wears a dove-gray linen suit that shows none of the bulges or sags from her recent body changes. Her walk is brisk, and her periwinkle-blue eyes sparkle with energy.

She is married to Michael O'Donnell, forty-three, an equally handsome marketing executive. Each has a six-figure income, and both enjoy the challenge and excitement of their careers. Their children, born when both parents were already well established in their respective fields, are Devon, 7; Cory, 6; and Mackenzie, the newest infant girl. They love these children passionately.

The O'Donnells live in a three-level, contemporary-style home perched on the side of a mountain that looks out over the majestic sweep of San Francisco harbor. The sunlit living room has one wall entirely covered with shelves crammed with well-worn books that sometimes spill over onto the off-white carpet. Even with their jam-packed lifestyle, the O'Donnells still somehow manage to keep up their reading. The separate dining room suggests many formal dinner parties, also a testament to a very full life. On the lower level is a small apartment the couple completed for live-in help before the first child arrived—the woman who takes care of their three children for much of those children's waking hours, when they are not attending private school.

The O'Donnells have investments. They are warm, caring people.

They lead the "good life." They are a modern success story, the kind the business journals and women's magazines love to write about.

But what will life hold in store for those girls?

By the late 1980s families like the O'Donnells were being churned out by the booming economy and the women's movement as fast as new pairs of Reeboks. Not even the stock market crash of October 1987 could make a noticeable dent in their goals or way of life. Although these sorts of couples had been around for years, they never seemed quite so noticeable or numerous. Professionals working with them and their children began calling them "fast-track" parents. An umbrella term covering a multitude of occupations and income levels, it was coined as much to identify an attitude toward life as an actual lifestyle. In most instances such parents are not only highly ambitious for themselves but for their children, too. In everything they do, whether for business or leisure or in their role as parents, most tend to be such strivers as well as such determined super-achievers that the personality label "Type A" seems inadequate. Many of them might be more accurately called "Type A-plus."

By the time they have a first child a majority of fast-track parents tend to be already in their thirties and have achieved a great deal. Some may be on second marriages, about to raise a second family without the financial constraints they suffered the first time around.

They are confident, optimistic, in-charge sorts of people. Their goal is to be outstanding and also to command a really strong income, which many have indeed managed to achieve fairly early on in life. They are understandably proud of the fact that they are part of the late-twentieth-century emphasis on professional success—a world where keeping up with the chairman of the board has replaced merely keeping up with the Joneses.

By the time the first child comes into their lives many are using that hard-earned money to enjoy a Gatsby-like life. This frequently means enjoying the comforts of a fine home located at a top-flight address, a Porsche or BMW in the driveway, live-in help, a winter ski lodge or a summer home by the beach, designer clothes, and (when there is time) foreign travel. Even if these couples are not particularly interested in such accoutrements they probably find themselves needing one or two to offset the social pressure and avoid feeling inadequate compared to their peers, especially in an age of "money fever," as *Fortune* magazine describes the late 1980s fascination with the trappings of wealth.

Moreover, it makes a statement like none other. In his book *Money and Class in America,* Lewis Lapham attributes this lavish living to the fact that in an egalitarian society possessions are the only yardsticks by which others can measure success.

There are other theories, too. "Maybe it's something in the Perrier water," observes Lucy Brodsky, the salty up-and-coming writer in the movie *Irreconcilable Differences.* The remark was actually not intended as a wisecrack. It was uttered more out of a fear of being caught up in a phenomenon that seemed inescapably linked to this new Gatsby age—a value system that equates net worth with self-worth. These parents are normally "beautiful people," too—ultra-thin, physically appealing, and with an innate sense of elegance and style.

In the nursery of these homes the tooth fairy is equally likely to be working overtime. For such adults spare no expense when it comes to their children. No wonder fashion houses such as Ralph Lauren, Esprit, and Laura Ashley have been able to launch successful lines of designer clothes for the younger set. And F.A.O. Schwarz, the ultimate in toy stores, can sell $500 pandas and $180 dolls.

Such parents frequently place as much pressure on their children to achieve as they have placed upon themselves. Second-rate doesn't rate in the vast majority of these households. It is absolutely, positively unacceptable. "I remember how my husband couldn't stand it when our son couldn't even win one swimming event at camp," recalled a mother who flies helicopters and is also a physician. The father is an equally high-powered property developer. "He kept ranting about it for weeks," added the woman. Is it therefore any wonder that specialists like Glenn Doman, founder of the Better Baby Institute, a learning research and development center in Philadelphia, have become the gurus of the group, offering to show such parents how they can gain higher achievement from almost any child, starting virtually from the cradle?

The children inhabit a world where "they learn from the start that they dare not be left at the bottom," observed Suzanne Prescod, former editor of *Behavior Today,* a monthly newsletter for therapists that has reported on the topic.

No wonder even minor personal shortcomings seem to trouble these children. When Dr. Anne Petersen, a professor of human development at Pennsylvania State University, conducted a study in the late 1970s of 355 such youngsters from two of the most fashionable suburbs in Chicago, she found that those who suffered most were those who were physically less attractive and mediocre in accomplishment.

"The parents set such perfect models it was hard to measure up," she told me.

Indeed, the children see their mothers and fathers placing such priority on perfection, on getting to the top, "that they worry their parents won't respect them or love them unless they do the same," noted Audrey Rosenman, a Manhattan psychotherapist whose practice is devoted mainly to prep school students.

Moreover, some parents unwittingly impart the idea—from their own lives—that it is easy to be "tops." And their children, not prepared to weather the defeats and disappointments that inevitably come along the way, become oversensitive to criticism or failure, particularly when evidence of shortcomings is clearly not acceptable at home.

When Dr. Petersen first interviewed her study group in 1978, the participants were around eleven years old. About three-quarters of them "felt okay" at that time. By 1986 only half were still functioning well as high school seniors. A third "had periods of great difficulty" and the remainder "were having serious mental problems," she said. The girls, she noted, had constant concerns about body image even though most were not overweight. Even some of the brightest ended up turning in poor grades. The chronic underachievement came, maintained Dr. Petersen, "because they saw the goal of meeting or surpassing their parents as near impossible. So they decided instead to have a good time."

Meanwhile, Petersen and other researchers were finding that those who seem to be turned on rather than turned off by the pressure became outstanding—almost formidable in their excellence.

With their heavy emphasis on achievement it is hardly any wonder such parents typically insist that these children receive a blue-chip education at the finest private or public schools, enriched by the best extracurricular activities money can buy—ballet, horseback riding, skating, gymnastics, music, or karate lessons. It used to be one or two of these. But more and more the children are taking part in all of the above, or at least almost all. Often very little unstructured playtime is left in any day.

The attitudes became so widespread that in 1986 Anna Quindlen, the former *New York Times* columnist, felt compelled to note, "Sometimes I feel that we've all entered a sweepstakes for the Most Accomplished Person in the world in the year 2025, and we've got to get ready *now.*"

In this sort of environment, noted a 1987 opinion piece in the *Greenwich* (Connecticut) *Time,* a daily newspaper, characters from literature might be rated thus: Huck Finn would be a delinquent; Tom Sawyer wouldn't be working up to capacity; and nobody would ever let Alice just sit there, doing nothing at all but dream through a summer afternoon.

These children also inhabit a world where they learn from infancy onward that if you can't get what you want legitimately, on your merits, there is likely to be someone there to use the needed influence, status, or connections to pave the way—from a place in a top nursery school to acceptance into the Ivy League. Certain teachers, fearful of offending a highly influential parent, told me they were being increasingly tempted to overlook lapses if schoolwork was not up to snuff. And the reward for helping out, several private school administrators confided, was no longer an apple placed lovingly on the teacher's desk. Today's thank-you was far more likely to come directly from the parents and be delivered by messenger. Among the gifts teachers and school heads mentioned receiving: an embossed silver tray, a vacation in the Bahamas, and a hefty donation to the school's scholarship fund (unsolicited). Though this sort of occurrence is hardly new, there was a rising concern among some of the educators I met about the value system such behavior imparts to the child as well as the temptation it poses for teachers to become less than objective.

Chances are strong that part of that child's upbringing will be traumatized by a divorce. By 1987 *New York* magazine was reporting that about 40 percent of the children in New York City's private schools had divorced parents, up from only 10 percent a decade earlier. And it was occurring, the teachers reported, when the children were at an ever-younger age. In addition, it seemed to often become an extremely bitter, protracted divorce since there were frequently large assets to fight over and giant egos that did not take kindly to being badly bruised.

Even if the parents do remain together, family life in the fast-track household will most likely be characterized by the parents' lack of free time. For instance, in order to fulfill their ambitions or retain that position in a highly competitive marketplace, both parents usually need to devote far more than the usual forty-hour week to the job. And timing is against them since the most intense years of child-raising tend to coincide with the years that are most critical to career advancement. Moreover, it is not easy simply to decide to cut back (as so many child guidance experts suggest) since this immediately sets up terrible internal struggles. It can be an agonizing call.

"My business was my first baby," I was told by a dark-haired, earnest, and pragmatic woman who had spent nearly a decade painstakingly fostering a following for her party supply store. "I had given it so many years of my life, I couldn't just let it go like that." Others who may wish to jump off the career carousel, at least for a while, talk of the financial need to keep going in order to keep up with the cost of a lifestyle to which they believe, with justification, that—by dint of hard work and long hours—they have become entitled to enjoy.

Still others spoke candidly about the "ego problem," the loss of status and standing, that gets in the way of slowing down, especially at a time when the whole country seems focused on success. Dr. Bettie Youngs, a writer on children and stress from Del Mar, California, remembers the jolt she suffered when she gave up a prestigious teaching affiliation at a local university—a post that was consuming most of her weekday evenings—to have more time for her teenage daughter. "Suddenly there was no identity," she said. "Nothing to put on a business card."

Close family members whose own identity is tied to that success suffer, too. John Couch, a former senior executive at Apple Computer who helped build the company with Steve Jobs, describes it well. Hardly having had any time to spend with his wife and his three children during their early years together, he was suddenly struck one day with the notion that perhaps he was jeopardizing a vital part of his life. His own father had died when he was only six years old and in a way he said he feared he might be passing along the same fate to his own children. So, in the mid-eighties, having accumulated enough money to last him virtually for the rest of his days, and having seen "the fun" go out of working for the company, now that it had become a major public corporation rather than a group of maverick tinkerers, he quit. Cold. And retired a millionaire at the age of thirty-six.

"When I told my mother I was going to leave Apple so I could spend more time with the family, she replied, 'But what will I tell my friends?' " said Couch with a warm grin.

Not many fast-track parents have that luxury. Nor would they take advantage of it if they could. Thus their lives, while exciting and challenging, frequently become draining. By the time both parents get home at night even the best intentions they might have had for the children—reading a story at bedtime, helping with homework, listening to events at school, cooking a meal together—may get postponed for yet another day. Often all that the child sees is an exhausted parent who seems to have no fun. If there is conversation, the children complain, it has the character of a cat about to pounce on a shoebox full of mice. For it tends to be of the "score card" sort—a moment when the child is supposed to recount the results of a test or the grades anticipated in math for the quarter.

Not all fast-track families fall into this pattern or create such a highly pressured environment. Indeed, some, like the O'Donnells, sensed the dangers in advance and are taking some of the precautionary measures spelled out later in the book. But it seems to be awfully easy to fall into that mold.

The question is: why?

# 2.

# The Making of a Fast-Track Parent

Why do so many fast-track parents get swept up into this scenario? To better understand the dynamics it is necessary to look at their own upbringing, the state of mind of *their* parents during their own formative years, and the kind of competitive pressures these fast-trackers must face each day in the business world.

The vast majority were among the 76.4 million people born between 1945 and 1965. Although they came from a diversity of ethnic and geographic backgrounds they were, for the most part, baby boomers—fortunate and frequently indulged children who grew up during the era of postwar prosperity in spanking new trees-and-grass suburbs built to eliminate all the hardships their parents or their parents' parents had lived through.

With the horrors of the Great Depression and World War II behind them, most of these parents threw themselves wholeheartedly into child-raising, determined that their children would never live as they had done but would instead inherit a Promised Land. And they made good on that pledge. It was a time of stay-at-home mothers, stable marriages, a car in every garage, and an expanding economy that made everything seem possible. Dr. Benjamin Spock's *Baby and Child Care* was the runaway best-seller. "Father Knows Best" and "Leave It to Beaver" were popular on TV. Being labeled "Mother of the Year" was neither a joke nor a slur. The nation as well as the parents considered their children top priority. Mom and Apple Pie were truly the watchwords of the era. And Father probably had no problem getting and keeping a job and bringing home plenty of bacon on a regular basis. It was, in truth, a Norman Rockwell world.

Thus, right from the beginning, many of these children absorbed the idea that they not only had the right to the Good Life but that the world would always give it to them. It was the kind of upbringing that psychologists today know can produce a deeply ingrained narcissism, a selfishness and a self-indulgence that are difficult to shake. Growing up during an era of steady economic expansion also seemed to indicate that dreams and desires could indeed become reality—provided you worked hard enough and persevered.

And the parents, eager that their children should be equipped to survive and prosper at a level they might never achieve, encouraged them on—urging them to go that step further and continue on the lineal progression of upward mobility that had always been so much a part of the American Dream. It was not hard for a majority of these children to believe they could do it, either, to believe they could surpass their parents. Educated most often on the GI Bill, many of the parents were still relatively modest folk—small businessmen, hometown accountants or lawyers, blue-collar workers, shopkeepers, salesmen. Few had reached the upper echelons of corporations or the high-status positions their children hold today. If they managed to do so they tended to arrive there after their children had grown up.

A number of those parents were also eager for their children to be super successful so that the youngsters might fulfill the ambitions that a depression or a world war had snatched from them, whether a secret desire to develop the Widget of the Year or become a movie star or a business mogul. If those parents worked late, or put in extra time at the office to save up for college tuition for a child, it was always "so our kids will have a better life." Rarely was the impression given at home that those hours had been invested so that the parents could themselves benefit from that glory or wealth. The focus, again, tended to be on doing it all "for the family." No wonder those children felt so special. Yet that very phrase, or attitude, also placed subtle obligations on the children—an obligation to become the best lawyer, doctor, or corporate executive, if only to fulfill the implied contract they had made with their parents in those early years.

Meanwhile, at school and at play, the children were being caught up in a demographic maelstrom that would also shape their thinking. Wherever they went, whatever they did, there were always too many of them—too many applicants for places on the team or at summer camp, too many trying to get into college. These were the days when public school systems would regularly cram thirty or forty children into one class or put the institution on double sessions just to make room for them all. Often it would take months before the teacher remembered their names. Some never did.

The feeling of being lost or swallowed up by a crowd can generate a fear that psychologists say is one of the worst anxieties facing any human being: nonexistence. "It's the idea that nobody knows who you are or if you are even there," explained Samuel C. Klagsbrun, a noted New York psychiatrist. It can create, he said, a compelling need for recognition and achievement that comes from deep within and is totally separate from any drive that might emanate from the home environment.

And in the suburbs, where so many of these children grew up, that anonymity was compounded by the homogeneity of the landscape—everyone seemed to dress alike, speak the same way, live in the same style of houses, watch the same TV programs, go to the same schools, drive the same make of cars. To be noticed, to gain recognition, you really had to stand out. And you had to keep on doing it again and again.

Thus it was a world that not only expected high results but was also highly competitive. "As soon as Sputnik happened in 1957 our generation was brutalized with ambition," recalls Dr. Terry Eisenberg Carrilio, a therapist in Philadelphia. But winning one's place in the sun was not easy to achieve. Someone always seemed to be lurking in the shadows, ready to elbow you out of the way if you faltered even for a moment. To be first in the class was not just a question of being smarter, brighter, harder working than a handful of your peers. It meant being smarter than hundreds of your peers, dozens of whom were also being encouraged onward and upward by their own parents.

A warm, jovial woman who is now a community leader in Connecticut has vivid childhood memories of those days. She grew up as the eldest daughter of an accountant and an at-home mother in a midwestern suburb. She recalled: "We lived in a three-bedroom ranch house in a new development. The school was brand-new, too. By fourth grade I remember it was already important to me to be competitive. We all went into the auditorium one day for tests to see what kind of musical instruments we would play. I knew that the ones who did the best would get the strings. So I wanted strings. I tried very hard."

She continued, "Looking back I realize that this drive was being reinforced in so many ways. We had a radio program called 'Charming Children' and it had a song which said that charming children 'smile instead of cry and never, never say they can't . . . they say I'll try.' The assumption was that if you tried you got the prize. It was the mode of encouragement that suggested you could do anything. It was the same at home. My mother wanted so much to be proud of me, of any achievement, that she kept putting my name in the local paper whenever I won something. Fulfillment for her would have been if I—her daughter—had made it as an expert on the 'Today' show. It would have shown that I had finally made it—become Somebody."

Then suddenly it was time for college. And for those who found themselves on campus during the late sixties and early seventies it was also time for rebellion from all that conformity and sterility of a postwar childhood. If you could not always gain a sense of identity and recognition individually you found you could do so collectively. If the world had seemed tailormade to indulge this generation of children, it became even more accommodating as these youngsters became adolescents and young adults.

When they put on their ragged clothes, rejected the materialism of their parents, tore apart the traditions and rules that had been part of established culture for years, many an administration conceded to their demands. True, there was normally a humanitarian motive behind the actions. But those demonstrations, for the most part, were also fun. In certain institutions the students were not even threatened by poor grades for their time out. When hordes of students began to skip class and go on a campus rampage, sitting in or marching in protest against imperialism, pollution, and other ills of society, a number of colleges even instituted a pass-fail system so grade levels would not be impaired. When the students rebelled against a rigid curriculum, many an administration loosened graduation requirements.

It was a time for breaking the rules, getting away with it, and loving it. Life was a great big party. It also had a surging sense of purpose. Nobody yet talked much about the long-term effects of drugs. Sex was not only available and uninhibited, it was also danger-free. Herpes and AIDS had not even entered the popular vocabulary. The economy was so strong there was the sense that even if you dropped out and "did your thing" for a few years you could always come back if you felt like it. Once again the world was indulging the baby boomers.

In hindsight the worst part of it all might have been that they got away with so much, an attitude that some social critics have since suggested may have only added to the narcissism of many from that generation. Too many also learned from those campus riots that if you challenged or broke rules you were not penalized but instead could emerge a winner. That view was certainly being underscored by a number of worried parents, many of whom were working behind the scenes in every way they knew how—paying for their youngsters to stay in school, subsidizing them to go off to Canada—in order to prevent them from being drafted and shipped to Vietnam. Besides, it was not part of the agreement. They were supposed to build a better life. Remember?

And when the parties, the communes, and the self-inflicted poverty became uncomfortable and rioting lost its purpose, that is exactly what a lot of those baby boomers did. They went back to fulfilling the contract. Besides, age was creeping up on them. The party was over and they were smart enough to sense it. Admittedly, some never moved back into the mainstream of society or abandoned those causes. Instead, they took the ideals they had cherished and started working from within for their goals, through special-interest groups rather than street confrontation. In other instances a great deal of the energy that had gone into organizing protests and setting up a commune went into creating yet another world that would fulfill dreams: personal career success.

It worked. Miraculously, as before, a great many members of this "jackpot generation" really did hit the jackpot. World events again conspired to make their timing just right. Except for a few minor setbacks, the booming economy was able to offer them the bounty they sought and had been told to expect—provided, however, they were willing to devote the backbreaking time and effort into making headway in an overcrowded fray. Their drive came from that original contract. It also came in response to their swollen numbers. And to the victors—those who have made it—have gone the spoils.

They have been shrewd, too. Many of them, particularly the best and the brightest, have capitalized on the skills learned during those student days. Several former campus activists pointed out to me that the managerial skills needed to organize a successful student riot are not so different from those required to run a corporate department. They also explained that if you could get yourself out of facing combat in the Vietnam War it does not seem so awful to "bend" a few of the rules in the business world that might get in the way of your goals, especially if nobody was getting hurt in the process. Keeping your eye on winning despite the hurdles had been a way of life since childhood. And for the most part it had worked.

But then came parenthood. And the agenda was really tough this time. For it was no longer a question of equipping a child for a better life as their parents, grandparents, or even great-grandparents had done. It had become a question of providing the tools to make sure that child could at least continue living at the elegant level you had reached. And that meant making sure these children were able to earn a lot of money and really be outstanding. It was terrifying to face the idea that they might slip back down. The notion was so new that it could not be viewed as a generational hazard. Instead, it had to be looked upon as a blow to one's own self-esteem as a competent, conscientious parent.

So now the stakes were much, much higher. While it had been relatively easy to surpass one's own father (or mother), a child of a baby boomer needed far more intense conditioning to be able to surpass, or even equal, one's own achievements. "We have two sons of astronauts in our school," the Reverend Mark Mullin, headmaster of St. Alban's School in Washington, D.C., told me as we discussed the problem facing such children. "How do you top going to the moon?"

Moreover, since these children now had much further to climb just to reach parity with their parents, it was not enough simply to foster independence. That child had to be bred for success from infancy onward and assisted financially well into adulthood.

There were other serious issues facing these parents. In 1940 only 35 percent of all high school graduates went on to college, according to the Bureau of Labor Statistics. By 1988, 63 percent of all high school graduates were doing so. Again, it was no longer enough to make sure a son or daughter got a college education. A conscientious parent had to be more selective than that: he or she had to make sure that child got into the Ivy League, no less than Harvard, if it was at all possible.

Frequently, added personal concerns underscored that agenda. Many high-achieving mothers, influenced by the women's movement, were determined to give their daughters the economic self-sufficiency and the credentials to overcome all the prejudice and setbacks they themselves had faced. One mother's story, told in Chapter 20 of this book, "Private Lives," is a poignant testimony to this concern. If those mothers had been divorced along the way, that concern became even stronger. Like the mother in the tale, many of the women who were left to raise one or two children alone became passionate about the need for a girl, in particular, to gain gilt-edged credentials of her own.

"My kid's not going to have to go through all that. She will go to law school or get a medical degree" is the way these mothers express their concerns to Howard Greene, a former admissions officer at Princeton who is one of the best-known private educational counselors in the Northeast. Other parents told me that by providing their children, through expensive educations, with an upper-class veneer, they could help those children have the patina of the well-to-do inbred from childhood that somehow opens all the right doors—something many of them, with their public school and state university backgrounds, felt had made their fight to succeed so much harder.

These fast-track parents also understood that our nation was increasingly becoming a meritocracy. Thus their children would have little chance of making it into the power structure unless they not only attended all the right schools but also gained the required grades and made the right friends—networking, as it were, from diaper days onward. Those parents, toughened from the tribulations of their own boardroom battles, knew what it took to get to the top. Why not make it just a little easier on their children?

Yet to do so, they soon found out, they had to start a program of academic and social preparation almost from the cradle—the finest nursery school, the finest public or prep school, the finest tutors. It became a tyranny of sorts, as if as parents they could not qualify for inclusion in the in-group unless they fulfilled all items on that rigid checklist. They had to be sure *their* child had what Nicholas S. Thacher, headmaster of New Canaan Country School, has described as "the edge." Besides, they had lived with competitiveness themselves from the beginning and understood the importance of having the right credentials. Thus as loving, caring parents, they were willing to spend what it took to provide that edge. Moreover, they had the checkbook resources to do so.

For some, the very giving of those advantages soon became a way to keep up with their peers. "The social pressure on contemporary parents to use their children as symbols of economic surplus and status is powerful, even if parents are not fully aware of it," noted Dr. David Elkind, the child-rearing specialist from Tufts University, in his 1987 book *Miseducation: Preschoolers at Risk*. "A successful child is the ultimate proof of one's own success."

Anna Quindlen, the *New York Times* columnist, suggests that this constant quest for the perfect child is a natural outgrowth of the way many of today's parents approach life in general. "I can understand why this is happening," she wrote in one of her columns. "We are a generation of people who like to play numbers: 750 on the verbal SAT, a starting salary of $65,000, two cars."

But to keep it all up soon became a frantic race, especially when a parent would spy a neighbor or colleague on the same track, able to offer the same advantages. "I see so much fear, anxiety and insecurity behind those elegant façades," notes Dr. Roy Nisenson, a New Canaan psychologist who regularly counsels high-achieving parents and their children.

Meanwhile, they couldn't let up at work because there were massive bills to pay for the high-octane lifestyle they had won. Besides, everything around them—in magazines, in newspapers, on TV—was reaffirming the idea that winning in the business world was the name of today's game. Status and success had become the epiphany of the epoch. Neither the contemporary culture nor their own upbringing had prepared them for the idea that settling for less or dropping back into the slow lane might not be so terrible after all. The 1980s has been described as the Decade of Getting Ahead. How true.

Others were haunted by the terms of that original contract. They had to keep on succeeding in order to continue receiving the love, respect, and recognition they still needed from *their* parents.

But in order to make it all work and be super-parents as well as super-achievers, accommodations had to be made. Help had to be hired to take care of the children. Spending on expensive toys and togs replaced spending enough time at home. The treadmill was carrying them around so fast that before they realized what was happening, they had re-created for their children an upbringing that was very close to that of the upper classes, the super-rich, Old Money.

Knowing more about the impact of that kind of upbringing was surely needed, some of them soon began to say. Others argued that by giving their children every advantage money could buy there could be no problems. The notion that privilege could promote pain seemed bizarre indeed.

But it happens to be true.

# 3.

# Children of the Rich or Famous

When I began searching for clues to the impact upon personality development of children who grow up in a fast-track family, parallels to the experiences of children of the super-rich became immediately apparent. Like the super-rich, many super-achievers were employing live-in caregivers for the child as well as housekeepers, gardeners and maids. Like the super-rich, the household staff, including tutors or a special teacher hired to provide private instruction in such refinements as music or sports, often spent more time with the children than the parents. As with the lifestyle of the super-rich, there was frequently more than one family home. And during school vacations it was not uncommon for the parents to remain in the city apartment during the week, coming out to spend time with the children at the vacation home only on weekends.

Like the super-rich, these children tended to be segregated from the mainstream of society by the privileged enclaves in which they lived, augmented by attendance at private day or even boarding school—what Kurt Hahn, founder of Gordonstoun, the elite boarding school in Scotland, has been quoted in the press as calling "the prison of privilege." Enrollment at public school in such sophisticated communities as Greenwich, Connecticut, acted to keep them within much the same sort of protected environment.

With all this in mind, it seemed helpful to take stock of what we already know about a super-rich upbringing, if only to try to mitigate the painful, limiting, or harmful experiences that can occur, as reported in autobiographies of individuals who grew up in such surroundings. I had been encouraged to turn to these sources after finding very little in the medical-psychological literature. Corroborating material also showed up in the histories of prominent families. Other insights were provided by the findings of therapists who have treated the children of the super-rich.

The overwhelming conclusion, contrary to popular myth, is that it's not easy to grow up rich. Being born into a wealthy family has obvious advantages—a beautiful home, the best education, lots of fine clothes, and exciting things to do. But there is a dark side, too. Ask Gloria Vanderbilt about it. She might well tell you she would have gladly traded the lap of luxury for a less-exalted seat. Holden Caulfield, the prep-school dropout, echoes the same mournful theme in *Catcher in the Rye*: "The first thing you'll probably want to know," he writes, "is where I was born and what my lousy childhood was like."

Even the identifying phrases "stinking rich," "rich kid," "richie," or that old-standby "poor little rich girl" carry pejorative overtones that have a way of throwing cold water on a lucky break. The United States is a republic and a meritocracy dedicated to equal opportunity. The notion that someone should start out so much ahead of everyone else seems somehow dirty pool, making that money unclean. We celebrate the self-made man (or woman), not the one who is given a Golden Sendoff. The children sense this even if they can't quite articulate their embarrassment and self-consciousness. There is even a phrase for it that seems even more fitting for the inheritors than the original creators of the wealth: an embarrassment of riches. The wealth can also make these youngsters feel guilty about admitting to having problems of any sort. "How in the world do you ask for sympathy when you've got all the things that are supposed to make you happy?" explains Laura Rockefeller, daughter of Laurence Rockefeller, in the book *The Rockefellers*, by Peter Collier and David Horowitz.

Such children may also be plagued by the idea that they may appear different from everyone else. A young woman on the Upper East Side of Manhattan confided about how, as a small child, she would always curl up on the floor of the limousine that her father had proudly hired to drive her to school each day. She had been terrified that other children would look in through the windows and laugh at her.

A story is also told around Los Angeles about the television crew that came to tape a segment about the youngsters who attend Beverly Hills High School. A small group of students from the school quickly gathered around the cameras. The TV reporter started the session by telling them that he wanted to ask them a few questions about themselves.

"If you were at a party," he began, "and someone asked you where you came from, what would you say?"

One of the boys in the crowd shrugged and said, "L.A." Everyone nodded in agreement.

"And if that person asked you, 'What part of L.A.?' "

The boy thought for a second. "West L.A.," he replied.

"What part of west L.A.?" continued the reporter.

And so the probing went on until it became abundantly clear that the last place the youngsters wanted to be identified with was a have-it-all neighborhood like Beverly Hills. Their parents, by contrast, were known to have a habit of slipping this famous address into conversation as early as possible, anxious that new acquaintances should know right away that they were successful people. It was a way of affirming their talent, energy, and drive. To their children, however, that money and affluence did not provide them with the same pride. They had not made that money.

What do we know about the impact of growing up rich? Only in recent years have physicians, psychiatrists, and others in mental health started looking at the childhood of rich people in a serious way. Much of this data is interesting, I think, because it does help to provide insights for those who may follow. Nevertheless, the pickings are slim for understandable reasons: foundations and other funding sources usually decide that their money could be put to better use than analyzing the problems of a group of people who have ample resources to take care of themselves. Rich people do not command the moral imperative that the poor do.

What is written up in the medical literature comes mostly from a skewed sampling—the combined experience of therapists who have been called upon to help wealthy young people with emotional problems.

Despite this limitation there does seem to be sufficient evidence in that material to suggest that wealth itself has the capacity to set up a difficult environment for a child. Clearly that silver spoon has the potential for leaving a very bitter taste.

Wealth has undoubted benefits, but it is not good for children. It distorts their functional relationships with the world, it belittles their own accomplishments, and it grotesquely amplifies their sense of what is good enough.

That statement is from the introduction to an article on rich children by Dr. Frank S. Pittman III, an Atlanta physician and family therapist. Published in the December 1985 issue of *Family Process,* a professional journal, it outlines for medical colleagues the prevailing opinion of those who have examined these children. And that opinion does not seem to differ whether the researchers gathered their information from wealthy families in the South, Midwest, West Coast, or Northeast. Dr. Pittman, for instance, examined fifty wealthy southern families, not all of whom were in need of counseling.

The difficulties seem to start from the way a wealthy household operates rather than conscious plan on the part of the parents (who are no doubt as well-intentioned as any other parents). Normally a child's daily care is placed in the hands of servants from birth. Unless the mother and father make a conscious effort to be closely involved in the infant's life, these babies will see very little of their parents, who rarely perform routine (yet nurturing) tasks—such as feeding, changing diapers, cleaning wounded knees, explaining why leaves fall off trees, reading about Little Red Riding Hood, or giving them a bath. "Almost all of the mother's usual functions may become delegated to a nanny, with mother-child interaction reduced to a minimum," notes Michael H. Stone, associate clinical professor of psychiatry at Cornell University Medical College in New York City. His observations, compiled for his professional peers in 1979 under the title "Upbringing in the Super-Rich" for the medical book *Modern Perspectives in the Psychiatry of Infancy,* were based on his own wealthy patients over a ten-year period.

If there is too great a turnover of maternal substitutes, these children may end up suffering from "maternal deprivation," according to Dr. Stone and others. Writing about children of the wealthy in the *History of Childhood Quarterly* in 1975, Dr. Stone recounted a series of bizarre stories that far outdo the shenanigans in "Dynasty" or "Dallas."

For example, in one case he talks about a child who had been living in isolated luxury on a large estate surrounded by acres of exquisite grounds. She was not allowed to "bother" her parents and indeed saw so little of them that she had no early recollections of her father or mother. Memories of her father began when she was eight years old and centered on the image of him emerging occasionally from his study to ball her out for playing the flute. Isolated and in desperate need of some kind of comfort, she spent her free time in a small cave on the property, reading comics by flashlight and guzzling soda pop.

Dr. Stone also tells a tale about the daughter of a southern aristocratic family whose parents took frequent and extended trips abroad, sometimes staying away for as long as six months. Even when they were home they were so aloof that neither the girl nor her brother and sister even ate with them. Conversation between parents and child hardly existed. The girl recalls rarely having the chance to tell either parent about her thoughts, feelings, or endeavors. Moreover, she soon gained the impression her life did not "matter" to them anyway. Though the household staff were supposed to take care of her needs, they were punitive and unempathetic.

The turn-of-the-century childhood of Peggy Guggenheim, a member of the famous philanthropic family, is replete with such examples. In the book *Peggy, the Wayward Guggenheim,* the author, Jacqueline Bograd Weld, tells how Peggy's parents rarely saw her. Instead Peggy and her two sisters were "relegated to the top-floor nursery, connected directly with the servants' quarters by a flight of steep, dark stairs." Peggy's sister Hazel observed, "I had no connection with my mother, who never read me a book or told me a story."

These examples highlight two potential dangers, the first being the effect on personality of an extreme lack of parental involvement—which, according to Dr. Stone, is likely to leave a child with low self-esteem. He writes, "If one has scarcely been the recipient of a parent's concern or interest, one tends to have little regard for oneself—even one's own life." Dr. Roy Grinker, a Chicago psychiatrist who has counseled some of these children in adolescence, adds another explanation for the low self-esteem often found in the super-rich: "The money that allows the parents to become absent parents is interpreted by the child as disinterest." Dr. Grinker calls such children "deprived children" who frequently develop serious problems caring about anything or anyone very deeply and who also lack values, goals, and ideals. There is even a new term coined by the popular press to identify a young person suffering from such a state of mind—the youth is said to have contracted "affluenza."

The second potential danger is the profound effect that the caregiver's attitudes and character can have on the child's emotional development. Dr. Sirgay Sanger, director of the Early Care Center of New York on the Upper East Side of Manhattan and author of *The Woman Who Works, the Parent Who Cares,* sees dozens of children who are spending their early years almost exclusively under the wing of a caregiver. Looking into what that experience does to the child, he has found that these caregivers may be "jealous of the privileged child." And when that happens, he notes, it becomes difficult for the caregiver to provide the genuine warmth needed for nurture. In addition, he warned, some caregivers purposely try to keep their young charges at an immature level in order to hold on to a well-paying job.

It is therefore not surprising that being surrounded by caregivers and other household servants hired to fulfill every whim (or who believe it is their job to do so) can rob these children of their sense of usefulness as well as make them genuinely helpless. "The chores kids perform in other families may be done by servants in rich families," writes Dr. Pittman.

Experienced in excess it can inhibit natural development. Dr. Sanger recalls the case of an eight-month-old boy who was brought for the first time by a nurse to play at the center. "The child would scream every time he wanted something that was out of reach," recalled Dr. Sanger. "He had been so used to the caregiver putting every toy between his legs that he expected this sort of service all the time." Added Dr. Sanger, "When we left a toy just outside his reach it took him ten minutes of crying before he realized he could lean forward and get it for himself."

Although seeming like paradise, too much pampering from caregivers and household servants can also create the erroneous impression in the child's mind that the world is set up to fulfill his or her every need. Most of us remember Tom and Daisy, the wealthy and self-centered couple in F. Scott Fitzgerald's *The Great Gatsby*. Fitzgerald, who understood the wealthy so well, writes disapprovingly: "They were careless people, Tom and Daisy—they smashed up things and creatures and then retreated back into their money or their vast carelessness, or whatever it was that kept them together and let other people clean up the mess they had made . . ."

That type of behavior, say the therapists, is typical of the wealthy and often comes from an early life surrounded by people whose job it was to "clean up the mess," whatever that mess or the needs of the moment happened to be. No wonder so many of them do not see their behavior toward others as exploitation. As children they didn't "have a give-and-take relationship with the world (like everyone else)," writes Dr. Pittman. That lack of two-way involvement has also been found to promote a numbing sense of ennui so characteristic of the youthful rich.

Dr. Pittman believes that children who spend too much time around servants allowed to do too much for them can also rob them of an opportunity to build confidence in their own abilities. "Even if there are chores," he writes, "they are [often] token character-building exercises imposed unnecessarily by the parents. Rich kids don't do useful work—they take lessons—music, dance, tennis, even charm, whatever will make them more decorative and socially acceptable. This reaffirms their belief that they are useless."

A further danger, say these professionals, lies in the relatively large amounts of money that are frequently placed at the disposal of these children. Though it seems on the surface to be a major advantage, it can distort their idea of what is needed to get by in this world, deprive them of the thrill of attaining material advancement, stunt motivation for career achievement (which normally includes the development of self-discipline and self-reliance), and often ill prepare them for the realities they must face as adults.

In his book *Privileged Ones*, Robert Coles, the noted Harvard professor and child development specialist, dubs this attitude "entitlement." Others have characterized it over the years as the mien of the dilettante.

Another difficulty stems from the limitations of wealth—a seeming contradiction in terms but a real pitfall. Dr. Pittman has found that some parents actually prevent their children from pursuing certain fields in which they may have a genuine interest for fear it will tarnish the family image. He cites as an illustration the movie *Private Benjamin*, in which the "parents" of Goldie Hawn rush to rescue her from the army and urge her to say she was in a mental hospital rather than let anyone know she had contemplated something as low-class as enlisting.

The family money or name is also used, note these professionals, to "buy" the child's way out of trouble, again distorting reality and never giving the child a chance to develop a separate identity or sense of accountability for his or her own actions—a pattern that can lead to irresponsible behavior throughout adult life. And buying a child's way out of trouble seems to be standard behavioral pattern among super-rich parents, notes Dr. Stone, in part because of the fear of scandal. Yet "a night in jail may accomplish more than a year in therapy," he comments wryly.

## CELEBRITY YOUNGSTERS

As some high-achieving parents may receive a measure of public renown along with affluence, I felt it was worthwhile to take note of the impact of parental fame upon the child as well.

And it seemed that even if that fame is limited—the person's name is only a household word in one particular town or county, or among professionals working within the same area of expertise—the impact can be profound. The daughter of the mayor of a small city told me that it mattered not that her father was only well known in the community where she was raised. It was the same as if he had been a national politician or a TV star, since her whole life revolved around that city. Everywhere she went people referred to her as the mayor's daughter. Though she was proud of her father it made her feel self-conscious and somehow not a real person in her own right: this feeling disappeared once she moved to the anonymity of a large city early in her adult life.

Indeed, what seemed clear, early on in my search, was that while such renown obviously offers children unique access to the corridors of power and possibility for their own ambitions, it must also be recognized as a mixed blessing. For those children could end up developing an even weaker sense of their own worth and identity as they grow up enveloped by an ever-present shadow—if care is not taken to find ways to boost their own sense of self-worth and independent identities.

Consider for the moment those subtle difficulties: In his book-lined suite on Sunset Boulevard, just next to the spot on the curb where a large blue and white bulletin board urges visitors to "see the homes of the stars," Dr. Charles William Wahl, clinical professor of psychiatry at U.C.L.A., regularly counsels the children of show-business celebrities. Dr. Wahl talks of the anguish that can occur when "you see your parents giving time to the multitudes but never having enough time for you"—a problem that Burton N. Wixen, another Los Angeles therapist, has noted can lead to desperate attempts by certain show-business children to gain that attention for themselves, even if it means resorting to illegal acts. "One such child stole a lace handkerchief," Dr. Wixen noted in his book *Children of the Rich.* "Only later did she realize it resembled a shawl Mother wore in her most famous movie role. She was searching for some part of an unapproachable mother she could hang on to."

In addition, the differences the child begins to notice between himself or herself and the famous parent can create feelings of inadequacy almost from the start. "The more you discover what Grandfather did, the littler and littler you feel," remarks Ann Rockefeller, daughter of Nelson, as she describes some of her childhood experiences in the book *The Rockefellers.*

The child may feel like an impostor, as though he or she doesn't deserve to be a part of all the adulation and esteem. When Carrie Fisher, daughter of Eddie Fisher and Debbie Reynolds, was asked by a *New York Times* reporter at the time of the publication of her first (and reputedly autobiographical) novel, *Postcards from the Edge,* about her allegedly difficult childhood, she explained: "I was world-weary at twenty. I had unlimited access to money, fame, and acceptance. How could I have felt I'd worked hard enough to achieve that. Something was off."

In addition, friendships become suspect. Dr. Stone, who has also counseled children of famous parents, notes that from a tender age the child may feel uneasy, wondering if friends are genuine or just trying to curry favor with the famed parent. Gary Crosby, son of the singer-actor Bing Crosby, recalls such an incident at the close of a summer he spent, as a boy, raising a calf. "One of the [local] cattle brokers, a nice man who was a friend of Dad's, bought him for so much a pound," he writes in his book *Going My Own Way.* "I should have felt a sense of accomplishment. I didn't. I knew the guy only bought it to please my father."

If the famous parent is a controversial figure, like a politician or a disgraced Wall Street trader, the child may become further disoriented, notes Dr. Stone, because he or she may become the target of ridicule or rejection for reasons that seem incomprehensible at the time. Then there is the danger that the child's own mistakes may become more than private foul-ups—they could be mentioned on the nightly TV news or appear in newspaper headlines.

Gary Crosby talks about this, too. He recalls the trauma he faced as a small boy when his father decided to have his son appear as a guest on his famous radio show. "There was no question in my mind that Dad expected me to perform my lines perfectly," writes Gary Crosby, "and would let me hear about it later if I didn't. . . . Just the fact that he was Mister Perfect in the world's eyes and I was his son was enough to make the thought of messing up absolutely cataclysmic in my own mind, the very worst thing that could possibly occur."

It is clearly not a problem if the child does have as much talent and ability as the celebrity parent. Indeed, that child has the advantage of using the name and the connections as a springboard to even greater success. Most often it is "a child of meager endowment born to such a family [who] will feel crushed by the difference between his capacities and those of the parent," notes Dr. Stone. What would be "normal" in any other family becomes inadequate in these households.

Adds Dr. Pittman, "If the children cannot see their way clear to being spectacularly successful, they may feel themselves damaged and give up any effort at all toward productivity."

All very well, you may say, but what about the glamorous stories of the ones who have sailed straight to the top anyway—Nelson and David Rockefeller, John and Robert Kennedy, Jane Fonda, John Quincy Adams, Winston Churchill, Henry Ford II, Clare Boothe Luce, Donald Trump, Antonia Fraser, Anna Freud, Alice Roosevelt Longworth, Margaret Truman, Senator Robert A. Taft, Liza Minnelli, Douglas Fairbanks, Jr.?

Therein lies the key. What makes some children of the rich or famous (which many fast-track parents have become or may become in the not-too-distant future) able to capitalize on their privileged status to enhance and enrich their own lives, and possibly the lives of those less fortunate than themselves, while others seem to wither under the glare and glitz of it all?

The answer to this tantalizing question was what I set out to learn as I delved further into my research. It turned out not to be simple. But I have tried, as the book goes along, to provide clues and insights that can be used as a starting point for any high-achieving parent anxious to plan a suitable and enriching childhood for a son or daughter, given what we are now learning about the impact of one's own success upon a child.

# 4.

# Parenting Is Succeeding in a Different Way

I t may come as a surprise to learn that the skills, talents, and lifestyle that have combined to make certain people so successful in business, politics, the arts, or the professions may get them into hot water as they assume the role of parent. Remember the troubles that beset the high-powered Manhattan management consultant in the movie *Baby Boom* when she was unexpectedly thrust into the role of mother? Though much of the film is a satirical exaggeration, it makes a powerful point: parenting can confound and confuse even the most accomplished individual.

In the old days the parent with the most highly developed marketplace skills—usually the father—was buffered by the mother, who had been encouraged to develop nurturing skills. Not so anymore. Both sexes are now urged to hone their marketplace skills. A woman's upbringing and training today may do little to prepare her for motherhood, so that the resultant sense of personal ineptitude may be an unexpected product of our times rather than a personal lacuna.

Indeed, after considering the following list, compiled from conversations with about a dozen educators and psychologists, one begins to understand why many fast-track parents are thrown off-balance when they discover that raising a child frequently turns out to be more difficult and frustrating than succeeding in a chosen field. It may not actually be more difficult; it may just be that child-raising skills are indeed very different from the skills needed to succeed in business— much in the way that an engineer may be brilliant at building bridges but may have never acquired proficiency in spelling and grammar. Or a writer may be able to produce exquisite prose but has never been able to master numbers.

Naturally, not all these characteristics belong to all high-achievers. The full list probably only applies to extreme types. But almost all high-achievers may recognize themselves in at least a handful of the items. Here is the list:

| QUALITIES NEEDED TO SUCCEED IN CHOSEN CAREER | QUALITIES NEEDED TO MEET NEEDS OF GROWING CHILD |
|---|---|
| A constant striving for perfection | A tolerance for repeated errors |
| Mobility | Stability |
| A need to be free from time constraints to pursue an independent life | Plenty of time for family activities |
| Impatience | Patience |
| A goal-oriented attitude toward the project at hand | An acceptance of the seemingly capricious nature of child-raising |
| A way of operating based upon consistent rules and procedures. | A way of operating based on the constantly changing nature of the parent-child relationship as the child grows |
| A total commitment to yourself | A total commitment to others |
| A stubborn self-will | A softness and willingness to bend |
| Efficiency | A tolerance for chaos |
| A belief that succeeding must always be the top priority | An understanding that failure promotes growth |
| A controlling nature that enjoys directing others | A desire to promote independence in others even if their ways are not your ways |
| A concentration on essentials | An ability to digress just to smell the roses |
| A concern about image | A relaxed acceptance of embarrassment |
| Firmness | Gentleness |
| A feeling that nobody is as smart as you | A true respect for your child's abilities free from comparison with your own |

| | |
|---|---|
| An ability to create a family that is supportive of your chosen career | An acknowledging that children have their own agenda |
| A preference for concise information | A willingness to listen patiently to prattle to help develop a child's articulateness |
| An insistence on high standards | A genuine tolerance for the lack of certain abilities |
| A need to maintain an executive role over others | A respect for a child's right to total independence after a certain age |
| An exploitation of others | An ability to put another's needs ahead of one's own |

Dr. Pittman, the Atlanta family therapist, is one of many mental health professionals who are becoming convinced that the ideal child-raising personality is at odds with that of the super-achiever. "People who get rich have a very special talent and an obsessive dedication to the marketing of it," he noted in his 1985 article in *Family Process,* a journal for marriage and family therapists. "This is usually associated with a single-mindedness that tends to leave out time-consuming relationships with . . . husbands, wives, and children. More often those who get rich are highly competitive and therefore intolerant people, who experience situations less as adventures than as opportunities and other people as either competitors or tools or obstacles."

Then there is the personal drain. In his book *The Executive Parent,* Dr. Stephen Hersh, a Washington psychiatrist who regularly counsels high-achieving parents, points out that many highly ambitious people become workaholics. Says he, "Extreme workaholism undermines physical health through a combination of inadequate rest and sleep, lack of exercise, and often poor diet, including an excess of caffeine from either tea or coffee." He also warns that unless care is taken to offset the drain, a high-pressure job can leave a parent "abstracted of mind and too short of time and temper to deal resourcefully with the needs of their children."

Another pitfall can emanate from the competitive drive. Even though the parent may be convinced that he or she is aiming only for "the best" for the children, that parent may actually be perverting the whole process. "On some unconscious level a highly competitive parent may need to see a child fail because such people can no more tolerate competition from within the family than they can from outside," warns Dr. Samuel C. Klagsbrun, the Manhattan psychiatrist who has many supremely successful individuals in his practice. It depresses their own sense of importance. Seeing a child become an independent achiever in his or her own right also means a loss of control over that child. And control is a major need of many powerful, successful individuals—a characteristic that might be dubbed the King Lear syndrome. In that classic tale from Shakespeare only the two daughters who swore the greatest loyalty and love for their father, the King, were deemed worthy to inherit his kingdom. That way he had hoped to keep control, but even this was not enough. The King stayed on, crowding the palace with his own people and constantly interfering. But by trying to hang on long after he should have let go—and putting his kingdom in the hands of two sycophants rather than the most able successor—all were destroyed in the end by his megalomania.

The same curious behavior shows up in *The Fords*, the story of the automobile dynasty. "Ford liked to create the conditions by which he could possess people entirely," observe the authors, Peter Collier and David Horowitz. "This was truer with Edsel [his son] than with anyone else. . . . He said he wanted his son to succeed, but whenever Edsel gave evidence of doing so Henry immediately undercut him, often humiliating him in front of Ford executives in a demonstration clearly, if unconsciously, meant to show who was boss."

This may appear as a paradox when one knows that a hallmark of fast-track parents is fostering high achievement in their offspring. But what seems to happen is that high achievement is often only acceptable when it can be directly attributable to parental efforts—the phone call to a trustee that gained the child a place at a prestigious school, an affluence that enabled the parent to pay for music lessons from a virtuoso. The danger is that if it is trumpeted too loud or the child is constantly reminded of this fact it may seriously undermine that young person's fragile self-esteem. It leaves little room for the child to feel proud. The tormented writer Franz Kafka might not have become so tormented had he not faced an identical problem. "You only encourage me in anything," he wrote in *A Letter to My Father,* "when you yourself are involved in it, when what is at stake is your own sense of self-importance." Continued Kafka, "What I needed was a little encouragement, a little friendliness, a little keeping open of *my* road."

Because super-achievers are so goal-oriented they are increasingly known by psychologists to view their children as "products" rather than people—expecting certain results as a consequence of the actions they choose to take as parents, much in the manner that they perceive an investment in their professional lives. Moreover, if this does not happen as planned their immediate reaction is to take the business approach, which means cutting their losses. But that can backfire in child-raising. I heard a painful tale from a psychologist about a ten-year-old boy, the youngest of three children, who refused to apply himself to his schoolwork. Eventually the father decided that it was no longer worth paying for the expensive private school the boy had been attending. The child just seemed to give up after that, turning in an even worse performance in public school.

So one sees how a business approach can be counterproductive in child-raising. The basic makeup of the child may not be suited to the goal set up for that child by the parent, or the child's own agenda for life may not match that of the parents. Take pregnancy, for example. The parents have no way of assuring that the baby will come into the world with a set of genes and a personality that will respond to their strategic plan for that child (however carefully charted and implemented) or complement their image of themselves as successful human beings. No wonder so many of them find pregnancy more frightening than anything they have ever faced.

"Suddenly there was something inside me I couldn't control and perhaps I couldn't even fix. It was terrifying." The person talking is Royal Kennedy Rodgers, a TV news correspondent. She compares that feeling to taking on a difficult assignment. No matter what would go wrong with that assignment she always knew she could find some way to make it work out. When it came to having a baby she found she was no longer so self-assured. There was something going on in her life that was very precious to her. Yet she had been excluded, as it were, from the decision-making and she felt uncomfortably out of control.

As the transition from career to parenting can be such an awkward one—at odds with career pursuits and even adult pleasures that may have been enjoyed for years—therapists now increasingly recommend that two-career couples analyze the changes that will occur in their lives before taking the big step. Such a rehearsal, suggest these experts, can help smooth the way for everyone involved, lessen the resentment or depression that can set in during those early months, and help set more realistic goals for themselves and their children.

Among the suggestions:

• Think carefully about why you are planning to have a child and whether, realistically, a child will be able to fulfill those objectives.

- Put yourself in a situation where you might have to put the child's well-being ahead of your personal agenda. How does it feel?
- Imagine the baby is already in the house; discuss what activities might have to be sacrificed and how you would react to those losses on a prolonged basis.
- Talk openly about the financial drain. Analyze the cost of help, schooling, clothing, and what this means in terms of cutting back on your personal lifestyle.
- Talk openly with each other about your fears and expectations and then weigh these against reality by talking with friends who are able to speak candidly about parenthood.
- Spend some hours—perhaps a day or even overnight—at the home of a close friend who has a small child; separate the myth from reality. There may be some pleasant surprises along with the sobering realities.
- Start practicing some self-deprivation: save more than usual, take a more modest vacation.
- Discuss how you might feel and act if a child of yours was plain and average instead of brilliant and beautiful.
- Discuss how you might handle matters if the greatest opportunity of your career meant relocating to a place that might undermine your child's scholastic career.
- Think about what you both might do if your child develops a dangerously high fever or if it is the day of the school play and you and your spouse both have important meetings to attend.
- Imagine yourself five years down the road with two children. Where will you live and how will you cope?

The experts have also found that certain high-achievers make child-raising more difficult for themselves by failing to use the management or professional skills that *are* readily adaptable to parenting. It is a pity, since some of them can do double duty. Here is a partial list. You probably have some of your own you could add.

| GOOD MANAGEMENT TECHNIQUES | THAT ALSO WORK AS GOOD CHILD-RAISING TECHNIQUES |
|---|---|
| Regular staff meetings for input on market/client conditions | Regular family meetings for input from children on concerns emanating from their daily lives |
| | *(continued)* |

| | |
|---|---|
| Delegating appropriate tasks with clear instructions | Delegating appropriate tasks with clear instructions |
| Inspiring subordinates | Inspiring children |
| Networking with colleagues in the same field | Networking with parents and others connected with child-raising |
| Helping a subordinate improve without giving offense | Helping a child overcome a weakness without destroying his or her self-image |
| Becoming a role model | Becoming a role model |

Preparing for parenthood is normally viewed as preparing in a more practical way, such as buying Big Bird wallpaper for a nursery. But clearly there is a great deal that can also be done on the psychological front. For high-achievers this is unquestionably a priority, as the transition can be so much more traumatic because of prior training and lifestyle.

# 5.

# The Challenges

It has often been noted that fast-track parents have three goals as they take on the role of parents: (1) their children should be happy, (2) their children should be brilliant, and (3) their home should be so perfectly managed that a career can still be pursued without short-changing the child.

The first two goals seem to be unquestionably true. The third may be an overstatement. Certainly many older fathers in second marriages (who have already attained a certain level of success) feel sufficiently content with their accomplishments to be able to cut back and enjoy their children more fully than the first time around. And a growing number of women are working out similar part-time arrangements, at least for the early years. A *Newsweek* poll conducted in 1986 found that more than 50 percent of the 1,000 working mothers they questioned had eased up or changed jobs so that they might have more time for their kids. Similarly, a poll conducted by the University of Michigan one year later showed how concerned many mothers had become over the effect of their multiple roles on their children. Clearly, everyone cares. And cares deeply.

But for a majority of highly ambitious people, cutting back is not an easy option. So much has been invested in getting this far it is terrifying to think that the momentum could be lost. The challenge therefore is to try to raise self-sufficient and happy children despite the difficulties and special pressures we are learning that these children—and the parents—face.

In subsequent chapters the intention will therefore not be to try to offer any quick fixes for any of the three goals listed (indeed, the second may not always be appropriate or even attainable). Rather, the aim will be to try to learn from what we already know about these households. I hope to accomplish this by opening a window on the lives of certain fast-track parents to see how they have managed to solve some of the more complex dilemmas.

We will also be looking at the techniques that therapists and educators have found effective with parents who became highly successful a decade or so ago, and whose children have already learned to deal with some of the issues. Above all, we will be speaking to the children themselves to see how they view their upbringing and what they have found helpful; conversely, what actions the children have found counterproductive even though the parents' gestures were well-meaning. This seems to be a particularly critical gap: it never ceased to amaze me how much of a difference I would find in the description of the same event or incident, depending upon who was relating it to me, parent or child.

Most people love a challenge. And I think that high-achievers are particularly prone to view difficulties as exciting challenges rather than impossible hurdles. Thus, based upon the sort of expectations and problems we know confront these households, I think it would be fair to say these challenges include:

- creating a loving, caring, and supportive environment even if the parents' actual time at home is limited
- knowing what kind of pressure acts as a motivating force and when pressure can turn a child off
- avoiding the pitfalls that can result from showering a child with too much money
- understanding in more detail why certain parents act the way they do toward their children
- preparing these children for the future in a realistic and compassionate way—a task that may necessitate a redefinition of what most high-achievers currently consider success
- consciously seeking ways to improve these children's self-esteem, which may need substantial bolstering in light of parental achievements
- developing in these children the sense of *noblesse oblige* that ideally accompanies the level of affluence they are fortunate enough to enjoy
- learning the subtle differences between hearing what these children are trying to say rather than just listening to them

A tall order, you may say. Nobody expects 100 percent fulfillment. Or even 99 percent. A parent can only try. Nobody is perfect. Parents are human with human failings like everyone else. But, then, so are their children.

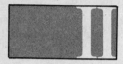

# The Early Years

*My child arrived just the other day,*
*He came to the world in the usual way*
*But there were planes to catch*
*And bills to pay . . .*

*—Harry Chapin*

# 6.

# Caregivers

Even before a baby arrives most success-oriented couples are likely to be having long discussions about the best way to rearrange their lives. Should the wife stay home for a while? Should they try to divide the responsibility by juggling schedules? Should they give up some of their social or community commitments? What if they could find someone wonderful to live in?

What can make this sort of conversation so frustrating is that real life tends to get in the way of what might, theoretically, be best for them and the child. Perhaps in some instances it is more beneficial for the mother to be home in those early years. But mothers who have stayed home, believing it to be better for the child, told me how frustrating it can be to pick up a magazine or newspaper and discover yet another early-childhood study stating that nobody can definitively prove this point—especially if the child has a particularly good mother-substitute. That finding was underscored by Dr. Ann M. Milne, an educational policy researcher, who analyzed the differences between the educational performance of children with stay-at-home mothers and those with working mothers. Her paper, "Family Structure and the Achievement of Children," was presented at a conference on education and the family sponsored by the U.S. Office of Education in June 1988.

Moreover, much may hinge on whether the couple can afford to give up one income or is fortunate enough to find a loving, affectionate caregiver. Furthermore, nothing is cast in stone: a change can be made later on. For instance, at some point the wife may decide she needs to stay home for a while or would be better off cutting back to part-time work. She might even arrange to work part of the week from home— as Mrs. O'Donnell, the executive recruiter from San Francisco, arranged to do. (My impression is that a highly ambitious man who agrees to do this is still a rare bird indeed.)

Even if she does, the couple is far more likely to hire live-in help, at least for the nursery years, than use daycare. There is a great deal of anecdotal evidence from people who run domestic-help agencies to support that view. The reason they have found this practice so prevalent today among high-achieving couples, they said, is primarily because of the parents' schedules. And it is usually only these parents who can afford the tab. This was confirmed in a 1987 article in *Time* in which career-oriented couples explained that it was the only practical solution among their peer group because of the long hours and frequent out-of-town travel they must face. And there was no question that a live-in helper seemed to offer the most individual attention and nurturing for the child when the parents could not be around.

No wonder I found the use of daycare virtually nonexistent among the high-achievers I met—although most of these parents did enroll their toddlers in preschool enrichment programs at least part of the time. Indeed, it seemed that every parent deeply involved in a career seemed to harbor a Mary Poppins fantasy at one moment or another— the secret longing that this wonderful British nanny would be blown in on the East Wind to *their* doorstep complete with her parrot-headed umbrella and carpetbag. And, in addition, she would have that unique blend of discipline, magic, and wisdom that would help *their* children grow up in just the right way.

Fortunately, a great deal of information is beginning to surface concerning the impact of caregivers on a young child. And this can help guide the parent in making a choice and directing the helper. Although I'll admit that too frequently the opportunities to be highly selective are few and far between—most agencies receiving far more requests than they can fill—it still helps to know the ropes.

## SELECTING LIVE-IN HELP

To provide some initial guidance in hiring help I talked to directors of specialized-help agencies that are increasingly springing up to supply live-in caregivers. I then spent time talking with a group of mothers who had used live-in help for the practical view. Among the most highly recommended books for background reading was *The Nanny Connection,* by O. Robin Sweet and Mary-Ellen Siegel (Atheneum, 1987). It is not only an excellent guide to the selection and ongoing supervision of help, but also provides a comprehensive state-by-state list of placement agencies and nanny training schools. Another good source is the International Nanny Association in Claremont, California, an advocacy group, professional association, and informational clearinghouse for anyone involved with live-in caregivers.

Most mothers I met said they felt it was more efficient and safer to locate the agencies they used through recommendations provided by members of their professional network or personal friends. Other parents said they had been equally successful asking trustworthy caregivers employed by friends or neighbors if they knew of anyone who might be interested in applying for the job. Advertising the position or checking the classified section in a local newspaper was, of course, another option. But again, I did not find it as widely used for live-in help as for daily housekeeping assistance.

Occasionally the parents said they did place "Nanny Wanted" ads in parts of the country, such as Idaho and Iowa, where other parents had found good caregivers. Some parents also advertised abroad, such as in Denmark or Great Britain. But anyone doing that should be careful about immigration requirements, since a sudden loss of a caregiver due to lack of papers can be devastating to the child, as well as wreck the parents' schedules.

The value of an agency is that it will prescreen the applicants, although there seemed to be a measure of cynicism on the part of certain parents concerning how carefully that always occurred in reality—all of which places the burden of careful selection squarely back in the parents' court, even if an agency is used.

There are usually three categories of choices: (1) an au pair, normally a young girl from Europe in her early twenties who is using the opportunity as a way to live overseas for a while. She will expect to be on call only part of the time while furthering her education in this country; (2) South American or American-born girls of similiar age who make a full-time commitment (twelve hours a day, five days a week); and (3) a mature woman, either locally born or foreign, who has raised children of her own. Much will depend on availability.

If it is possible to interview the candidate personally do not overlook the reaction of the child or baby. Doris Elliott, president of Help!, an agency in Weston, Connecticut, who has placed over 1,000 caregivers since April 1983 (and limits placement to people who can be interviewed in person), recommends a selection technique used by a psychologist client. In addition to her own enquiries, the client would place the baby in the caregiver's arms and watch how that baby reacted. "Sometimes the baby would recoil," said Ms. Elliott. "At other times that baby would seem content." Older children can be quizzed for their reactions. Added Ms. Elliott: "They do not have any preconceived notions. They give you a gut feeling."

Sharlene Martin, president of Helping Hands, a nationally known agency specializing in live-in help, has analyzed over 800 placements she has made.

She found that a caregiver who came from a family where she had been the oldest sibling turned out to be the most comfortable accepting responsibility. Those from single-parent families did best in single-parent households, while those from two-parent households likewise did better with two-parent employers. Similarly, matching someone from a small town with an employer who lived in a small town, and a city caregiver with a city family, seemed to lessen the disorientation and dissatisfaction that often emanates from being tossed into an alien environment. Based on the findings, she also recommends looking for job stability if the person has been employed before—at least one year at any one home and a good explanation for any significant gaps between assignments.

The group of mothers I met had eight preschoolers between them and a combined total of twenty years' experience in seeking and evaluating help. The women have learned that when the interview has to take place over the phone, which happens if the applicant is thousands of miles away, it is vital to find out in advance why the person is eager to take this sort of job and whether she really understands what she is undertaking. To do so, they suggested asking the following questions:

- Have you ever lived away from home before (since they had found that first-timers frequently had problems with homesickness)?
- What has been your caregiving experience? Was it just the occasional babysitting job or more comprehensive? Have you taken any child-development or baby-care courses?
- What activities do you like to do with a child?
- Have you ever spent a night alone in a house with a small child?
- Describe your family life (see if her accustomed style of living complements your own).
- What are you planning to do with your life? (The helper's plans may indicate a more rapid departure than you had been led to believe, and that could be disruptive for you and your child.)
- Do you have a personal relationship? If so, how do you intend

to handle the separation? (These separations have been known to result in abrupt departures).

- Do you like children? (This question can reveal some hidden misgivings or confirm enthusiasm.)

If the applicant is in her late teens or early twenties the mothers found it helps to also talk to the parents and find out if they are equally enthusiastic about the idea. Otherwise those parents may undermine the helper's feelings about the job, which again may result in a premature departure. Care should also be taken to explore the physical and emotional health of the applicant through a family doctor. In addition, tell the applicant something about your own family life to see if it sounds compatible. Naturally, check references. Some agencies may cover many of these points on the form the applicant is asked to fill out. But asking again, in person or over the telephone, may help provide a deeper sense of the nature of the person.

If the caregiver seems more keen on cooking and serving a meal or cleaning house, this might be a warning that the individual is not too keen on children. By contrast, if the applicant is a woman who has raised competent children of her own, so much the better.

Give the caregiver a one- or two-week trial period before making a commitment. If possible arrange for one parent to stay at home at least part of that time to get a sense of the person's caring style and competence. Many of today's caregivers are inexperienced young people who are barely out of their own childhood, so it is critical to be cautious. You may also need to be highly detailed in your instructions concerning the daily routine and include certain safety issues, such as yard play. "I even take a new au pair to the doctor's office so I'm sure she knows where it is in an emergency," said one of the mothers. Another said she likes to take a ride in the car while her helper drives to make sure that the person's driving habits are safe (other mothers seem to prefer to find ways to lessen the amount of driving a helper has to do). It may also be a good idea from time to time to ask the helper what plans have been made for the child that day.

Even if the mother has decided to stay home for a while it is better not to wait until having the baby to seek help. "You will be too busy. You won't feel so well. You probably won't even be thinking as clearly," warned Gloria Andujar, a West Coast textbook publisher and mother of two who has used helpers for nine years. Gloria found that having the caregiver in the house during those initial weeks helped the caregiver gain an idea of how she liked the baby handled before she left to return to work. It may help, too, to be candid about all the chores that helper will have to do and also to let her know upfront if you are seeking a long-term commitment. "You might say, 'I want someone to grow with my child,' " said Gloria, who feels particularly strongly about a young child's need for stability.

Therapists told me repeatedly that preschoolers seem to be more relaxed and less anxious when a constant turnover of caregivers has been avoided. Carlotta Miles, a child psychiatrist in Washington, D.C., who counsels the younger members of some of the country's most distinguished families, was emphatic on this point. Little wonder that requests for older women—fifty years or over—have become more common among many of these mothers. It can be comforting to have someone who has already raised a family of her own. And with good reason: she is used to the frustrations and is probably less likely to panic in an emergency.

Even if you do have a helper in the house, it is probably wise to have a backup system in place. One suggestion is to become personally acquainted with your helper's friends (who might fill in if there is a crisis); or offer to take someone else's child for a day or so in order to establish some system of reciprocity.

## IMPACT OF THE CAREGIVER
## ON A CHILD'S DEVELOPMENT

What we are learning about the impact of a caregiver on a small child suggests that a parent needs to consider, perhaps more carefully than had been previously thought necessary, the likely results of that constant and close contact with a mother-substitute.

Nicholas Thacher, headmaster of the New Canaan Country School, is one of a number of educators who are finding that the increased reliance upon young women from abroad is causing more and more of his kindergarten students to arrive with limited vocabulary skills. Even regular viewing of such venerable educational masterpieces as "Sesame Street" does not develop language skills in quite the same way as interaction with another English-speaking adult or child. Solutions might include encouraging that caregiver to get together regularly with other caregivers and their charges so the child not only has companionship but is forced to communicate verbally with children of the same age. Attendance at a play group once or twice a week might also help, since playing with other children requires higher linguistic performance than conversation with an adult.

Another manifestation of the increasing number of infants and toddlers being raised by caregivers and a household of servants is the unrealistic expectation, mentioned earlier, that there will always be someone there to attend to their every wish and need. At La Jolla Country Day School in Southern California, for example, a growing number of youngsters have been coming into the preschool program in recent years still expecting to be fed and dressed and assuming somebody else is supposed to pick up their toys.

"We've had children who were so used to being fed by a Mexican maid that they couldn't function at lunchtime," reported Moreen Fielden, the school's lower-school director. On other occasions she has found that caregivers are so convinced it is their job to make sure the child knows how important it is to stay neat and "nice" that those youngsters come to school afraid to mess up their clothes. Compounding the dilemma is the delight that many parents take in buying the newest designer-label clothes for their children—encouraged by a fashion industry that is putting out extremely expensive and irresistible garments even for toddlers. Nursery and kindergarten teachers in some parts of the country have become so concerned about the current craze to dress small children like the youngsters in a Rembrandt painting that they are sending flyers to parents alerting them of the dangers of inappropriate garb. "It can make small children feel inhibited as well as guilty if they smear paint or spill water on this sort of clothing," warns Karen Manuel, founder and director of Toddler Time to Five in New Canaan, Connecticut. "And that's an unnecessary burden."

One reason many small children are arriving at school so behind in basic skills like dressing, feeding, and cleaning up after themselves may be due to a lack of clear parental instructions. Certain caregivers can be warm and loving to a point where they become oversolicitous of their tiny charges. And unless a parent instructs the helper to behave otherwise, the child will not acquire the expected skills until considerably later than normal. The caregiver may therefore need to be told to encourage the child to feed himself or herself, even if this creates a fearful mess and delays the completion of the meal. The same instructions might have to be given for dressing. The caregiver might be told that the child should be permitted to make some of the choices— even if, on occasion, that youngster does end up wearing a bizarre and inappropriate combination like a purple T-shirt with short red pants on a wintry day. "One of the skills we work on in our preschool program is learning to make choices," says Ms. Fielden. "How can a small child learn that unless he is given a chance to make some mistakes?"

Those who have monitored the behavior of caregivers, such as child psychiatrists and agency managers, offered another cautionary observation: a caregiver may not wait around for a child to pick up his or her own toys. And there seems to be a good reason for this. One should not forget that the caregiver is likely to behave more like an employee than a surrogate parent. This could mean that she worries more about how she comes across as an efficient servant than fostering the emotional or intellectual growth of the child. For example, that caregiver may be convinced that her employers, the parents, would not want to walk into a house that is in disarray. "So she will rush to tidy things up," said Ms. Fielden. "And the child gets to believe that this is the way the world is." The adjustment, Ms. Fielden has found, can be quite upsetting when those children finally get to school. Again, it may be necessary to remind the helper, telling her that you don't mind an untidy house; you are more concerned with having the child learn to take care of his or her own things.

No parent intends to turn over the entire job of child-raising to a caregiver. And some moments in the child's life definitely require a parent to be present. The middle of the night and bedtime are considered the most emotional times since these can be moments of terrifying fear for a tiny child. Darkness envelops his world as the sun goes down and the lights are switched off, and nightmares come in which illusion cannot be separated from reality. "I know many parents who make the decision to get up in the night even though they have live-in help," said Dr. Elena Lesser, a family therapist in Brooklyn who treats many high-achieving couples. "They know it is essential to that child's sense of security." This may be even more important if there is likely to be a regular turnover of caregivers. By the same token it may also be wise to postpone going out in those early years until after that bedtime story has been read or you have tucked that two-year-old in for the night.

Other psychologists suggest creating "boundaries" so that the caregiver knows in advance which activities are reserved for the mother and father. A bedtime story could be one; at least one meal together a day might be another. It's a way of creating a pattern that will help the parent stay very closely involved.

The same sort of structure might be used to create ways of checking up and guiding the happenings at home between caregiver and child without seeming to be overly intrusive, or lacking faith in that helper. A regular meeting time, such as after the child has been put to bed or just before the evening meal, would help both employers and helper feel more comfortable about raising even the most sensitive issues than if those conversations were left to occur only on an informal basis. Viewing the caregiver as a surrogate teacher is something else to con- sider for those early years. Certain learning tasks might be assigned, such as recognizing the letters of the alphabet or numbers. This way the loss of the intellectual growth that would have otherwise come from the presence of a highly educated mother in the early years can be mitigated by direction from the mother to the caregiver.

The way the family treats the live-in helper can also have an impact on the child's personality since this may well be his or her very first exposure to the treatment of outsiders. If the child senses that all outsiders are simply paid servants for whom he or she should have a certain degree of contempt, the child could develop that arrogant at- titude toward subordinates characteristic of certain privileged people. Dr. Sirgay Sanger, the New York child psychiatrist, recalls a sad en- counter with a four-year-old girl already well on her way to having such an attitude:

"What shall we play?" the girl began by asking him, in a demanding fashion, as she knelt on the carpeted floor.

"I can't think of a thing," said Dr. Sanger, sitting down beside her.

"Well, everyone tells me what to play. And you will, too."

"No. I can't think of a thing."

"My mommy *pays* you to play with me! You must!"

Clearly it is important to treat that employee with respect—"just like you would a visiting relative," recommends Dr. Nisenson, the New Canaan psychologist. He goes on, "It may seem a burden to nurture her, too. But she will be grateful and your child will learn from that." Failure to do so could have other repercussions. If the caregiver be- comes resentful of the parents she could start taking that resentment out on the child.

If space is available, it may help to provide that caregiver with a small apartment of her own, preferably with her own entrance. A pop- ular method among families I visited is to convert a ground-floor family room or create a unit above or at the side of a garage. In this fashion the sense of unity of the family is preserved, and both employee and employers retain highly cherished privacy. "Separate quarters become an oasis for the helper and lessen tensions inside the family," said Dr. Nisenson.

Be prepared, the mothers say, for a surge of jealousy if the caregiver and the child become so affectionate and attached to each other that it seems to push the parents right out of the picture. Dr. Roy R. Grinker, Jr., the Chicago psychiatrist, has noted that it is not uncommon for a parent to fire a helper under such circumstances—a move that can create severe emotional distress in that child. Mothers admit it is a subtle but very real problem. A physician in the South spoke of sitting at her desk during the day counting the hours she spent with her infant son versus the hours her caregiver had with him. Friends would tell her similar tales of how they could not stand being in the same room where their child was cuddling the family's caregiver. The result can be false charges about inadequacies as a way to provide the mother with a reason to fire the helper (often not even knowing herself why she feels so strongly about getting rid of the person). "I was fully prepared to feel guilty," said the physician, "but nobody prepared me for jealousy."

Discipline is yet a further issue that these experts now insist should be resolved in advance. Too many parents are making only vague references to discipline when they take on a helper, which result in two different approaches for the child—one used by the parent when he or she is home and the other by the caregiver. The style of discipline may also change as helpers change. This can be confusing and unsettling for both caregiver and child. Nor do the parents necessarily check up unless the child has complained. Not until there is a crisis—where discipline has been meted out in a totally inappropriate fashion—do the parents wake up to the problem. At that point the parents' fury may be so great that the arrangement with the caregiver falls apart, exposing the child to yet another disruption in his or her young life.

Take, for example, what happened to Gary Crosby. "It never occurred to us to complain," writes Crosby in his childhood memoirs. "We assumed the grown-ups were all in it together." He was referring to the practices of one particular nurse who had been unusually harsh in the way she had punished him and his brothers. He recalled, "If she caught any of us talking in bed or getting up too early in the morning she hustled the guilty party into the bathroom and ordered him into the tub. When it was filled with two feet of water she grabbed him by the hair, plunged his head down to the bottom and held it there awhile, then brought it back up so his face went under the stream still gushing from the faucet. . . . I was so relieved when Mom happened to walk into the bathroom one morning and caught the nurse in the middle of her routine. She exploded in rage. She fired her on the spot and threw her out of the house."

A detailed briefing needs to be given, in advance, of the methods preferred in your household, the situations that warrant action, and the standards that prevail. Consistency helps the child learn more easily, too. Yet curiously, too many American parents, particularly women, still admit they are uncomfortable about giving instructions to domestic help—possibly because they are unaccustomed to the practice. This may explain why so many caregivers are not adequately trained by their employers. Perhaps it is time to realize that such an attitude can actually end up doing more harm than good.

The caregiver also needs to be taught about the routines that must be followed if she will be taking her young charges to and from their preschool program. Like many other school administrators, Ms. Manuel, the nursery school principal, has become so frustrated with the difficulties she has had with caregivers who are either not told or do not understand the regulations that she is considering holding regular orientation sessions for helpers. Among her suggestions:

- Make sure the helper is aware of all the rules, even seemingly minor ones like holding a child's hand in the parking lot.
- Be sure the caregiver is fully aware of all information contained in the flyers that come into the house.
- Encourage the caregiver to talk over any concerns she might have about the child with the child's teacher.
- Check each day to see if any special clothes or items will be needed.
- If you are not picking up or dropping off your child, call the teacher regularly; it is the best way to keep in touch.
- Try to make a regular habit of sitting down with the child from the very first day and asking about what happened in class (if you cannot be there to hear about it right after school ends).

Above all, if live-in help is preferred, then the parents should do everything possible to balance the child's exposure to the single caregiver with outside play groups or nursery centers—and with their own prearranged, constant participation in the child's daily routine. Though this is usually the intention at the outset, that resolve can diminish even among the most conscientious parents when workplace pressures mount. And that can be a danger for the child. Tighter parental and auxiliary attachments formed by a small child provide greater emotional stability and lessen the trauma that so often accompanies any change-over in help during the preschool period. "That is one of the most important messages I try to get across," said Sharlene Martin, who has placed hundreds of caregivers in these families and watched the results.

# 7.

# As Baby Starts
# to Grow

If an observer were to peek into the nursery of a baby born to super-achievers it would beckon with the promise of a storybook child-hood—at least from an initial glance. Typical of those that I saw was one that had an imported white Italian crib with a matching chest of drawers; a toy chest and rocking chair that had been decorated with pink-and-blue stenciling; a changing table that could later be converted to a bookcase; personalized appliquéd crib sheets; wall hangings custom-made to incorporate the baby's name inside a pastiche of nurs-ery rhyme characters; and a large stuffed teddy bear and a colorful musical clown hanging from special mounts on the ceiling.

On closer observation, however, there was a more controversial side to the adorable setting. Attached to each end of the crib were hand-carved figurine mobiles enhanced by a "learning-center" clipped to the slats—all of which had been cleverly designed to develop ob-servational and motor skills.

In addition, on a small desk in a corner was a scattering of the educational tools now deemed vital to the baby's future: the book *How to Multiply Your Baby's Intelligence*, by Glenn Doman, and an article about learning activities for a toddler that can help improve perfor-mance on tests increasingly used by private schools as an independent measure of a tiny tot's intellectual prowess and potential. There was also some correspondence with a top-rated nursery school. Like other knowledgeable parents, this couple had heard from friends that the better schools are inundated with applicants. Thus it had been necessary to get that child's name entered on an advance list immediately after birth.

To call the years from zero to five the "preschool years" may thus be a misnomer in these families. The fear that the child will not gain a place on the overcrowded fast track can turn babyhood into a chronic dash for achievement. The concern has a certain validity. *New York* magazine noted not too long ago that it had become harder to win a place in the nursery school at Horace Mann—one of Manhattan's most prestigious educational institutions—than to get an older child into Harvard.

However, too often the necessary achievement levels are being gained at a fearful price. The possible long-term impact upon healthy emotional development is now being viewed as such a serious concern that pediatricians and child psychologists are beginning to sound the alarm and recommend a less extreme approach.

Consider a sampling of their observations:

Nursery school teachers are finding that at three or four years of age, certain youngsters are developing trembling hands or facial tremors. It is a phenomenon that has been highlighted by Dr. David Elkind, the professor of child study at Tufts University, mentioned earlier, and author of *Miseducation: Preschoolers at Risk*. He maintains that excessive pressure for academic achievement frequently produces apathy, constant complaints about headaches and stomach aches, and aggressive behavior. Resistance can become so marked, he insists, that the reaction of the child becomes very similar to the youngster with a learning disability.

Dr. Elkind maintains that the highly pressured preschooler is in danger of losing his or her natural enthusiasm for learning. The child's innate friendliness and trust in other children may also be inhibited since a highly competitive atmosphere sets up the idea that others are adversaries, not buddies.

Some youngsters are now so overprogrammed—enrolled in so many different activities—that teachers find they will forget even the most basic rules of that particular group. "One girl's mind seemed so weary that after a year she still couldn't remember which ladder in her classroom jungle gym was for Up and which was Down," one teacher told me.

Dr. Peter Czuczka, who has been a pediatrician in Westport, Connecticut, since the early seventies, finds more and more of his preschoolers developing sleep disorders. "I see a lot of emphasis on achievement," he said sadly. "But I don't see a lot of loving and holding anymore."

Teachers also say that many of their preschool and play-group students are now so worried about not giving the "right" answer to a simple question that they are constantly "seeking approval for every-thing they do," as one Manhattan teacher put it. They no longer dare to trust their own judgment.

At an exclusive nursery school just north of San Francisco, a teacher told me that some of the three- and four-year-olds have become so fearful of being labeled a failure that "they hate to be included in any group activity where there will be Winners and Losers. These sorts of children also resist playing the fool—like dressing up like a bunny rabbit," she said. "Then there are those who can read at two and rattle off the names of famous explorers. But they seem unable to readily socialize with the other kids." A handful, she said, cannot even create their own games or amusement because they are so accustomed to having an activity or learning project carved out for them.

When such pressure for early academic achievement is added to the parents' own business concerns, it is easy to see why so many observers are finding that in the early years in such households the children often see experimentation as something to be feared rather than an exciting adventure.

Warns Dr. Elkind, "We put our children at risk for short-term stress disorders and long-term personality problems when we ignore their individuality and impose our own priorities."

Added Dr. George Sterne, head of the American Academy of Pediatrics Committee on Early Childhood in the fall, 1984, edition of the organization's newsletter, "Is that type of lifestyle going to produce a better child? I don't think so. Though this type of instruction may make the child a perfectionist, it may also burn him out. Doctors often see more psychosomatic illnesses in children who've been raised this way."

Having too much academic pressure placed upon them at such an early age may also set the pattern for internalizing that pressure to the point where they cannot slow down later on or genuinely enjoy life, say these doctors. Moreover, there is no evidence whatsoever, writes Dr. Elkind, that early academic mastery is "crucial to the attainment of eminence" later in life.

Concerns are also being voiced by the medical community over the long-term implications of the Doman regime of early-childhood home instruction, especially when not used in moderation and with the cautions Doman himself weaves into his recommendations. Glenn Doman, a physical therapist by training, first became widely known for the seemingly miraculous way he was able to teach basic living skills to brain-damaged children. He maintains the brain develops so rapidly during the first six years of life that a child's mind can absorb far more than had previously been thought possible, much of it by stimulating the development of other sensory systems, such as sharper observational skills; and making learning something the child enjoys by providing him with a lot of loving encouragement and attention from a caring adult. So Doman later began training mothers of children with normal intelligence levels, teaching them how to carry out regular learning drills (regular repetition of the words or numbers on a flash card is one example) and how to stimulate response.

Though Doman has chalked up an impressive record of intellectual development and academic mastery through various repetitive learning techniques and instructional tapes, there are those who wonder, once again, about the potential cost. One critic is Dr. Sara Sparrow, director of research at the Yale Child Study Center. In a controversial article published in the August 1978 edition of *The Journal of Pediatrics,* Dr. Sparrow argued that little work had been done to compare Doman's achievements with a control group that had not been exposed to his methods. She then set out to do just that. She and a group of colleagues conducted a comparative study looking at the accomplishments of three different groups of fifteen seriously retarded children—Doman having developed many of his original techniques for disabled children. One was given Doman training for two hours a day, five days a week, for a year. Another participated in activities with foster grandparents. A third was offered no special stimulation. At the end of the test period the research team could find no differences among the abilities of the three groups. The study thus questions whether Doman really gets some children to do something out of the ordinary—or just sooner. For example, as Dr. Elkind has pointed out, "The issue is not learning to read early, but learning to enjoy reading."

What, then, to do? Whiz kid or woe? How does one balance the demands of the scholastic marketplace with emotional well-being? Unfortunately there are no simple solutions. But it might help to pause and consider whether outstanding intellectual accomplishment is really that important at such an early age.

Parents might also question whether it is their *own* self-esteem that hinges on which school the child attends. An unusually close identification with that child's achievements or failures was a constant pitfall that I found afflicting high-achieving parents. For instance, would that child really be at a disadvantage by going to a less-prestigious nursery or elementary school? It might also be a good time to begin to question whether the child needs to achieve in the same manner as the parent in order to lead a fulfilling, productive, and happy life, or whether the development of other traits and goals, such as the pursuit and mastery of a creative talent, might not be equally or even more fulfilling, especially for the youngster who is clearly not comfortable in a highly competitive environment. And we can also ask if being relaxed and joyful and good with others might not be equally important "achievements." For these attributes are also critical to professional and personal success later in life.

The parents I met also seemed curious to know if—bearing all this in mind—there were ways to separate positive pressure that could challenge and stretch a child from the excessive sort that creates emotional problems. Time and again the experts have insisted that it is often as simple as carefully watching that child to see when excitement turns to fatigue, and to be responsive to those cues. For instance, reading to a child or finding interesting places to visit is an obvious way to stimulate learning. But insisting that the child sit still and listen long after attention has waned—or that child has lost interest in the place he or she is visiting—may turn such opportunities into occasions to be feared and even resisted. "A truly gifted and talented child will lead *you*," said Dr. Elkind.

## TOYS

A further issue that possibly needs evaluating and exploring at this early stage is the question of overabundance—too many toys, too many expensive gifts, a desire that is too readily satisfied because a parent is tired (and it becomes so much easier to say yes than no).

Audrey Rosenman, a therapist who counsels private school youngsters and their parents, has found that boredom sets in sooner—not later—when there is a constant influx of new toys. The barrage also robs the child of the warmth of "favorite things" by blunting that child's ability to feel in a caring way. "These children are never forced to make a real connection," she said. "There is no point in working to master one toy if another one is right there waiting to be picked up. How can a child learn to care about something, anything—like an old teddy bear—if he knows a new one will always be put in its place if it gets broken or lost?" That lack of depth, say psychologists, can translate into a difficulty in forming caring relationships later on—something that Dr. Miles, the Washington child psychiatrist, has also found in younger children who have faced a constant turnover of caregivers, especially when the father and mother's involvement was minimal. It can also lead to problems with "frustration tolerance"—the self-defeating trait whereby a person repeatedly abandons a venture, friend, or course of study the minute a problem or hurdle begins to surface.

Ironically, these children are also being cheated out of the ecstasy that follows a long wait for something very special—like counting up the days to that moment when they will get a shiny new bicycle. They also never get to learn much about tolerating and surviving loss. "How can you ever really feel grief and mourning if you know whatever you lose will be instantly replaced?" asks Dr. Sanger, the early-childhood specialist. Thus using gifts as a metaphor for love and time devoted to that child may actually be harmful. Dr. Sanger has also found that too many gifts given out of guilt set both sides up for defeat: the child does not necessarily see that constant cascade as an expression of love and caring; meanwhile, the parent expects a level of gratitude and adulation that the child does not comprehend to be a part of the deal.

"Instant gratification may be the worst thing you can do for a child," said Ms. Rosenman.

Since we saw from the previous chapter that self-esteem, that fragile but critical ingredient in a well-balanced personality, may come less easily to these children than most—because they are likely to consider themselves inadequate in comparison to the super-achieving parent or because of the excessive attention seemingly given to everything else in the parent's life—special care may need to be taken right from the start to bolster self-esteem whenever possible. Some suggestions include:

- Give a child plenty of opportunity to succeed at small endeavors. Let that child make his or her own peanut butter sandwich, even if it makes a mess. Give small responsibilities that are age-appropriate, like filling the water bowl for the dog each day.
- Rearrange the house so the child can manage without the constant assistance of an adult. Put a stool in the bathroom so he or she can reach the wash basin. Add a towel rail at the child's level. Put cereal boxes and some bowls in a low kitchen cabinet. Encourage the independence that this arrangement affords.
- Arrange for the child to get up about half an hour earlier than normal at least two mornings a week so he or she has enough time to make it through the morning dressing routine without assistance.
- Start a pattern of formal family meals—only on weekends at the beginning, if that is all that is possible. But try to include several weekday evening meals, too, when you are not too late, so the

youngster feels a part of your daily routine. And make it a time for talking about family matters together (even a baby can participate by observing from a highchair or infant seat).

- Praise every small achievement. Praise and praise again. Find at least one praiseworthy item to mention each day even if everything else has been a disaster ("I liked the way you placed those napkins" instead of "How come you always forget the salt?"). But remain sincere. A child quickly sees through hypocrisy.

- Emphasize the positive accomplishments and avoid highlighting the child's shortcomings, much in the manner that you avoid continual criticism of a subordinate or employee. If the child gets more attention from the parent for the good rather than the bad, he or she will be more interested in continuing the positive behavior and gain self-confidence.

- Treat even the smallest child with the same courtesy you would give an important client or superior. The way they hear you speak to them is the way they will speak to others. If plans must be canceled, set up another date to show you care. Explain. Mumbling something suspect like "I had to work late at the office" can be as devastating and deflating for a child as it always is for a spouse.

- Avoid expressing criticism in terms of the way the child's behavior may be jeopardizing your professional or social life. For instance, instead of saying, "Hurry up, I have an important meeting to go to this morning," put it another way. Try saying, "See who can get dressed first—you or me!" Or make it into a game, perhaps a race.

- Avoid comparing your child with a sibling or a neighbor's child in a negative way. ("How come you can't write as neatly as John?") It reinforces fears that he or she is not measuring up and lessens interest and eagerness in trying to master the skill.

- Take a few minutes to ask about any project or drawing that is brought home from play group or nursery school. Why was it done? How was it made? Hang the best of them on a wall—somewhere, anywhere. Stacy O'Donnell, the executive recruiter mentioned in the first chapter, had her small daughters' drawings professionally framed and mounted for her downtown office (where they look surprisingly like designer items).

- Try to drop off or pick up your child from play group or nursery school at least a few times each week. The child can proudly "show off" the parent and begin to feel more important.

- If you are looking for an activity you can do together, do not rely upon shopping or going to movies since these are not activities that promote closeness. Instead, try hiking, swimming, fixing something together (like cooking or painting a fence). Read a story out loud. Even without a lot of conversation these activities breed warm memories and a sense of caring.
- If there are several siblings in the house, take one out alone at least once a month for a really special evening—dinner at a restaurant or overnight in another city. If a new baby comes into the house make the older sibling part of the process with small jobs. And continually remind that older child that he or she is as special as the new baby.
- Have you hugged your child today?

# The Middle Years

# 8.

# Telling It Like
# They See It

"When you live somewhere like this you want to believe you can stay here forever." The eight-year-old redhead with the ponytail twisted her slight frame around in the Windsor chair. She continued: "You can go surfing. You can go horseback riding. You belong to the beach club. When you picture yourself older you don't picture yourself struggling. You already have everything. You have the best job, the best home . . . but really it's scary because maybe it isn't true and you might have to struggle. And you don't know what it's like down there . . . struggling . . . and maybe if you can't keep up that's what will happen to you. . . ."

We are sitting in a cozy living room of a private house late on a Sunday afternoon. There are four children in the room of varying ages, two boys and two girls. We had gathered together to talk about what it is like to spend your childhood in a Garden of Eden. It was one of dozens of encounters I would have with youngsters from fast-track households throughout the months that I was working on this book. We met in private houses, in skyscraper apartments, in church halls, in school classrooms, on the bleachers in sports fields, in the offices of counselors, and occasionally even on a one-to-one basis in the privacy of my own home or theirs.

The children represented a wide cross-section of parental occupations and incomes. All had parents who made a substantial amount of money or had incomes bolstered by family wealth. The youngsters were growing up in various parts of the country—the Northeast, Midwest, the West Coast, the South. Their ages ranged from ten to sixteen years old. (Later I would talk to older adolescents and young adults.)

Their parents' occupations ran the gamut—corporate executive, investment banker, entrepreneur, physician, mental health professional, college professor, lawyer, real estate developer and broker.

Some of the children were as competitive and high-achieving as their parents. Their enthusiasm and optimism for the future seemed infectious. Others were more cynical, complaining their subculture represented a distortion of all that was good in the human spirit by worshiping status and success beyond all other qualities. Still others were having difficulty coping academically and socially with standards and expectations that seemed overwhelming. Whatever their age or perspective it became crystal clear from the outset that regardless of all that the parents might or might not do for these children or how sensitively they structured home life, the attitudes, expectations, and values of peers and society at large played as significant a role in shaping their outlook and image of themselves, from a relatively young age, as the happenings in the home. Listening to them describe their lives became in itself a way to begin to learn how to create a more hospitable environment.

Take, for example, the impact of moving into a fast-track community. It may seem like a dream come to life for the parent, but it can be daunting for the child who may be faced with competing with a seemingly endless array of super-achieving kids, many of whom are also exceedingly good-looking.

Take Lisa (a pseudonym), a pudgy girl with liquid brown eyes and unkempt, choppy hair. She wore the obligatory stone-washed jeans and monogramed polo shirt. But there were little bags and sags in all the wrong places. "We came to this town when I was six," she began. "Before that everything seemed okay. But when I got here it seemed like you had to be a superstar to be accepted. And I was just a regular kid, not even very beautiful. I never got very good grades either. Suddenly it became very important for me to get those grades and do all the 'right' things and look right if I wanted friends. I remember in fourth grade when we all got to pick instruments. I wanted to play the drums. It seemed like fun. But my parents wanted me to get the strings as they mean, well, you're the best. So I was given violin lessons even though the teachers told them I was tone-deaf."

Competition rather than cooperation seems to characterize many of their friendships, making it difficult to unload vulnerabilities and weaknesses to friends or enjoy close bonding. "I had a friend in math class," said a sixteen-year-old boy, "and we would always keep track of who did the best, all through the year. Usually we were about the same. But whenever he did better than me he would always rub it in. How could I talk to him about how I really felt?"

Clearly, the kids were constantly struggling to maintain an edge over their peers (just as they saw their parents doing?). "From the first day I went to school it was, like . . . everyone was trying to put everyone else down," said a thirteen-year-old girl who looked like she had jumped out of a glossy ad for designer jeans. "It became a habit. You found yourself doing it even with your best friend."

Then there were those who seemed thrilled by the excitement and challenge of their privileged lives and could not get enough. "When you see that you are starting halfway up the ladder you know it's going to be easier," admitted one boy. "You know you will have someone behind you in case you mess up . . . I know I'm luckier than most. And I'm going to go for as much as I can get."

Burnout was an ever-present threat. Many spoke of having too much to do each day although they seemed torn, sensing they'd be out of step if they slowed down. "I feel panicky when everything starts to pile up," said a rather plump boy. "Take tonight. I've got chess club. Then swim team. Then some homework to do. Sometimes I'm so tired I forget things. All I want to do is sleep. But when my mom says to give up something I think about what I might miss. I like to experiment with lots of things, be like everyone else. . . ."

Comparison with siblings seemed inevitable among them all, with achievement the only currency that counted in many of the homes. "I have two older sisters, each very different," a ninth-grade girl confided. "The oldest is a super-achiever. Everyone's always saying how great she is. The next one is an artist. She can draw anything. But her grades aren't so great. And she feels it. I think creative people often get lost in these sorts of places. . . ."

There were also poignant tales of high achievement being so much a part of parental expectations for these youngsters that nothing was ever good enough and there was very little praise—just criticism when they did not perform as required. "By the time I was in eighth grade I'd become the local chess champion," a scholarly young boy told me. "I was constantly bringing home trophies. But I never remember either of my parents congratulating me. Instead my mother told me the trophies were ugly. And she made me keep them in my room."

Early on, the youngsters also seemed to absorb an accurate reading of parental expectations, despite what might be said to the contrary. "You have to be careful what you say you want to be when you grow up," a seventh-grade girl told me. "Your parents say they will support you in anything you want to be. But when my sister said she wanted to be a jockey my parents made it very hard on her. They made jokes in front of her. . . ."

"But you want so much to do something for yourself, by yourself, without your parents being involved, even if it's selling used cars," noted the boy sitting alongside her, interrupting, and beginning to articulate the dichotomy that seemed to permeate all their lives. "A part of you wants to be totally different than your parents. But another part wants to be just like them because they have such a nice life. . . ."

"But if you try and argue and say you want something your way they immediately say, 'Look how I turned out. I know!' And what do you say to that," acknowledged the girl sitting across the table. And with that she began talking about the frustration, frequently expressed, of trying to make any headway with individuals who always seemed to have all the answers *and* the results to prove the correctness of their vision.

Quite a number did not seem as proud of their parents' success as the parents might have expected. Rather, they feared its toll. Said one boy, "My father never has any fun. Maybe he's a big lawyer. He's made a lot of money. But I don't want to be like him. I want to experience other things. When I grow old I would rather have lived a good life than become very important."

Nor could possessions alone make up for lack of expressions of love and affection. "Perhaps making a lot of money isn't so important," sighed a girl whose parents were on the verge of breaking up. "I have a friend whose family doesn't have much. But there's so much love in that house it's wonderful . . . just to be there. I often wonder what it would be like to live there."

Clearly these children were facing a multitude of concerns. Yet, as I was soon to find out, none were insurmountable provided care was taken to acknowledge their difficulties inside or outside the home, provisions were made to assist where assistance was clearly warranted, and attempts were made to be sensitive to their fears and needs. Often all that was demanded was more time to listen, an honest look at the world from the child's viewpoint, some good old TLC, and a little confidence-building instead of criticism at low moments.

# 9.

# Building
# Family Life

If there was one theme that constantly emerged from my conversations with the children it was a surprising undercurrent of aloneness—feelings of isolation from peers as well as parents despite their busy lives. This was certainly not true of all of them or all of the families. But it did suggest that family time was important to a majority of them—the sharing and the caring.

Certain parents I met were clearly worried about this and had taken quite dramatic action. Having one parent work from home, even if it was only for part of each day or week, was a favorite (and statistically growing) option. Between 8 and 11 million people were running offices from their homes by 1988, according to the National Association of Home-Based Businesses, up 30 percent since 1970.

Among fast-track people this was clearly easier if that parent was a professional, such as a lawyer, college professor, accountant, or consultant, rather than a corporate executive. Others had found it more practical to lock in family time by purchasing a weekend home—a place where the family would be brought into closer contact with one another, physically and mentally removed from the responsibilities that kept them apart during the week. In this chapter we will be looking at a number of ideas such families have worked out for spending time together, despite their heavily scheduled lives.

Some of the children's difficulties pursuing peer friendships were clearly due to the geography of communities where they lived. In many places the houses were set as far apart as befitted half-million or million-dollar homes. And until these children reached driving age it was nearly impossible to hang around with friends unless prior arrangements had been made and there was someone willing and available to do the driving. The traditional "kid down the block" was simply not there. Even in higher-density, high-rise settings like the Upper East Side of Manhattan, the gathering of friends after school was rarely ad hoc (at least for younger children) as safety on the streets became the big issue. Those attending private school faced further obstacles. Private institutions tend to draw from a wider geographic area than public schools, so it is harder to get together with a friend who lives in the next town, or even on the other side of town. Nor did it help, some of them told me, that friends were seen as competitors and therefore often best kept at an emotional distance.

Adding to the sense of being on one's own much of the time was the fact that there was often nobody in the house until the dinner hour or even later, once the children had passed the age (usually about eight or nine) where a babysitter was needed. I found this confirmed by a study of 60,000 households undertaken by the National Institute of Child Health and Human Development in 1987. That study found—surprisingly—the largest measure of unsupervised children among wealthier and better-educated families. And when the parents did come home they often seemed so worn out and hassled they were almost unapproachable. Kenneth Howard, head of clinical psychology at Northwestern University, added yet another reason for that sense of aloneness—a tendency among such families to lead separate leisure lives rather than arrange family outings as had been the pattern a generation or two ago.

Yet another factor that seemed to contribute to personal isolation was distance—geographical, cultural, and economic—from the extended family. One of the hallmarks of high-achievers is that they can normally afford to move into a town or neighborhood that is far too expensive for relatives or parents with considerably more modest achievements. The setting may even intimidate those relatives. Thus high-achievers create, in a way, a diaspora of like, kind, and quality rather than one based upon family or ethnic grouping. In sum, such an environment seemed to lack the natural support systems that normally act as a buffer for a child from the hurts, setbacks, and normal tribulations of growing up.

As a result—and this may be particularly necessary for younger children—parents may need to make a conscious effort to build parent surrogates as well as family time. Studies of resiliency in children have shown time and again that the consistent emotional support of at least one loving adult can help them overcome all sorts of chaos and deprivation. Parents may also need to create opportunities for the casual kind of nurturing friendships that are not tied to a structured activity where a child feels in competition with his or her peers. In short: redesign family life.

Here are some of the ideas I gathered from parents and the professionals who counsel them. I have separated them into two sections. The first shows ways to build an extended network of kin and other support people to give the child a sense of belonging to more than just a nuclear family; the second examines ideas that parents themselves might act upon.

It may be possible to build a broader family network by drawing more fully upon:

*Grandparents.* Once upon a time grandmothers and grandfathers came with predictable images: she was that wrinkled old lady who loved to cook, and he was that bent-over old gentleman who had trouble making himself understood. No more. Better educated, better looking, better off, and far more likely to be in good health throughout a child's growing-up years, they can be wonderful resources even if they are not living over the river and through the woods. Distance does not have to spell deprivation.

Grandparents give a child a sense of roots and the idea of being part of a continuum. My own children have grown up very close to their grandparents even though they live in London. We do not jet over for the weekend. But through repeated visits over summers, special family events, and holidays they have developed a sense of being part of an ethnic group they would otherwise have never known.

Grandparents are great for a child's self-esteem because they tend not to be judgmental. Who else is convinced you are marvelous even when you are having fights with parents and perhaps not behaving as you should? Grandparents (even today's kind who often have more crowded calendars than people half their age) may take children on trips and to places the parents are not anxious to go. Grandparents may be persuaded to do something wonderfully old-fashioned like write regular letters to a grandchild. Or they could be encouraged to send tapes telling about their lives or even family tales. Grandparents can even be "reached out and touched" (as the telephone company loves to remind us) by phone without parental intervention if the idea is fostered. Grandparents can replace parents at school events. "On many occasions Grandpa Fitzgerald stepped in, faithfully appearing in the stands for their games in school," writes Doris Kearns Goodwin in *The Fitzgeralds and the Kennedys*—the Kennedys, of course, being one of the early examples of fast-track parents. Grandparents often have very different lifestyles and interests. Thus the world of the grandparents can become real-life education.

Dr. Harold Bloomfield, a psychiatrist in Del Mar, California, who studied the interaction of adult children and parents for his book *Making Peace with Your Parents,* found that too often grandparents are kept at a distance because their children have not yet come to terms with the resentments left over from their own childhood. "You lose out on a lot of goodies if you are not prepared to accept the fact that some friction and tension may come with it all," he says. A young couple who are both practicing physicians admitted this to me. They were troubled by the fact that one of the grandmothers always likes to bring expensive toys when she visits their two preschoolers. But in the end they accepted the trade-off for the companionship and sense of belonging that grandparents provided. They also found that the involvement of the grandparents was valuable as an extra source of support for the caregiver—to drive a child over to a friend's house, for instance, or to help out with an errand.

What may therefore be required, said Dr. Bloomfield, is to work on a conscious strategy of involvement—what he calls "family life by appointment"—in which both sides openly discuss and negotiate the type of role a particular grandparent might best play. Ditto for aunts, uncles, cousins.

*Sisters or brothers.* The youngsters in several of my focus groups mentioned the value of the companionship and genuine help they had gained from older siblings. These were contemporaries who really understood life from their viewpoint. These were older people conveniently under the same roof whom they could approach for advice and even a ride, if that older sibling was of driving age. Though some parents are uneasy with this sort of arrangement it should not be lightly discarded. The older sibling certainly learns responsibility and passes along the idea that the children in a family should not always be on the receiving end—they should be helping one another out.

*Religion.* Close ties to a parish or congregation are family indeed, providing a strong attachment as well as underscoring those roots (despite a child's groaning to the contrary). "Rose established certain times of days as constants . . . including shared religious exercises . . . which she deemed essential for the maintenance of a secure, ongoing home life," writes Goodwin in her Kennedy book. A similar respect for the cohesive as well as ethical value of religious ties and the balm of ritual permeates the childhood tales of the Rockefeller family—a dynasty that has had remarkable success providing society with successive generations of valuable, achieving individuals despite its wealth and prominence.

*Coaches, private teachers, helpers.* Stories of families that have been well off for generations are also replete with tales of the value of such an adult to the general development of the child. These families saw the value in encouraging friendships beyond the lesson. You can, too. A piano teacher told me how one of her students would linger after the lesson was over. The girl clearly needed to unburden herself in a private setting where she had no need to impress anyone—not the teachers at schools, not her friends, not even her parents. Eventually the teacher started taking her along to concerts, on occasion, and also inviting her to stay for dinner. Even when the girl grew older and left for college she would enjoy coming back, "just to visit and say hello," said the teacher.

*Pets.* A dog, cat, or other animal provides a home with life and warmth when nobody else is around. And who else provides quite as exuberant a welcome and is never moody? A pet also teaches responsibility.

*Reciprocity.* Some parents have early schedules; others work late. A recruiter in Philadelphia said she had great success forming a reciprocal arrangement with a friend who works in the local school system. That woman finishes her day very early and so takes in the recruiter's children late in the afternoon. The recruiter starts her day relatively late and so can see those children off to school with her own. Going back to a house where there is a mother and other children on a regular schedule, even a few times a week, may be better than coming home alone or attending an after-school program. Having a housekeeper around late in the afternoon can also help. One woman in Maryland told me how she arranged to have her housekeeper start late and stay late just to be sure someone was around well into the evening, even though the children were already in middle school and perfectly capable of looking after themselves. Caution: after-school activity programs may solve the problem of leaving a child alone. But they rarely substitute for the closeness of being around family or surrogate family members for at least part of each day.

Parents can themselves help build that warmer family life, despite the seemingly impossible odds, with just minor modifications to their usual schedules and habits. Among ideas I gathered:

*Phone contact.* Though it may appear a poor substitute, the telephone can be a valuable tool for keeping in touch with a child's world at key times during the day—provided the emphasis is upon maintaining interest in the happenings in the child's life rather than just a checkup that everything is okay. It also lets a child unload a fear, a hurt, or a triumph while it is still fresh. If feasible, it may be useful to teach that child as early as possible how to reach you at the office.

*Travel.* If the job or career requires regular and lengthy travel, some thoughtful preplanning can help alleviate that pit-in-the-stomach aloneness a child may feel when a parent is not around. Dr. Bettie Youngs, the writer on children and stress, recommends leaving a "trail of access" every time to ameliorate the fear of the unknown and sense of abandonment that can occur. This might include a written itinerary that lets a child known where he or she can reach you each day, a steady stream of daily postcards with the implied message "I'm thinking of you," a regular phone call at a prearranged hour that brings the child up-to-date on your travels and lets that child visualize your surroundings (but diplomatically avoids being turned into "grilling hour" when the child has to give an account of homework or grades). Or the child can be taken along occasionally—something a Connecticut lawyer told me he has been doing for fifteen years. "I choose a resort-style hotel," he said, "where they can stay independently by the pool for several hours. Or I take them with me to a client's office where we can usually find something for them to do." If necessary, in the evenings, he hires hotel babysitters or has his children spend time with a client's children. Other parents create a going-away ritual like a dinner at a favorite restaurant the night before departure as a way of saying, "I will miss you, so it's important we spend time together before I go."

A word of warning: even with the best of planning do not expect a warm welcome upon return. The child may still feel sufficiently deprived so that he or she tries to express that displeasure in a way that seems to a parent like rejection—refusing to be kissed, not budging from that television show. This *is* rejection. The child is simply returning in kind the treatment he or she believes was received from the parent. And it does no good to explain how important the journey was. It only makes the child feel even less important—certainly less valuable than the task that took the parent away. Bringing back a gift may also be counterproductive. It sets up unrealistic expectations of gratitude that the child cannot feel.

*Reentry.* One of the most brittle moments can be the arrival of that parent at home each evening. Like that moment of return from an out-of-town business trip, the child may have built up some resentment of the lengthy absences, especially if the parent is consistently late home each evening. That child may therefore need a "quick fix." A suburban mother who spent years commuting to Manhattan confided that home life became much smoother after she stopped rushing into the bathroom upon returning home each night and acknowledged that "at least the first ten minutes" needed to be set aside for the children to unload. If, however, her children happened to be engrossed in TV or on the telephone she also stopped expecting them to get up just because she walked in. Instead she would touch them on the shoulder lightly as a gesture of affection, acceptance, and contact. And she would always try to show respect and caring by calling ahead if she was delayed, rather than simply by showing up an hour or two later than expected.

In a foreword to Dr. Stephen Hersh's book *The Executive Parent,* T. Berry Brazelton, the Harvard Medical School pediatrician, talks about the value of having the parent recount tales of his or her day upon returning at night. After telling how much he enjoyed seeing this sort of sharing at the home of Dr. Hersh, Dr. Brazelton noted that it also made the child feel a part of the parent's life rather than an outsider. From the child's viewpoint what may seem dull to the parent may, in fact, sound like yet another juicy episode in the real-life soap opera ("How the Office Turns"?). If, in the process, the child begins to pick up some career skills and a deeper understanding of the dynamics of a parent's profession or business, so much the better. That child may form a closer bond with the parent—and become better informed

*Rituals.* It may also be important to designate a consistent pattern of "at home" nights (off limits for meetings or other-than-emergency business calls) or a certain hour set aside for listening to the child. One parent I met felt it was particularly important not to let a child of any age go to bed without having been able to talk over a problem, since it seemed somehow to loom larger overnight. Others insisted upon a family meal once each day where a sharing of one another's lives in a nonjudgmental way was the staple on the menu. "At our family meal everyone is given a chance to talk about what happened that day," the senior editor of a woman's magazine told me. "We take turns. Even the little one is included," she added, referring to her six-year-old son. That meal does not even have to be at home. Taking even young children out to eat is a growing trend. The number of children under six patronizing restaurants other than fast-food chains rose 43 percent between 1982 and 1986, according to the National Restaurant Association.

Encouraging young children to write a diary each day is another way of keeping in closer touch because the child will begin to discuss what has happened as the words are being put down. This has been the experience of one Asian-American mother I met. The mother is a social scientist, her husband is a college professor. Their six children have all had outstanding academic records. Among them the children have four Harvard degrees, two MIT degrees, one Yale degree, and two Radcliffe degrees. Because of her exemplary record as the mother of scholars and the exceptional way she had handled the pressures of a two-career family, officials at the U.S. Department of Education invited her to give some advice at their 1988 conference on Education and the Family. In the paper she prepared she talked about those journals. "It was a valuable way to teach and share ideas with our children," she wrote, even though it was "time-consuming." The mother also underscored the importance of the family meal, although she and her husband chose to have everyone rise extra early for a sitdown family breakfast. That breakfast meal was a moment when everyone, in turn, was invited to lead morning prayers out loud, including the children. And through those prayers, she said, she often learned about the joys, frustrations, and worries her children were facing—emotions that might not otherwise have been voiced.

Occasionally it may also help to let the child visit your office or become part of a business or research project. (In my own life I remember having a lot of fun when I was running for elective office in England. My children helped me sort and fold flyers.) Psychologists say it is important to do so because it shows a child you enjoy your work and your lifestyle. Otherwise they may resent that work or even shy away from following in your footsteps because all they see is the toll it has taken by the end of the day—not the excitement, sense of accomplishment, or fulfillment that makes all that effort so worthwhile.

The Asian-American mother emphasized this. One of the steps she took was to encourage her children to take a leadership role in helping the older generation understand young people and vice versa within a friendship group she and her husband founded for Asians living in the United States. She and her husband also set up a pattern of regular family meetings, with each child given the opportunity to convene and lead the meeting in rotation. "The meeting also served the purpose of allowing each member of the family to voice his or her opinions, reach joint decisions, and participate in family responsibilities," she explained to participants at the conference. "Thus the importance of communication and the cohesion which is often a result of communication were introduced to them at an early age." For private chats she found it useful to give each child a turn at helping prepare the evening meal with her. Cutting the children's hair at home (originally begun because of lack of time and money) became another much-cherished, one-on-one family ritual between mother and child.

In sum: the aim is to find a way to make sure the child is not inadvertently forced into silently carrying problems (or even triumphs) alone because there seems no ready access to the parent. And it is vital to build those access bridges before the child decides it is not even worth bothering to get through. Otherwise the communication gap can grow to the point where parent and child cease to really know each other—and that can lead to bitterness, misunderstandings, and alienation.

*Siblings.* Any family of high-achievers that wants to stay close may have to be especially sensitive to the needs of the least-accomplished member of that family. In addition to comparing their own meager accomplishments with those of their parents, such children also feel excruciating pressure from their peers. "I have seen them become so discouraged," noted Elaine Mazlish, co-author of *Siblings Without Rivalry.* "They feel inadequate. Some feel the family does not belong to them and they don't belong in the family."

"I worked with a lovely girl whose brother and sister were both Merit Scholars," recalled a senior counselor at a high school in suburban Chicago. "She could not keep up with them. She was more on a B level. She had such a difficult time because the model was so high. It took several years of counseling before she understood why she felt so bad. This was so even though her parents hadn't pushed her."

Donald Trump, the developer, mentions the same problem in his autobiography, *Trump: The Art of the Deal.* Speaking of his older brother, Freddy, he tells how fun-loving Freddy could never excel in business in the way their father had anticipated. Eventually Freddy became discouraged and drank heavily, dying at the age of forty-three. Writes Trump: "In many ways he had it all, but the pressures of our particular family were not for him. I only wish I had realized this sooner."

Listen, for example, to twelve-year-old Diane describe the feeling from personal experience. Dubbed a "space cadet" for her outrageous behavior and zany way of dressing, she clearly had a desperate need to stand out in some way—any way. The evening we met she was wearing gold rings on each of her fingers and heavy black mascara and eyeliner around her chestnut-brown eyes. Her white sneakers had no shoelaces.

The daughter of an electrical engineer and the owner of a small retail business, she was a member of a family of math whizzes. Both her brother and sister were brilliant math students. She was not. In fact, her grades all around were decidedly mediocre. "I felt like I had been cheated out of something," she said. "It was almost like I didn't deserve to belong to that family. Sometimes I feel that I don't. Honest. It's lonely. I feel frustrated. I remember one night my dad tried for two hours to help me with a math problem. I just couldn't get it. I went up to my bedroom and sat on my bed and cried. It makes you feel like you never want to be around people who are 'A' students because you feel so stupid. But you know? I have this feeling I have to stand out some way so my parents won't feel they missed out . . . like I have to make it up to them for not being good at school."

Thus it is no wonder that so many less able siblings often end up dressing or acting in an outrageous way by the time they move into adolescence—the most common stories being told about those who gravitate toward the world of blue-collar stereotypes: riding motorcycles, wearing leather clothes with studs. When you think about it, it is the obvious way for them to distinguish themselves and place a safe distance between their own lives and family values that somehow do not work for them.

In addition to that search for the area where the less able sibling can feel accomplished, parents may need to caution more gifted siblings that they must not taunt a brother or sister with their achievements— not say things like, "See, I bet you couldn't do that!" The interaction could even become an important lesson in compassionate behavior and the richness of individual differences. One mother I met would regularly make a pattern of complimenting a less-able sister on something she had done well, whenever her older daughter, highly accomplished academically and also an athlete, brought home yet another award. She would use everyday occurrences—such as how much care the less-able sister had been taking lately with her appearance or something praiseworthy a friend or relative might have said about her.

*Discipline.* The busy parent with heavy career obligations faces a formidable challenge trying to monitor or impose discipline while away from home. And too often a failure to make it work and the resulting buildup of resentment on both sides only increase the chasm between parent and child. With school-age children this usually means the maintenance of standards and expectations without adult supervision, since by this age babysitting is usually over. If there are still babysitters, the same rules should apply as with early childhood caregivers: the helper needs to be given a detailed briefing of the way the household operates and the kind of behavior that is not tolerated, as well as the disciplinary measures that will be imposed if the child gets out of line. Maintaining a consistent pattern is less confusing for a child. It also avoids mislabeling the child disobedient when in actual fact the child is unsure of how to behave because there have been so many different standards. Moreover, the child should be reminded that the caregiver has been instructed by the parent, since this adds clout and thus is more likely to minimize behavioral problems while the parent is absent.

Dr. Bernard Guerney, professor of human development at the University Park campus of Pennsylvania State University, has found that with an older child it helps to leave precise instructions. "Don't just say, 'I want your room cleaned up by the time I get home,' " said Dr. Guerney. "The child's idea of clean might be very different from yours. And that starts the arguments. Say instead, 'I want the clothes in the hamper, the bed made, and the records in the rack.' " If the chores and obligations have been fulfilled satisfactorily do not ignore that compliance. "Show your appreciation," suggested Dr. Guerney. "Say how good it feels." In short: show the child he or she can get as much or more parental attention for compliance than for a transgression.

If, however, the required job has not been done, or the child has disobeyed instructions, try to hold back your rage and listen to the excuse before erupting in a storm of abuse. "Perhaps there was a good reason and you need to change the contract a bit," said Dr. Guerney, referring to the agreement that might have been worked out concerning what should have been accomplished while the parent was absent.

Incentives coupled with removal of privileges also seem to work well. A university faculty couple with an eleven-year-old boy told me how pleased they had become with the effectiveness of posting a "job list" on the front of the refrigerator. The paper provided spaces where the boy could check off the items as they were accomplished. Rules were as follows: full compliance would result in full pocket money at the end of the week. Each item missed cut down that amount by twenty cents. "He's at an age where he wants that money for tapes and baseball cards," said the mother, "so it works well." Checking the veracity of the sign-off sheet was no problem, she said, as the jobs were easily traced. This idea also helps begin to tie money or goodies to the work ethic, something Old Money families have always been keenly aware of the need to foster.

It is usually more effective if a child knows specifically, in advance, the kind of gains that could be won or losses of privilege that would be jeopardized for noncompliance. "It's what I call the Golden Rule mode," added Dr. Sanger, who also recommends a trade-off program for older children—"the kind that implies, 'You like me to fulfill your expectations of me, like buying special clothes or taking you out,' " he said. " 'So how about your fulfilling some of mine?' "

*Community obligation.* "In my younger and more vulnerable years," writes Fitzgerald in *The Great Gatsby,* "my father gave me some advice I've been turning over in my mind ever since. 'Whenever you feel like criticizing anyone,' he told me, 'just remember that all the people in the world haven't had the advantages you have.' " That idea, together with a sense of obligation toward those less fortunate people, has traditionally been started early on in wealthy families, and is as applicable whether the money was made a generation ago or is only now being earned. It can be as simple as remembering to explain why you contribute time or money to various causes or serve on a board, or by encouraging the child to do his or her share, even in a small way, through a school, church, or community venture, especially if you can persuade them to use some of their pocket money for such a purpose now and then.

Writing to his grandson, Steven, on his tenth birthday, which fell in April 1945, John D. Rockefeller, Jr., enclosed a check along with some even more valuable insights. "Money is a useful thing to have," he told the boy, as recounted in *The Rockefellers,* by Collier and Horowitz. "You can buy candy with it and tops and marbles and boats . . . But it has other uses. When there are children who are hungry or who need clothes or who have no homes, it helps to get for them what they need . . . you will enjoy the tops and marbles much more when you have given something to another boy who has less than you."

Actual participation can also be valuable. An eleven-year-old girl told me how she loved to go along when her mother regularly visited certain old people as part of a community volunteer program. It felt so good, said the girl, to see the pleasure these visits seemed to give. Such concern or giving also helps build an important sense of purpose for the child, another way to enhance self-esteem. Studies of the super-rich show time and again that those involved in philanthropy—especially those who give their efforts rather than just their dollars—feel far better about themselves.

*Down time.* Finally, do not forget to fold in plenty of "down time"— the unstructured time when a child can unwind, much as a parent needs to unwind, for a certain number of hours each day. The more obsessive youngsters may even have to be coaxed to do so. Without down time, the teachers warned me, children never learn how to amuse themselves, never figure out what it takes to unwind (an inability that, by the teenage years, can lead to a reliance on harmful relaxants such as alcohol or drugs in order to make that transition), never develop their creative instincts free from the specter of adult judgment, never have time to develop a love of reading (the unassigned kind), never learn how to really have fun in an unmeasured setting, never have a chance to take a catnap or get extra sleep they so often need to recharge those batteries for that busy and demanding life. Were it not for "down time" for tinkering and dreaming, Henry Ford might never have dreamed up the Model T or Steve Jobs the personal computer.

But using the time to generate original thoughts and ideas should certainly not be the intent. On the contrary, it is important for a child to know that it is permissible and even important for the body and soul to do absolutely nothing once in a while, and not feel guilty for having "wasted" time. One mother I met was especially concerned that her own frantic, achieving lifestyle—"where I always seem to be doing three things at one time"—would give her three children the impression that it was important to be always on the go. So she began talking about her way of life to them, suggesting that it was not necessarily a good thing to be so busy too. "If I can't change the way I am so easily," she confessed to me, "at least I can tell my children why it may not be good to act the same way."

# 10.

# Thriving Through Those Golden Rule Days

Chatsworth, in the San Fernando Valley just outside Los Angeles, is an elegant residential town rimmed by the naked brown mountains of the surrounding desert. Horses graze lazily in fenced-in compounds. Exquisitely tended stucco homes, shielded from the street by giant palm trees and thick grasses, sport swimming pools and the ultra-neat flower gardens that exude a sense of wealth and privilege. Johnny Carson has a home here. This is also the valley that spawned the famous "valley girl" culture—a way of speaking, of dressing, and an attitude evocative of children who had a tad too much money to spend ("fer sure!").

In one corner of this golden oasis is the Sierra Canyon College Preparatory School, a six-acre campus of chocolate brown ranch-style buildings set amid a lawn so lush and green that it appears painted onto the desert landscape. Like dozens of other private schools that have sprouted in affluent suburbs throughout the United States in recent years, it grew out of the frustration of many upwardly mobile parents with the local public school system. Political in-fighting, a decline in academic standards, and a general malaise sent hundreds of these families fleeing to schools such as this one which offer small classes and glittering academic opportunities—in this instance from prekindergarten through sixth grade.

Indeed, one of the great joys of being a child of a fast-track parent is the exceptional education such a birth guarantees. If these children are not enrolled at the local private school at least they can be assured an education in one of the designer-label school districts of the nation, such as those in Scarsdale, Chappaqua, and Great Neck, New York; Greenwich, New Canaan, and Westport, Connecticut; Wellesley, Brookline, and Newton, Massachusetts; Fairfax County, Virginia; Beverly Hills, California; Grosse Point and Bloomfield Hills, Michigan; and New Trier in Winnetka, Illinois.

Thus these children are growing up more sophisticated, more cultured, and certainly more widely traveled than most of their parents at such a tender age—an early sophistication that unquestionably provides them with that critical edge, both socially and academically, when measured against peers from less advantaged backgrounds. "Those who rise to the occasion are becoming even more accomplished than ever in the past," the Reverend Mark Mullin, headmaster of St. Alban's, a prestigious private school in Washington, D.C., told me. "And often in a multitude of fields—an excellent lacrosse player, for example, who can also do magnificent carvings."

## CHOOSING SCHOOLS

Having the means to pay for private education or to buy a home in one of the outstanding public school districts of this nation also means that fast-track parents have more control over where and how their children will be educated than parents of lesser means. They can pick and choose even within the same family. They may find that the child with high academic potential and strong social talents may thrive in a top competitive public school or a well-known private school with a reputation for academic excellence. Another sibling, possibly more shy and less academically oriented, may be better off in the more sheltered atmosphere of a smaller, less competitively oriented school.

But though the parents may be intellectually aware of this, the hankering after the school with the prestigious name is powerful, right from the start, probably because peer pressure among the parents is so strong. But, curiously, the choice of school, at least in the elementary grades, may have less of an impact upon the future of that child than one might suspect. Certainly one fear can be put to rest: that the children in these communities tend to segregate themselves early according to the schools they attend. In the fast-track communities I visited I found little segmentation in fashionable neighborhoods among the children regardless of the schools they attended—public or private, highly prestigious or less well known. In the smaller towns where socioeconomic backgrounds tended to be similar they all seemed to know and feel perfectly at ease with one another.

Where possible, youngsters who clearly do not thrive on competition may do best choosing a school that has built-in protections against scorecards—at least for those elementary years. It allows such a child to gain self-confidence in a more relaxed atmosphere. The New Canaan Country School is one highly regarded school that does not grade a child until the middle of the eighth grade. Nicholas Thacher, the headmaster, has found that it is thus possible to shift the emphasis from competition with peers to an excitement with the progress of a child's own abilities, which is often healthier. "Teachers also become more precise in their written evaluations," he said.

If such a philosophy goes along with an excellent record of admissions to the top-flight schools on the next rung of the ladder, all well and good. If not, the school may unfortunately be shunned for the wrong reasons. In the fast-track parents' culture a school quickly gains status not by the nature of its program but based upon the kind of high school or university it feeds, something that these parents call a school's "track record." And too frequently, maintains Howard Greene, the private school consultant, parental choice is made based more upon that future potential than the program itself. And if the program is not right for the child, Greene has found, that child may be worse off in the end because he or she gets off to a start that seems so fraught with failure that the child loses interest and enthusiasm.

Greene is one of dozens of educational counselors who have begun offering a service that was relatively rare a decade ago—advice about independent education at all levels, from elementary to graduate schools. One group to which many of them belong is the Independent Educational Consultants Association in Forestdale, Massachusetts. Another is the National Association of College Admission Counselors in Skokie, Illinois.

This may therefore be an ideal moment to start to be honest about the differing talents and abilities of each child and begin to reevaluate educational goals accordingly. Those who can readily gain admission and cope with the curriculum and pressures of a highly competitive school should face little trouble in these families. By contrast I found that high-achieving parents seem to have particular difficulty in coming to terms with a child who cannot cope well in school, probably because a majority had been A-level students themselves and never knew what a nightmare it can be to know you may never be more than a second-rate student. It is a blind spot that can be likened to the trouble many highly intelligent people have always had coping with the shortcomings of anyone less able than themselves. ("If I haven't walked in your shoes," as the saying goes, "how can I feel your pain?") Teachers in particular expressed the concern that such parents often unwittingly do considerable damage to a child's self-esteem by labeling that child "lazy" or "stupid" before discovering (to their embarrassment and anguish) that the difficulty stems from a disability or simply a less stellar IQ than their own.

It might therefore create less tension all around to face the fact early on that not all children of fast-track parents are equally equipped for fast-track life themselves. Some may be creative types, or have a weight problem or a reading difficulty that suggests a less intense path. And if they can shine along that path while they are growing up—say, as an ace swimmer or in music—so much the better. They still have an accomplishment that can gain them accolades with parents and peers. Among high-achieving families this may be critical to self-image.

One East Coast family told me how they realized early on that one of their daughters would probably never be a super-achiever like her siblings. Anxious for her to develop some area that would bring her a sense of dignity and self-worth they discovered that she had a natural talent for playing the violin. They found an excellent music teacher who invited her to be part of a small ensemble. The performances made her feel special and gave her a unique standing in the family and at school. The parents did not expect her to become a famous musician—just develop the kind of self-confidence that would help her grow into a well-rounded adult.

Even so, remarkable achievements can emerge. Consider the childhood of Norman Rockwell, whose classic illustrations of American family life continue to brighten our lives. Rockwell was thin, poorly coordinated, and needed glasses and corrective shoes. His only sense of mastery came from his sketches. "All I had was the ability to draw," he later wrote in his autobiography, My Adventures as an Illustrator, "which as far as I could see didn't count for much. But because it was all I had I began to make it my whole life. Gradually my narrow shoulders, long neck, and pigeon toes became less important to me. My feelings no longer paralyzed me. I drew and drew and drew."

How can you tell if you are pushing your child into an area where he or she is not going to thrive? Naturally there are as many subtle differences as there are ways of smiling. Children blossom at different ages and stages. And they can change. But talks with educators and psychologists produced this outline that might help as a broad indicator for a child in the elementary years.

| CHILD WHO NATURALLY THRIVES ON COMPETITION AND AN ACTION-PACKED SCHEDULE | CHILD WHO FARES BETTER FOR THE MOMENT ON A LESS DEMANDING OR MORE CREATIVE TRACK |
| --- | --- |
| Fiercely independent and at ease with studies | Less academically gifted or more tuned into nonacademics like music |
| Highly coordinated | Clumsy |
| Ability to map out and keep to a schedule with little prompting | Not concerned about missing sessions or tardiness |
| Insists on being signed up for activities of his or her choice | Reluctant to participate to the point of rebellion |
| Able to balance a full schedule without showing signs of wear or tear | Constantly falling behind and feeling sick |
| Maintains good grades | Has trouble with schoolwork |

Greene constantly finds himself having to emphasize such variables to parents who come seeking guidance and help in placing their child in an appropriate school. Within minutes he says he frequently realizes that many have set their sights on a highly prestigious school, irrespective of whether the child will be happy or can handle the academic environment.

A visit to his office in Westport, Connecticut, one spring morning shows how it all occurs:

His office is a testimonial to aristocratic elegance. The obligatory Harvard degree hangs in a simple frame on the white wall. Windsor chairs, standing on an Oriental rug, are placed around a wooden sea chest that acts as a coffee table. Beams span the ceiling, interspersed with skylights that add sparkle to the room. At one end is a working fireplace decorated with an old milk churn. At the other stands his antique desk. Greene, a quiet-spoken, slender man in his fifties with salt-and-pepper hair, is sitting facing the desk in a high-backed chair, puffing on a pipe. The telephone has just rung. At the other end of the line is a mother frantic about her daughter.

"You *are* having problems?" says Greene. The tone is sympathetic. Someone speaks fast on the other end.

"Then I think you would fare much better with X school," suggests Greene.

Silence on the line.

"I know you feel that way about Y," continues Greene after the pause. "It's obviously a bigger, more diverse, and better-known school. But we are thinking about Beth. She will get what she needs in terms of structure and attention in a smaller school. The best that could happen for her right now is to go to X for at least a year. There will be children she knows. The program will be similar. Then she will be ready for the bigger institution. We have found she needs a lot of structure and support. We can count on that at X. If she goes to Y too soon she may not do all that well. Put your plans on hold for a while," he urges. "And I am saying that with the greatest respect.

"It is a big problem," says Greene, slowly replacing the receiver in its cradle. "The mother is feeling a lot of peer pressure. Her own self-esteem is at stake. She knows that child is having difficulty so she is also saying to herself, 'Am I doing the right thing or the wrong thing for my child?' Underneath she is feeling guilty. So I am helping her handle that guilt by saying, 'It's okay to have ambitions for your child. But let's take an easy strain. Maybe it's the way to make it work.

"It's a pity in a way," he continued. "In any other group this girl would have been just fine, not feeling like a failure. She is the sweetest little blond girl you ever saw. A sort of miniature Doris Day. She deserves to be voted the cutest girl on the block. A generation or two ago a family would have been thrilled to have a girl like this. Today she's got to get straight A's, too."

Some counselors have found it helps to let the child have a say in the ultimate decision on which school to attend, even at such a relatively young age. During a rap session I held with four Manhattan private school seniors who were high-achievers *and* very positive about their childhood experiences, one boy mentioned how good he felt when, at eleven years of age, his parents let him make the final choice between three schools they had preselected. After visiting all three and monitoring classes he chose one on the Upper East Side. "I felt it was 'my' school from the beginning," said the boy, a charming young man with porcelain-blue eyes, curly red hair, and freckles. "It made me feel proud of saying where I went. I was also determined to make it work for me." And he did: in his senior year he ended up president of the school's student government.

## THOUGHTS FOR SPORTS

Whatever school is chosen, the yearning for their children to become as outstanding in sports as in academics, right from the beginning, seems to be very strong among high-achieving parents. The same desire to maintain the competitive edge emerges. Moreover, sports creates stars. And wider recognition as a winner is important to such parents, whether for themselves or their offspring. That goal may obscure the fact that sports can offer a child other important lessons, too.

First, sports may be the ideal arena where a child can learn to value the process as much as the outcome. It is one of the fundamental lessons that seem to separate those who rise above their failures to become stronger and more likely to succeed (in their personal as well as professional lives) from those who are diminished by every setback. In their book, *When Smart People Fail,* Carol Hyatt and Linda Gottlieb dub those who value process "fireproof" people who are "able to pick themselves up and keep going after what others consider a defeat." This is because for them "the real joy, the real 'high' was ... the minute-by-minute, day-to-day quality of what they did, not its end results," they note.

But to do so the child must be in a sport that he or she loves for its own sake, insists Dr. Robert Goldman, chairman of the Sports Medicine Committee of the Amateur Athletic Union, the organization of competitive youth sports. And it might differ from the ones favored by the parent. That child, he said, must also know that the parent will neither mock nor become abusive whenever the youngster loses. Indeed, if the competition results in a loss the child should be encouraged to talk about his or her feelings, since that child has to face shame in front of peers as well as parents. Dr. Goldman suggests this might be a good moment to share one's own childhood sports memories of similar debacles.

Possibly the worst impression a parent can convey is a "win-or-else" attitude. It lessens the chances of enjoying the sport for its own sake, and certainly does not encourage the less able, or the faint-of-heart, to even dare to try. Sports may therefore be a perfect place to learn about coping with defeat in addition to savoring the thrill of winning. The trouble with growing up in a household with successful people is that defeat and failure tend to be viewed as disgraceful states, a subject that is taboo rather than an occurrence that enters everyone's lives at some point or another. Lack of that exposure appears to create some of those unrealistic expectations that later in life have been known to unhinge a child of fast-track parents. A psychologist in Southern California told me how he had coached one father, a navy jet pilot, to flounder purposely on some do-it-yourself projects around the house so the son could see how a disaster is not always a defeat. be a temporary setback as well as a way to learn.

Dr. Goldman has found that sports are especially good regard because the coach can point out some of the ways that ch might improve his or her performance to be in a better position to win another time. And when that win happens, the value of having gone through the defeat becomes even more apparent. The only people who never benefit from their failures, say the authors of *When Smart People Fail,* are those who refuse to examine the contributory factors and also refuse to acknowledge that they may have gained more in the long run by suffering the defeat since they are forced, as a result, to make needed adjustments. Failure, add the authors, also teaches compassion for others and humility—something privileged children of high-achievers are not confronted with very often in their daily lives.

Sports can also provide an excellent setting where parent and child can be together while both getting their workouts—say, by cross-country skiing or hiking with one another. Some of the newer preschool exercise groups have made this feature part of their marketing pitch, suggesting it is an ideal way for the harried parent juggling career and family to fit in more time with the child. All too true.

## MOTIVATION

Whether for sports or academics I was constantly bombarded by parents anxious to discover the magic secret of motivation. How indeed do you motivate a child to do well?

The best kind of motivation, teachers told me, seems to come from a learning environment that the child finds friendly and comfortable, neither boring at one end nor frightening and intimidating at the other. To want to succeed a child must know he or she can find success in everyday challenges and also be able to take some risks without being chastised for failing. "It also helps if the child has adults around— teachers, parents, counselors, private instructors—who seem genuinely interested in that youngster," said William Clarkson, headmaster at the Potomac School, a prestigious private school in McLean, Virginia. Exceptionally bright children with good self-images, he said, are motivated by environments where "they can soar."

Less academically gifted children or those with weaker egos thrive best when their "little talents" or abiding passions are applauded and fostered, like cartooning, acting, or a delight in raising animals—a fact

, published in 1986, of 700 children from the
...ai, directed by Emmy Werner, a psychologist at
...rnia at Davis.

...nt with the school also stimulates a desire in
...ccording to Laurence Steinberg, professor of
... at the University of Wisconsin. In 1988 Dr.
...,...ieu a comprehensive analysis of available literature
on the impact of parental attitudes on academic achievement. He found
that parents who maintained close ties with the school produced children with stronger academic records.

The MacArthur Foundation, an organization that regularly selects
individuals of extraordinary promise and gives each a grant of around
$40,000 a year for five years to pursue whatever projects they wish,
similarly conducted a study on what may contribute in childhood to
outstanding achievement. Support and encouragement from parents
were mentioned consistently—not necessarily demands for superior
standards.

The same conclusions were reached by researchers at the Stanford
University Center for the Study of Families, Children and Youth which
has also been looking into the way family behavior affects academic
achievement. "Only encouragement appears to be associated with
higher grades," wrote the center's director, Professor Sanford Dornbusch, in an early draft of the team's findings prepared for the 1988
U.S. Department of Education conference on education and the family.
"Parents expressing negative emotions and being uninvolved are both
associated with lower grades." Parenting styles also made a difference.
Families that expected mature behavior, set firm rules, and made sure
there was open communication between parents and child, as well as
a respect for the rights and views of each family member, had children
with the best academic records, reported Dr. Dornbusch. Highly per-
missive and authoritarian parents (parents attempting to shape and
control every aspect of the child's life) did not fare as well.

Possibly unaware of this, some fast-track parents have apparently
become so grade-hungry they will virtually take over the child's work
to assure success. Ann Gillinger, the director at Sierra Canyon School,
tells of a "show-and-tell" project where each student was supposed to
bring in a favorite pet and talk about it. One mother was so eager for
her daughter to be voted the one with the most interesting pet that
she bought the child a small tortoise at a nearby pet shop just for the
occasion. When it came to talking about the animal the child did not
even know it was her pet. "Education has become a product, not a

process," said Mrs. Gillinger. "And it is taking away from the intellectual pursuit for its own sake."

When inappropriate or unrealistic expectations are expressed either directly or implicitly at home, Mrs. Gillinger has also noticed that by fourth or fifth grade the child is in danger of "signing off" (starting to lose interest entirely). "They see how much work it takes and there seems no end to that work. It becomes overwhelming," she said. "They say to themselves, 'I've tried so hard to be good enough. But it looks like I may never be good enough. So why bother.' "

Others internalize that parental anxiety to excel. For those with naturally outstanding academic abilities this may work as a motivating force, spurring them to truly outstanding achievements that promote self-esteem and pride. For the rest it may outwardly provide the required grades; but teachers say that it can create a great deal of internal pressure on that child. An early warning sign of this internalized pressure is a child who is able to produce academically but is clearly having difficulty with relaxation and the social world of his or her peers. These are the sorts of children, teachers have discovered, who have a constant, almost obsessive, need to seek approval from either parent or teacher, no matter what they are doing, or intending to do. Interestingly, psychologists have found that the parent who is most likely to push a child too hard and not heed warnings is the one whose own parents could never be satisfied. "That sort of parent has to have a model child because he is still proving his own worth to his parents," said Dr. Martin Buccolo, a psychologist specializing in troubled adolescents of high-achievers. "It makes them judgmental and overly critical."

Mrs. Gillinger is among many teachers who maintain that long-term results will be much better if a parent genuinely values the accomplishments of the child and is prepared to accept that he or she may be pushing too hard or that the child is facing a temporary setback. "We now know so much more about learning," she said. "We know that every child has a learning curve. There are peaks and valleys. We can help put what is happening into its proper perspective, if the parents will only let us do that for them."

## PARENTAL ATTITUDES

Indeed, as the years progress Mrs. Gillinger is finding—like almost everyone else serving the upscale end of education—that there can be a troubling side to being raised on the gilded edge of society. Because many of these children have been showered with so much so early it seems difficult for them to appreciate the value of what they receive. Increasingly, for instance, the lost-and-founds at these schools are being filled with $150 jackets, radios, and other similarly expensive items that seem to mean so little they are not even retrieved. Exposure during vacations or as part of community-involvement projects to people less fortunate than themselves was repeatedly suggested to me as sorely needed in these youngsters' lives—from an early age.

In addition, parents are placing increasing emphasis on class rank and achievement rather than the value of learning. Again, the sense among the professionals is that the pressure emanates either from a fear that the child will not continue to enjoy such bounty in adult life or from a concern that the image of the parent will be tarnished if the child is not up to snuff.

Some parents are so uptight, said the teachers, that they now go overboard—constantly questioning what is going on in school to determine if that child is on the "right" path, and are not above stepping in even when it is not necessary. Moreover, because they are so educated and successful themselves, these parents will even insist they know better, overriding recommendations of teachers.

It is a syndrome that Robert Coles observed with alarm in his 1977 study of wealthy youngsters called *Privileged Ones*. Such a parental stance, he warned, can evoke a tension between teacher and child that is not conducive to good learning. The child picks up the parents' impatience or scorn for the teacher and the teacher in turn feels a certain fear and resentment of the parent—something that Coles believes occasionally leads to a less-than-honest evaluation of the child's progress. The result is that the child, knowing full well the truth of the matter, is undermined. Says Coles, "It is as if they (the children) never quite believe in themselves; they are always contending with their families' wealth, status, connections, always wondering whether they can really trust any compliment or take seriously any criticism at school."

Michael Reagan, the adopted son of President Reagan and Jane Wyman, comments upon the effect of such intervention in his book *On the Outside Looking In*. At one point he tells how he was spared expulsion from a parochial school because he was the son of a film star. But he was not sure that that was really such a good thing after all. He writes: "Unfortunately, like so many children of famous or rich parents, I was not being held accountable for my actions. The school had no intention of letting me fail because it was a black mark on them. They were able to use the fact that Jane Wyman's son was a student in their sales pitch. . . . I stored away the knowledge that no matter what I did I could get away with it because the school and my parents would clean up the mess after me."

Many such parents have also gained the reputation of pestering teachers to advance a child to a higher grade, with the notion that it is a sign of accomplishment. Yet in *Miseducation,* Dr. Elkind cites a study that showed that the older children in a grade regularly outperformed younger ones. Thus if a parent is looking to have a child shine among his peers the reverse may actually be more effective.

One more but important word on failure: teachers frequently told me how concerned they were that children from high-achieving families were not being allowed to face sufficient situations where they might fail. For instance, they would be urged to take only the elective courses where they could shine. If they did stumble, the parents would immediately jump in to minimize the damage, such as speaking to a teacher about modifying a grade. Such intervention (irrespective of the ethical implications) might improve class ranking. But constant shielding from the vicissitudes of life can turn out to be poor preparation for the real world as well as a distortion of what it really takes to succeed.

## VALUES

Many of the teachers I met were also becoming concerned about the kind of values that the pressure to excel instills in the children. For instance, those who seem to absorb the parental anxiety often look for ways to produce those results without the heavy workload. In effect, they learn early on that it is easier to manipulate the system than to provide substance. Teachers are finding they will produce papers that are beautifully finished, a joy to behold, and exactly the length assigned. But they often seem to have spent more time on the presentation than content. Others will find ways of staying in a less competitive group so they can be sure to bring home the expected A's rather than B's or C's. Many have learned that if you raise your hand regularly (even if you don't always have the right answer) you will get the points needed to maintain a high ranking. "But I wonder," says Mrs. Gillinger. "Are creativity and honesty being stifled as a result?"

Parents might also be surprised to learn how their own approach to life—those candid remarks dropped in the privacy of the home— can affect the way their children behave in a school setting, the school being synonymous in the child's mind with the office. Dr. Nisenson, the New Canaan psychologist, tells how he was called into an elementary school in an exclusive town near where he lives after repeated complaints by parents that children in the fourth grade were coming home in tears. Many had been telling their parents that they were being ridiculed or ostracized as "nerds" (although they were not quite sure what a nerd was except to suggest it was something quite awful).

"After speaking to the children I found an undercurrent of tension," said Dr. Nisenson. "The parents were all very successful and physically beautiful people. And it soon became apparent that the children were unwittingly and unknowingly transmitting the same hierarchical values that the parents used to judge the people in their professional lives. Being a nerd meant you couldn't compete—not good at sports, not verbally facile, not good at grades or even socially adept. The other message was that you were an idiot if you discussed your feelings. Even being part of the 'in' group was no protection because you could get kicked out at any time for the flimsiest of reasons—just like in a corporation. No wonder these children were feeling anxious and upset."

Though it is not the sort of exercise adults go through very often, it may therefore be necessary, early on during the raising of these children, for the parents to reexamine their own values. It might be a way of analyzing how the parent might be inadvertently passing along messages that were never intended. Or if values are being compromised—as happens in a business setting—it could be helpful to explain to a child why a certain action had to be taken.

## TUTORS

It also seemed to me, as I continued my group sessions and individual interviews with the children, that no child of high-achieving parents ever managed to grow up without being offered a tutor at some time or another. How parents handled the timing of that tutor and their expectations of the experience seemed to make all the difference to the child's self-image as well as his or her attitude toward the work.

The four highly successful Manhattan prep school graduates I met were quite vocal on that score. According to them a tutor is bad news on all counts, so the parent should not expect the offer to be greeted with gratefulness or joy, even if it is supposed to be helpful. Said one boy, "Having a tutor is an insult in the first place and a drag in the second." However, all agreed that the overture feels much less of a slap in the face if it comes from the teacher. "That's the person who is supposed to be in charge of your schoolwork," said one of the girls. "If it comes from the parent it's like . . . well, you've let us down." One of them complained that his mother tried so hard to be helpful she would "jump the gun," rushing to get that tutor at the drop of a C-plus. "I remember giving her a sarcastic answer like, 'Gee, I never thought of that.' I wanted to stay in control of my own successes and failures," he said. "I knew I could ask her for a tutor. She told me that enough times. If I felt I needed one I wanted it to be my choice." However, the group conceded that it was nice to know the opportunity was there.

Do not allow a tutor to do the child's homework or do it for them, warn the professionals. It blunts initiative and prevents them from becoming self-starters. Moreover, the child cannot enjoy the fruits of his or her own success because that child knows it is false. Dr. Sanger tells of one boy who was sent to him for therapy in adolescence. The parents insisted he was lazy. The boy also had a low self-image. What had happened, said Dr. Sanger, was that the boy had never felt the surge of confidence that came from handling anything on his own. He had been so used to his parents organizing his life and his schoolwork that he simply did not know how to start a project without adult direction. "If you never feel your own competence or learn to trust your own competence you wind up a hollow, frightened person," said Dr. Sanger.

It is better to have the tutor do other exercises that will help the child master the assignment when he or she does it later on alone. Parents can help in a similar way—explaining the lesson rather than doing the actual work. Parental interest in school work is clearly beneficial for the child. But there is a vast chasm between interest, encouragement, and a show of confidence in the child—and actually taking over the job.

"Looking back, I think the best thing my parents did for me was to let me know all along that they had confidence in my abilities," said the boy who became school president. "They made it clear I was a good kid. I made them happy. They were proud of me. And that they loved me even when I came home with that B-minus."

Who said it was easy to be a parent?

# IV

# The Teen Years

# 11.

# Adolescence in the Fast Track

Teenage life in a fast-track household is unquestionably a study in contrasts, a time when those who have the innate talents and right kind of support get deeply absorbed in all the exciting educational, travel, and cultural opportunities offered to them. These are the ones who early in life take on the panache of the well-to-do, moving about with quiet assurance and an understated style that lets you know *they* know (but no longer have to prove) they are part of the elite. Others, who are somewhat weaker and struggling with personal failings, may begin to lose confidence because they see themselves as slipping further and further behind. "When you know you have so many more advantages than everyone else you feel exposed," a sixteen-year-old New York boy explained. "You don't have many excuses left."

Adolescence is a pressured time for any youngster. And clearly these teenagers are not spared any of the anguish, despite their elite status. While some worries, such as paying for college, may be less, other stresses are intensified: the sort of grades your parents expect you to get, how socially adept you must be and how you must look to reach even a modest level of popularity, the need (if you are a girl) for a superlative body image which means super-thin, super-elegant, tanned, and gorgeous—not just simply attractive. "For us, these sorts of things are the norm," said a slender, thirteen-year-old girl I met in California. The boys admit, somewhat self-consciously, to an added stress point of their own, one that most of their fathers were spared: knowing they will have to compete for the few places at the top with super-achieving girls as well as boys.

Though there is probably no way to prove such a conclusion statistically, it seemed to me from my conversations with teenagers and teachers that adolescence in a household of super-achievers was thus a time of polarization: the youngsters saw themselves as either winners or losers. The winners made the Ivy League, became Merit Scholars, played football or lacrosse for the school, dated the most-sought-after guys/girls, had the best looks. The self-labeled losers (even if it was not true in the context of the wider world) who couldn't compete on any or most of these levels blocked out the pain. And they normally did it with the customary substitutes for a genuine sense of well-being: drugs, booze, and quickie sexual thrills. "I wanted to feel on top like everyone else," explained a chubby fifteen-year-old boy—a C-level student who smokes, does drugs, and brags about his high tolerance for alcohol. At least this way, he said, he felt sufficiently cool to be assured a measure of popularity.

Few had the extraordinary inner strength or the needed peer and parental approval to see equal value in filling an important middle ground—vital cogs in the giant economic or cultural wheel rather than its chrome-plated superstars. Exceptions were those with unusually laid-back parents or those who had spent time outside the Garden of Eden. There was, for instance, the girl I met who had gone to France for a year as an exchange student. She said that only when she started living overseas in a far more modest community did she realize just how far ahead she really was. "Because your parents are at the top you grow up thinking of the top as standard," she explained, "and everything else as below." Those with creative talents similarly seemed to weather a no-frills status better. A boy from the Midwest talked about the boost he got from being editor of his yearbook. A southern teenager, a pretty redheaded girl, talked about her involvement in her junior year with a local theatre group as having changed her life. Again, there was another world with less exalted standards by which the youngster could judge personal performance.

Adolescence in a fast-track household is a time when money gushes forth as if from an underground spring. "I know a kid whose parents gave him $100 to take a cab from the Hamptons to New York City because he didn't want to take the train," the boy from New York continued. "I have another friend who is allowed to use his father's company limo to drive him to his tennis game. You see it all the time."

Parents admit this is true. But they say they give in because they are often tired and it is easier than getting embroiled in a drawn-out argument. Besides, if they have the spare cash or an office perk—such as a personal chauffeur—why not pass along that benefit to their children? Often, they said, such largesse also gives their child an edge with peers. How could that be bad? Only those who had come from wealthy backgrounds and knew the corrosive effects of having "too much, too soon" seemed to feel strongly about resisting.

The teen years in such households are also a time when the young-sters themselves begin to have the maturity to see their parents in sharper focus. And sometimes what they see comes as a shock. No wonder they are eager to tell you how that parental success was gained at the expense of cheating or exploiting others. They complain about being told to do one thing and seeing their parents do exactly the opposite, about parents who never really try to understand what the child is facing. "What was the use of trying to speak to them?" said an unusually bitter young woman who has since become a graphic de-signer. "They couldn't hear."

Perhaps so. But I also sensed a compulsive need among many of these youngsters to exaggerate their parents' shortcomings and even, at times, find ways to unhinge their parents, if only to help bolster their own fragile egos in light of those exceptional parental achieve-ments. In his book Michael Reagan writes: "Like many children of famous parents I wanted to show my parents failing at something. I wanted to bring him [President Reagan], Nancy and Mom down to a common level. . . . All my life I had grown up hearing how great my parents were. My dad had seemingly never failed at anything."

Further, it is only when they reach their teens that these youngsters really begin to appreciate just how far their parents have climbed—a realization that is disturbing because of a fear they will not be able to make it that far themselves. As Michael Reagan goes on to observe, "For Dad and Mom it had been easy to overshadow and rise above *their* parents. Yet how was I to rise above the Presidency and an Acad-emy Award?" Clearly, that expectation, so deeply a part of the American cultural heritage, can be devastating because the concept of downward mobility has not yet become acceptable, except as a manifestation of personal failure.

"It's hard for people like my mother (a highly successful psychol-ogist) and my father (who built a billion-dollar business) to know that their kids are scared of those accomplishments," an Ivy League graduate told me as he reminisced on his teenage years. "Take my father, for instance. He expected us to be proud. He even made sure right through our childhood that we heard all about his accomplishments, all the time. True, he worked very hard for what he has today. But every time he did something special—got his name in the paper for taking over a company or being elected to a board of trustees—he had to remind us of it. That made him look even more powerful. And it became harder and harder to deal with him as a person or feel good about what I might do with *my* life."

Others are so convinced that they can never surpass or even equal their parents' achievements that they lose the motivation to try. "I looked around and I thought, 'There's not a lot of room left for rich people,'" said that chubby, fifteen-year-old boy who calls himself a "druggie." "So now I think about living in a hut on a beach in the Bahamas. Unless you are perfect you think, well, why bother."

I found peers as demanding as parents. At school or around town the youngsters had to contend with a highly selective social life that—mirroring the world of their parents—paid homage to the handsome, the beautiful, the outgoing, and the achiever but had little time or compassion for the plain, the plump, the pimply, the skinny, the in-articulate, the shy. "When I see those girls standing around the wall at our seventh-grade dance, my heart goes out to them," a retired private school teacher told me.

On top of it all, these teens face the very same obstacles that haunt all teenagers today: school and activity schedules that frequently run from dawn (getting up early for swim team practice) to the time that child climbs into bed (to study for tomorrow's Latin test); the academic day of reckoning when those college acceptance or rejection letters arrive in the mailbox; a need for friendship yet a concurrent fear of getting caught up with the drugs and alcohol that are often the ticket to the "in" group; a longing to experiment with sex yet a fear of the AIDS epidemic; parents divorcing; parents remarrying; parents who seem so wrapped up with their busy lives and so out-of-touch that they cannot be counted on when problems arise.

Increasingly among high-achieving families I sensed that brothers and sisters were filling that void. They had become the favorite aunt, the kindly grandmother, the ever-present mother of former genera-tions. So many of the teens I met spoke lovingly of the supportive role of older brothers and sisters. "My brother had been through it all," a sixteen-year-old overweight girl told me. "He understood." Besides, unlike friends, siblings were deemed far more reliable—less likely to tell someone else that secret you had just confided.

Arrogance and a sense of entitlement were evident among many I met, mirroring the observations that Robert Coles has made about privileged youngsters. Dr. Coles maintains it often arises because these children grow up in households where they constantly hear their par-ents ordering others around and acting superior. They really do take for granted—and expect as their due—so many of the perks they get, like brand-new cars, foreign travel, designer clothes.

The competitive climate is now so overheated and academic achievement so much a mark of self-worth that cheating appears epidemic, no longer even carrying a stigma. Need someone else to take your SAT exam? No problem, said the kids. Call in sick on the day your own school holds the test, then (for a fee) round up a smarter friend to take the makeup test for you by using a fake ID. It is possible to do so without detection because that makeup test is usually held two or three weeks later at a nearby school where the teacher cannot make the distinction between the ID and the real person.

Need the perfect college essay? Take your pick of tutors who (also for a fee) will write your college essay. If not, a parent can usually be persuaded to take over the job. From the way so many of the youngsters I met talked (almost bragged) about using a surrogate, it is a wonder the colleges can still use these essays as an accurate barometer of any applicant's skills. Did it matter that this strategy might be dishonest? Apparently not, because this way you retained the competitive edge. "But you don't feel good about yourself," admitted one boy.

## FRACTURED EMOTIONS

Particularly—although not exclusively—among the more nihilistic and decadent groups there also seemed to be a free-wheeling belief that it was okay to exploit others. Along with that attitude came a lack of ability to feel deeply or care about others. The problem is described brilliantly by the young writer Bret Easton Ellis in his highly acclaimed first novel, *Less Than Zero*. Set in Beverly Hills during Christmas vacation, it is about a bunch of rich kids who are left alone with too much money and too much time on their hands. It is unquestionably an example of extreme behavior, but certainly includes families that could comfortably be described as fast-track. These youngsters sense a problem with their ability to form caring relationships with one another. Take, for example, the passage describing the attitude of the guy who has just found out that his current girlfriend has become pregnant. He is about to ask a member of his crowd for a loan to pay for an abortion. They meet in an upscale shopping mall.

"Do you have any money?" I ask.

Julian looks at me quickly and says, "Um, not now. But I will and, oh, by then it'll be too late, you know? And I don't want to have to sell the

Porsche. I mean that would be a bummer." He takes a long pause, fingers a cheeseburger. "Just for some abortion?" He tries to laugh.

Not exactly sterling values! In another passage the narrator's father is depicted as someone who is physically present but so wrapped up in his world of moviemaking he purposely avoids facing the fact that his son has problems. The mother is similarly distant, preoccupied with a new boyfriend.

When he wrote the novel, Ellis was twenty years old and a product of the Buckley School in Sherman Oaks on the outskirts of Los Angeles—arguably the toniest private school in the area, he says. Ellis clearly worries about his generation and says, "The book was supposed to be a kind of warning.

"When you are overprivileged," he observed, thoughtfully, "you become jaded. You have too much. Life holds no surprises. You don't get the kicks from saving up for something special as other people do. So you are constantly looking for other kinds of thrills." Moreover, when you are used to having the funds to replace anything you damage or lose, he added, you get to feel that human beings are readily replaceable, too. "If you have money," he added, "you know you can always buy new friends. You have a car to take them out. You have the money to go places."

Therapists who have worked with privileged youngsters suggest that early emotional experiences may be equally responsible. If these children were raised by a series of caregivers, with little parental involvement, they were probably never made to feel special by any one sustaining person. Therefore, they grew up unable to care deeply about the fate of others. Such an upbringing may have also left the lingering notion that people close to them were there to serve their needs rather than become equal partners in a relationship. In some instances such children may have also seen parents exploiting others, so using people is seen as a perfectly legitimate practice. Further, as most of them become aware by this age that their lives *are* different from those of ordinary people, "They may also feel quite above or at a remove from so-called middle-class morality and customs," notes Robert Coles, commenting on the roots of similar behavior in his book *Privileged Ones*.

Parallel attitudes have been detected among the so-called winners in this group, too. However, in this case the apparent lack of concern for others seems to emanate more from the fierce competition that pervades their lives at school. "It is as though they can't afford deep loyalties any more," observed the Reverend Mark Mullin, the head-master of St. Alban's School.

The youngsters agree. "To have a sense of yourself as viable in the world, everyone tells you that you need to tolerate failure as well as success . . . but somehow you know you don't have the license to fail," said a fifteen-year-old boy from New York. "So winning becomes everything."

Drugs are as readily obtainable as a glass of Pepsi. No wonder; the market is so strong. "These kids have the money to buy all they want," said Ellis, the writer. "They also have the kind of liberal parents who are likely to go along with it." He continued, "I knew three guys whose fathers supplied them with marijuana so they would not pick up 'bad' marijuana. Those parents rationalized that their kids would probably do it anyway. And the arguments would cause an unavoidable rift, which would be worse in the end," he added.

Is it that, or is it that the Children of the Sixties, themselves a product of a drug culture, now have trouble saying no to the *children* of the Children of the Sixties?

Certainly not all adolescents follow this path. I met some youngsters who were determined not to let their values or their behavior slip and indeed were extraordinary human beings. But the stresses and temp-tations are very real. Adolescence may therefore be a time when these children need their parents more, not less, to provide them with an alternative haven. They may also need limit-setting if only to give them a socially acceptable excuse if they don't feel comfortable around the drinking, the drugs, or even the sexual pressures. But the problem is how to do this while still giving them the personal space they need to develop into independent, well-adjusted adults with decent values.

## WAYS TO HELP

Bettie Youngs, the child development specialist from Del Mar, maintains that the first step is an acknowledgment by the parents that their teen-ager may be under enormous stress despite a privileged status, and that nonjudgmental communication rather than an overly generous supply of cash or a hands-off attitude is what is really needed. "I worked with a mother who could not cope with the idea that her child might be having a rough time," said Dr. Youngs. "She said to me, 'I don't understand. He has his own room, his own telephone line, a car, a TV in his room. We've given him everything he could possibly need.' "

Listening, says Dr. Youngs, is probably the most valuable assistance a parent can provide at this age. "But it must be active listening," she says. "The kind that shows a sincere desire to clearly, honestly hear what the other person is saying." Listening, she adds, "tells our kids they are valuable, that they are worth our time. And that we are concerned—not out of a sense of duty but out of love. It also builds a sense of self that is one of the most important defenses against the negative sort of peer pressure we worry so much about."

A teenager who has a parent willing to listen in such a manner may also find it easier to bring his or her problems to the parents instead of relying so heavily upon friends for counsel. This then provides the parent with an opportunity to help that young person develop confidence in personal judgments. "But to do so you need to help that child figure out a solution for himself," said Seymour Mund, a former consultant with the Connecticut State Department of Education. "You must avoid the temptation to tell that youngster what to do." If a potential solution necessitates doing anything that might jeopardize that teen's standing in his or her peer group, continued Mund, this might be an ideal moment for the parent to share similar times of self-doubt. For instance, perhaps there was a time when *not* following the crowd turned out to be an advantage for the parent. It may also be a way for the child to learn, said Mund, that being turned down by a person or a group is not necessarily the end of the world. Rather, it happens to everyone sooner or later.

Expressions of love are also helpful, Dr. Youngs has found, even though we all know that teenagers squirm at this kind of parental behavior. "Don't be afraid to tell them 'I love you,'" she says, "or put an arm around them. Pat them on the shoulder. Show excitement about their activities. Praise what is going right." Other therapists have suggested that a teenager may feel more respected and valued when the parent makes an effort to know some of the child's friends by name and spend some time talking to them when they visit the house— despite the clear message from the teenager that he or she wants those parents completely out of the way.

For the parent who was part of the drug culture of the sixties— and who may have now decided it was not a very smart move—saying "no" to a child may appear hypocritical and extremely difficult at best. For them the solution may be candor of the sort supplied by Judge Douglas H. Ginsburg. Ginsburg was the Supreme Court nominee who was forced to withdraw his nomination when it was discovered that he had smoked marijuana when he was younger. In his parting public statement he declared simply, "I hope that the young people of this country, including my own daughters, will learn from my mistakes and heed their message."

Try also to avoid having your children go into overload—something they may view as normal when parents are so multifaceted. While in Del Mar I sat one afternoon with a teenager who was in tears because the day before she had been fired from her first job—selling ice cream at a small outdoor stand. She had not been showing up on time and had been leaving early. She had taken on that job (twenty hours a week, evenings) in addition to cheerleading (two hours a day), driver education (one hour), and her normal studies. "I kept trying to tell myself I could handle it all because my parents always coped with a lot of different things," she said. "I thought I could, too. Now I know you should not try to do too much."

Teenagers are helped—not hurt—by the establishment of clear boundaries, Nicholas Thacher, the private school headmaster, has found. "If there are no boundaries it makes them uncomfortable and insecure." Lack of boundaries also leaves a child without any defenses against peer-group pressure. Even so, certain boundaries, like a curfew, often become difficult to enforce unless other parents adhere to the same rules. Thus there has been a growing enthusiasm among parent groups at both public and private schools for the idea of parents getting together as a group and drawing up guidelines they all pledge to honor. Such action also lessens the resentment a teenager might feel for being saddled with what may seem to be ridiculous standards. Many private and suburban high schools now have such groups. Montclair, New Jersey, has been a leader in this area. In the fall of 1986, over 100 parents signed an agreement promising to be home when parties were scheduled and guaranteeing that no alcohol would be served. To make public this pledge and give it more clout, all agreed to have their names published in the local newspaper. Such groups are normally formed as an activity of a high school parents' group. It may be well worth joining one.

Group action also provides support for parents, maintained David Elkind in an interview with me on the topic. And it makes them feel less like the bad guys, especially if they are "torn between enforcing rules and worrying about doing anything that could jeopardize popularity." Boundaries also help take a teen off the hook, he added. "If they don't want to stay out late or go to someone's home they can blame their parents. It helps them save face."

Parental standards also provide a child with a set of opinions by which to test his or her own theories. "I find I have far more meaningful discussions with students about sex when I have opinions of my own I want to express," one headmaster said.

Maintaining and enforcing rules and standards develop a respect for other people and avoid encouraging that teenager to "dump" on the parent by acting irresponsibly. For instance, Mund has found that if the teenager knows he will have to pay out of his own pocket for repairs to a car—or not have it to use until he does—he will be less likely to do anything that will harm the vehicle. A wonderful tale is told concerning the way Franklin Roosevelt was trained to take personal responsibility for his activities. As a child Roosevelt was never permitted to start anything without finishing it. At one time in his early teens he reputedly became fascinated with taxidermy—the art of preparing, stuffing, and mounting the skins of animals so they appear to be alive. Though he would sometimes feel sick while preparing a bird he had no choice but to finish, once he had started. And he later admitted that such an upbringing helped give him the dogged persistence to see a project through, and to take responsibility for a venture rather than dumping it, unfinished and in disarray, in the lap of others as soon as ennui or frustration sets in.

Trust is important, too, at this point, provided the freedom for independent action is given in an atmosphere of continued caring and concern and in a manner that shows confidence in that child—for example, not constantly having to report to parents concerning what went on during an evening out with friends. "My parents are really busy," said a sixteen-year-old from a fashionable Northeast suburb. "So they aren't able to keep up with all that goes on in my life. But telling me they trust me to make the right decisions makes me feel good. I feel kind of obligated, too. It also seems to take away the urge to go out and do something bad because there's no reason. And anyway, I'd feel I'd be letting myself down."

Teenagers from whom a lot is expected also seem to thrive best when they feel they have a loving home where they can retreat from all the turmoil, stress, and demands of the wider world. As William Clarkson, headmaster at the Potomac School, pointed out, "If parents can give a child a sense of having that 'contact point' no matter what, a place of rest for soul and spirit, that child is far more likely to withstand the negative influences of peers and make sensible judgments."

A longtime teacher and administrator at another private school made the following suggestions:

- Be particularly sensitive to the child with late puberty development since this adds to a feeling of inadequacy among peers.
- Try to keep up with the prevailing teen culture by talking to other parents of teens and by keeping in close contact with school administrators; have your opinions ready so they can help place what is going on in a broader perspective.
- Learn more about teen temptations and turmoil by reading books on teenage difficulties (such as *Helping Your Teenager Deal with Stress,* by Bettie B. Youngs, or *Talking with Your Teenager,* by Ruth Bell and Leni Zeiger Wildflower); attend parent-teacher forums on teens and be prepared to do something quickly to help your own teen if a crisis erupts, such as calling in professionals or going to community meetings that discuss drugs, drinking, or sex among teens.
- Accept the fact that self-esteem—fragile at best among this group regardless of outward bravado or sophistication—may be at its lowest point at this awkward age and thus in need of extra boosting (for example, you might remind the youngster he or she is looking good, or you might encourage the youngster to obtain a job or get involved in a project where small successes build confidence).
- Try to keep family rituals or traditions, like birthdays or major holiday celebrations, alive despite grumblings or activities that seem to get in the way; this helps "center" a teenager, acting as a soothing oasis of stability in that teenager's churning universe.

It is not an easy balancing act.

# 12.

# Teens Talk About Parents: What Helps and What Hurts

As I continued my dialogue with the young people, in groups and individually, I would suddenly be told about a seemingly minor incident that for one reason or another had taken on a special significance in the youngster's mind. Frequently it concerned words or actions taken by a parent that had either wounded that child deeply or had been surprisingly uplifting and meaningful to the individual.

Uttering a silent *mea culpa* on several occasions when I was reminded of verbal arrows I may have unthinkingly tossed at my own children, I decided it might be useful to gather together a selection of those remarks. Their value, I believe, lies in their enabling us to see the world a little clearer from the other side of the great generational divide. Their comments might even spur some interesting discussions over the dinner table.

| WORDS OR ACTIONS BY PARENTS THAT HELPED | WORDS OR ACTIONS BY PARENTS THAT HURT |
|---|---|
| ". . . making me work summers because it helped sort out what I wanted to do. I also got to meet people I might never have met . . . it gave me a different perspective on life." | ". . . they never listened to understand, they listened to find out what I did wrong. It made me feel I couldn't go to them. Sometimes I don't even want to explain anymore." |

". . . the little games my father liked to play at home, like making us do multiplication in our heads or starting a spelling bee between me and my sisters or showing us a new card trick . . . it was just nice, healthy fun."

". . . insisting that I go away to summer camp, because being away from home made me feel grown up and able to manage on my own."

". . . my dad and my mom, sure they're important people, everyone knows my dad's name. But they always let me and my brother know the family is very important to them, too, even that it comes first. Having that at the back of my mind made a big, big difference. And they didn't just say it. I know they mean it because I've seen my father come back early from a lecture tour, or Mom cancel a meeting, to come to back-to-school night or see me in a show."

". . . my dad always told me that in order to do what you wanted to do in life you had to achieve at each level. There were no shortcuts. It was all up to you. I thought about that a lot and I think it's helped me want to do well. They don't have to nag me to do my homework anymore."

". . . traveling abroad together. That meant a lot. We saw different people and different ways of living and I learned to deal with people who were very different from us. We were all together, too, for a time."

". . . when my father yelled at me for spending too much on clothes and then went out and spent $400 on new things for his New York apartment."

". . . when my dad told me not to smoke and drink. And then he came home drunk or smoked packs of cigarettes. . . . I get kind of confused. . . . it gives me an excuse to do the same."

". . . when they expected me to be so perfect that I couldn't go to them with my problems . . . so I'd go talk to a friend."

". . . when I got into high school they seemed to get less interested . . . I was so busy, they were so busy. . . . I wish we would have shared more."

". . . when I came home with an 'A-plus' in English and all my mother said was, 'Well, what about French?' I mean, you could tear yourself up."

". . . I don't want to be told what I *should* want or what I *should* be."

". . . when parents want you to become a copy of them . . . I know they want me to enjoy the success and happiness they've gained . . . and I know they want to brag about me to friends . . . but I want to choose my own life."

". . . I would have done a lot better if they stopped yelling at me *all* the time."

". . . they never, ever said, 'Why can't you be like your brother?' They just encouraged me to do the best I could. If I was having trouble they would ask if they could help . . . I'm not afraid to come home with a 'C' . . . I feel bad, sure. But not having them yell makes it easier."

". . . I made this little animal, once, I think it was an alligator . . . in pottery when I was small. . . . My mother put it on a shelf in the kitchen and it's stayed there ever since. . . . I know it sounds silly, but it makes me proud."

". . . it's good when they emphasize your good points, and not make such a big deal about the things that go wrong."

". . . when they help you stick to something and then it works . . . you get that great sense of accomplishment."

". . . when they make you feel good about who you are . . . and are not just pleased because you got the 'A.'"

". . . when they were able to convince you to make the right decisions . . . without making those decisions for you . . . like showing you what might happen if you do drugs."

". . . whenever my mother sits down and talks to me . . . and I like it when she asks my advice about something she doesn't understand, like how to use the computer."

". . . whenever I made a new friend my mother immediately asked, 'Is she from a good family?'"

". . . when my mom said, 'Your best is not good enough.'"

". . . my parents did not encourage me in sports because they said it wasn't something I did very well. . . . If they'd only been honest and told me it was really because they were afraid I'd get hurt. . . ."

". . . when my parents made me give up drama club because they said I had too much to do. . . . If only they'd waited until my grades had slipped it would have been easier to take."

". . . my parents made me stay in the same small private school from kindergarten through twelfth grade . . . it was too sheltered, too much of the same people from the same background . . . I mean, is that really good?"

". . . whenever they refused to think of school as work and came in and told us how *they* had a rough day and so could we do this, and could we do that. We may have had a rough day, too. But they didn't want to hear about it."

". . . when my mom needed a step-by-step itinerary of where I'd been and what I'd done . . . it came across as zero trust in me. If only she'd have a little faith in me."

". . . when my dad kept saying, 'You gotta get better grades if you want to go to a good college' . . . it hurt

". . . I knew my father had taken a lot of chances in his life . . . and sometimes he had failed . . . so when there were openings for cheerleading and I tried out, I wasn't afraid to fail."

". . . what really helped was when my parents told me stories about what they did as kids and how they screwed up."

". . . when they listened without criticizing, at least for the moment, without saying anything, and you knew they were really listening."

because it made me feel dumb. Maybe he wanted to think I'm smarter than I really am. He won't believe I'm doing my best."

# 13.

# Dollars and Sense: Money Issues

Searching through the biographies of wealthy and prominent families who produced a fistful of equally accomplished children—the Lodges, the Roosevelts, the Mellons, the Kennedys, the Rockefellers—I was continually struck by the deep concern all of them had about the impact of their wealth upon their children. Unlike many newly affluent parents of today who are only now getting used to the idea of large incomes and family trust funds, most of these Old Money families did not rush to shower wealth upon their children. Sure, they made certain their money purchased the finest possible educations and cultural enrichment. But beyond that those parents went to enormous lengths to make sure the children learned how much hard work and effort had gone into making a dollar. Mindful of some of the excesses of young European aristocrats, they also seemed fearful that those children would be wounded later in adult life by unrealistic expectations and the lack of resolve characteristic of those who have been showered with too much too soon.

The biography *John D. Rockefeller Jr.: A Portrait,* by Raymond B. Fosdick, tells how almost from the start young John was required to earn his own pocket money. His account books (yes, he was even required to keep account books) show that in the year 1887, at age thirteen, he was able to earn one dollar by "mending a vase," a further twenty-five cents for "fixing a fountain pen," and an unspecified windfall for "killing flies, 2 cents a fly." The ledgers demonstrate that by fifteen he had a clothing allowance and had to keep within that limit or find auxiliary ways to supplement that sum through work on his father's estate. He was also required to donate some of his pocket money to charity, no doubt to underscore from an impressionable age that obligations accompany privilege—the biblical notion as expressed in St. Luke 12:48: "Every one to whom much is given, of him much will be required" (an appropriate notion on a number of levels for children of fast-track parents).

There was apparently no stricture on the philanthropy John Jr. might choose. This forced him to begin to think early about whom and what he wanted to support rather than have the choices made for him. By the time he was sixteen years old an entry suggests he favored giving to someone he knew to be personally in need—"10 cents for a poor man, 5 cents car fare for an old woman." His father also believed in giving him responsibilities for larger purchases and money management at an earlier age than most of us might think suitable today. "Before going to college John was already buying horses for his father and running the Rockefeller stable at 21 West 55th Street in New York," notes the author.

What we see from such an upbringing is that a great deal of thought and planning went into training that child so that:

- He came to accept from a tender age that it takes time and effort to work for what you want; and if you don't bother you may never fulfill your material desires.
- He was able to feel a solid sense of accomplishment, the sort that built confidence in his own abilities to cope.
- By the time he realized there might be sufficient money so that his basic needs would always be met, regardless of his efforts, he had begun to develop a sense of purpose through his philanthropies that would make him feel his life had value and meaning.

And indeed this did occur. In adult life John Jr. grew to be widely respected for his advocacy on behalf of less fortunate people, in particular for his progressive attitudes toward labor. A quiet and unobtrusive man, he was also admired for his careful and sensitive channeling of the family's excess wealth for the benefit of society. It also became his way to exorcise the taint and guilt that he, like so many beneficiaries, feel about the money they inherit.

How can parents translate these principles into a contemporary context, giving *today's* privileged child a strong sense of purpose that builds constructive lives and leadership and a sense of money management that will strengthen them amid the vicissitudes of life?

## TOO MUCH OF A GOOD THING

I doubt if anyone would be foolhardy enough to think that money is something a parent need not discuss. Money, like sex and drugs, is so much more available to kids these days that understanding how to handle it has to be a fundamental part of any upbringing. Yet it rarely is. A random sampling of 613 teenagers conducted in 1987 by *Money* magazine found a severe lack of sophistication about such basic matters as investments, taxes, and debt-service costs. And with credit as available as crack, noted the magazine, that could pose a problem. Coming from a relatively wealthy family did not seem to lessen the oversight. Teenagers from households earning at least $35,000 a year did not score any better on the questions than less well-to-do youngsters.

Perhaps parents should therefore begin by trying to avoid the idea that they are actually doing a child a favor by giving him or her all that they can. They are not. "One of the biggest mistakes we make when we give our children too much," Grace W. Weinstein, author of *Children and Money,* warned me, "is that they come to believe our pockets are bottomless. Learning that you cannot have everything is part of learning what it will be like when you grow up."

Interestingly, several therapists cautioned me that the indiscriminate largesse we see among so many fast-track parents may sometimes come from narcissistic motives rather than true generosity—the pleasure the parents are anxious to bestow upon themselves by showing their friends or neighbors how well they have done through the amount they can afford to spend on their children. Guilt is another reason for the bounty: a seemingly ideal way to compensate for the time not spent with the family. But, as we see, it can backfire.

Instead, the experts suggest (as do the actions of those dynastic families) that hard work and thrift are what such parents should be instilling in their children. In some instances it may mean linking pocket money to work right from the start. In younger children the tasks can be as simple as making a bed, tidying a room, or helping with the dishes even if there is domestic help in the house (with money withheld when such tasks are not completed satisfactorily). By the time those children reach the teenage years, however, it all starts to get more complicated.

## RESISTING PRESSURE TO CONFORM

How should a parent react, for example, when a twelve-year-old daughter wants a Benetton sweater just like the one all the other girls (she assures us) are wearing to class? Or when a sixteen-year-old son is pestering us for a car or a new set of skis because all the other guys have them?

Since most parents do not wish to make their teenager feel different and left out, it often helps to start by finding out just how much of the demand is coming from peer pressure and how much from a genuine desire for the item. "When parents say their child is coming home complaining that 'everyone else has such and such,' I say check it out with the other parents before doing anything," says Audrey Rosenman, the Manhattan private school psychotherapist. "The kids tend to take their cues from the one or two children who are being overindulged, not the majority. And once the parents have established that not everyone does have the sweater, or maybe those skis, it's far easier to say no."

Some parents may be tempted to say no anyway, because they consider the purchase a needless extravagance. But rather than turn the idea down flat and trigger (yet another) argument, Judy Barber, a family therapist in San Francisco who counsels many wealthy families, suggested that the child be asked to earn that amount, either at home or from an employer. The point is that the child is entitled to a different set of priorities provided he or she is willing to put in the effort needed in order to get what he or she wants. "You might even say, 'Let's think of some ways you can earn the money,'" said Ms. Barber. That not only drops the challenge back in the lap of the child, she added, but should help foster the kind of autonomy the teenager is anxious to have.

## CARS

A teenager's own car—and who pays for it and when—is one of the more volatile financial issues that erupt during adolescence. Yet looked upon as a teaching tool it could be an ideal way to begin to develop real financial independence. For that child can learn firsthand how much toil and tedious saving are needed to buy certain big-ticket items. A popular compromise used today is to match the funds, dollar for dollar—the parent providing half of the cost of that car or whatever fraction seems practical. One father used this method to encourage his son to save part of every paycheck by doubling whatever had been saved at the end of each summer's employment. This can turn a major purchase like a car into a reasonable goal. Financial assistance offered this way becomes an incentive and a statement of confidence rather than undermining that young person's initiative or drive.

Moreover, the teenagers themselves concede that they are far more likely to take good care of that car if they have had to save up for it, even more if they know they must pay for the repairs. Being able to tell others they helped pay for their own car is also a great boost to morale and self-esteem.

Giving adolescents too much too easily also robs them of the chance to challenge themselves and enjoy finding out how competent they really are. This was the view not of parents or teachers, surprisingly, but of a group of thirteen-year-olds I met at a small private school. "I remember when I wanted my room redone," said one girl. "But my mom said she would not spend the money unless I learned to keep it clean and tidy. I had to prove I could." Surprisingly, she added, she soon started to enjoy the challenge, figuring out ways to arrange her belongings so they were not just lying all over the place. And she became proud of her ability to improve the looks of that room.

Said a boy from the group, "You feel so good when you finally get what it was you wanted, like you've accomplished something, like perhaps you could do more than you thought you could." Besides, he added, "When I get something too easily—like for a birthday or Christmas—I seem to get tired of it more quickly."

The Girl Scouts have a badge they can earn called Money Management. Some of the tasks they must perform are interesting and could be copied by almost any household. They include opening a bank account and handling all the accompanying jobs like writing checks and keeping a record of credits and debits; preparing a budget and sticking to it for a period of time; obtaining part-time employment; attempting to prepare a tax return under guidance from an adult; saving up or raising money for a class or group trip as well as preparing the budget for the trip and finding thrifty ways to do the traveling.

Schools have increasingly begun offering money-management courses. Parents might want to encourage these activities and even offer some guest appearances of their own where appropriate.

## INVESTING

Most children who are born into a family of high-achievers are likely either to inherit money at some point in their lives or earn enough so that investments and the handling of personal capital become more than a theoretical exercise. Several studies have found that children who are taught or given some experience in financial fundamentals during childhood take charge of their capital much better as adults. Indeed, one of the major complaints of the women who join The Women's Foundation, a support group in San Francisco for women who inherit money, has been that they were ill-prepared for such an event. It does no good, it seems, to push the delicate matter of money under the (Persian) rug and then complain later that the child acted irresponsibly. Rather, it might help to start such youngsters on the idea of sound capital management as early as the teen years.

I collected a host of wonderful and even amusing ideas of how that might be done when I raised this point with high-achieving parents who had already amassed or had inherited quite a tidy sum. A father in the Midwest told me how he introduced his three children (then aged ten to sixteen) to the idea of stocks as an investment by assembling them all around the dinner table one night and telling them they would each be allocated a few thousand dollars. It was up to each of them to choose a company. A week later the children returned with their choices: the youngest favored Smucker's, the jock of the family bought Reebok shares, and the eldest daughter, who was anxious to become a journalist, chose *The New York Times*. Watching the dividends come in, and their profits soar and then nosedive in the crash of 1987, made them keenly aware of the dangers and the potential in the market, and they received more than a casual education in how to function under such volatile conditions. Noted the father: "When I was a boy money was a forbidden subject. I knew I would get a portfolio someday. I knew the money was there. But whenever I brought up the subject my mother would say, 'Stop! We don't talk about these things in our house.'" His lack of preparedness had been traumatic for him, he said.

John Levy, executive director of the C. G. Jung Institute in San Francisco, who acts as a counselor to wealthy families, favors the idea of a children's investment fund made up of any sum, large or small, that the parents can afford to set aside for the purpose. The children then meet regularly with the parents—say, once a month or so—to talk specifically about the progress of the fund, the kind of investments that are to be made, and the reasons why certain strategies are working or failing. That fund might invest in stocks, bonds, limited partnerships, real estate—anything.

The purpose, said Mr. Levy, is not to insist on certain ideas that the parent might know to be sound, but to gently guide the children and help them learn from experience and understand the various options. They will have to deal with a proxy request. They may even decide they want to attend their company's annual stockholders' meeting and vote on some of the issues. A certain date might be set when each child gets a share of whatever has been accumulated (or alternatively has to suffer the disappointment of the loss if his ideas proved to be off base, also an important lesson).

Mr. Levy also urges parents not to dismiss questions, when they arise, about investments the parents might have made, but to talk candidly about the underlying strategies and risks, using analogous examples from the child's world, such as sports events. Such a moment could also become another occasion to remind the child that the prospect of failure is present in many enterprises along with opportunities. While this sort of enterprise may seem a frivolous use of money, it is probably a lot less costly, in the long run, than seeing that money slip through their inexperienced fingers later in life. Think of it as tuition. Besides, what tuition bill ever had the possibility of reimbursement or even profit?

## THE VALUE OF GIVING TO OTHERS

As we have noted before, there are disadvantages to being advantaged. One is growing up feeling guilty and uncomfortable about the money that you do have. Another is not really comprehending what life is like outside the Garden of Eden. That sort of parochialism is probably responsible for the callous and often arrogant attitude that certain affluent young people display toward their less fortunate peers. But I think it is wrong to blame the kids or their parents entirely. Many of the parents do not readily concern themselves with mitigating such behavior or feelings because they probably do not easily identify with either the guilt or the parochialism, having grown up themselves under very different circumstances.

How, then, to behave? Giving a fortunate child a chance to help others should be as fundamental a part of an upbringing as, say, learning chemistry or calculus. Why so? It helps foster a healthy personality by being yet another way for that child to feel valuable. It helps the teenager develop a more compassionate outlook. And it genuinely accomplishes some good. Insisting that a small portion of that child's own money be donated to a charity or a cause is one way. Said Mr. Levy, "I tell parents that an important lesson is learning that the money is not there only for yourself. You have a responsibility toward others." One idea is to set up a small family philanthropic foundation (or at least calling it that). The parents can supply some of the money with the children contributing, too. The amount need not be large. Certainly it does not have to run into the thousands or even the hundreds. The family could then meet to discuss and vote upon which organization should get a check that particular month or quarter—and why. Causes could include the local church, a soup kitchen, a conservation center, or cancer or AIDS research. The children should be required to put in something of their own each month.

That has been the way each generation of Rockefellers has been raised. "From the time I was five years old I got an allowance that gradually increased from fifteen cents to five dollars a week," noted Alida Rockefeller, daughter of John III, in *The Rockefellers,* by Collier and Horowitz. "There were three little jewelry boxes. I got fifteen cents to spend, fifteen cents to save, and fifteen cents to give away. Every Christmas my father would sit down with me and we'd decide who I'd give the one in the third box to . . . it was a real ritual, one of the times we were closest."

If the child prefers to donate time instead of money, then this might be encouraged, too. Several private-school children told me how good they felt about themselves after they had worked directly on something like this—whether it was a fund-raiser for the school's scholarship fund or personally making gifts for underprivileged children for Christmas. Certainly it is a way to get teenagers, who tend to be egocentric anyway, a little more interested in others. It also gives them a chance to meet people in other circumstances.

Some schools foster this by making community service a graduation requirement; the Dalton and Brearley schools in New York City have done this. When a group of teenagers from those schools were interviewed by *The New York Times* about their feelings after working in a soup kitchen, all admitted that they had never really felt the direct impact of poverty before. Said one, "You know how sometimes you open the refrigerator and complain there's nothing to eat? I'll never do that again." A few conceded it was the first time they had ever had a chance to get to know someone who was down on his luck. And that changed their feelings quite a bit about the poor. Others said they hoped that one day they would be in a position to really help. And this would enable them to better understand the needs of others—the beginning, one hopes, of the notion that privilege can put someone in a position to further social justice. Though this may all sound condescending, it is certainly a way to foster the realization that some of the great satisfactions in life come from giving and doing for others, a concept to which these children rarely appear to be exposed.

"There is just so much room in a child's heart for compassion toward others burdened by problems never actually seen," writes Robert Coles in *Privileged Ones*. "When a moment of reflection has come or when a crisis has prompted uncertainty, sadness and worry, I have heard these quite fortunate boys and girls remark regretfully upon their own provinciality, their lack of awareness, their all too self-preoccupied days." In other words, a privileged upbringing, untempered by reality and an involvement with others, has the capacity to provide yet another blow to fragile self-esteem because it can make a child feel inadequate when dealing with the "wider world."

# 14.

# Derailed: Causes, Conditions, and Solutions

The discreet sign FOUR WINDS attached to a low stone wall is all that identifies a particular fifty-acre estate in a pastoral section of Katonah, New York. From the road a passerby sees nothing behind the stones but neat lawns and shade trees. A closer look confirms the initial belief that this is just a tranquil rustic retreat. For beyond the lawns lies a cluster of gray-shingled cottages with carefully tended windowboxes that sprout crimson geraniums and pastel-colored impatiens.

The reception area inside the main building similarly suggests this is probably a country inn or maybe an elite prep school. For it is decorated with antique furniture upholstered in green-and-pink-striped brocade.

In actual fact it is a psychiatric hospital of a very particular kind. It is here that a significant number of teenage casualties of fast-track households end up when neither they nor their parents can manage alone any longer. Despite good intentions something has gone seriously wrong. Drugs, trouble with the law, a drinking problem, promiscuity, suicide threats, or violence has caused a breakdown in the family's ability to cope. Professional help is sought. Among the teens that are brought here the difficulties have become so severe that inpatient treatment is needed for three to six months.

Growing up can be tough in any environment. But the fast-track world seems particularly difficult for some children, as we have seen. Not all thrive on the challenges, material advantages, and excitement. Only a very few need hospitalization. A number do well attending therapeutic sessions at the outpatient clinics that many of these hospitals operate. Less serious emotional difficulties can be treated in the community by a therapist in private practice. Other youngsters seem to thrive after they have been moved to a less-competitive day school or go off to a boarding school, away from the fast-track world where peer pressure may have been as difficult to handle as anything that might have been going on at home.

What kind of kids from high-achieving backgrounds get into serious trouble and how are they treated? Dr. Martin Buccolo, director of adolescent services at Four Winds, says they are typically youngsters who have had trauma in their young lives—the loss of a parent, parental separation, an alcoholic parent, physical or sexual abuse. Or they may have been adopted at some stage of childhood. Affluence and a top-drawer education do not lessen the emotional impact of such events. Others are the product of overanxious parents or a parent who needs to hold onto that child for his or her own self-definition. Still others have parents who seem unable to set limits or who are constantly at odds on how to raise that child, thereby confusing him or her. But the parents should not rush to assume blame. The child's own personality may be responsible, too. Some children inadvertently create more tension and trouble because their nature is more demanding. "We learn to look for these things regardless of our initial perception about the educational level, income, or the sophistication of the family," said Dr. Buccolo.

Other mental health professionals suggest that the beginning of an extreme downward cycle can often be traced to acute boredom. These are kids who could not seem to grow enthusiastic about anything, and unfortunately nobody had either the time or ability to spark their interest. They thus feel unworthy compared to their achievement-oriented peers. And this can turn into self-destructive behavior. Loneliness may be another factor, especially in families where the parents are heavily committed to an exceptionally demanding career. Moreover, by the time a child reaches the teen years, parents assume that they do not need to be around the house quite as much. Not so. "These kids end up feeling unwanted and unloved," said Cloe Madanes, co-director of the Family Therapy Institute of Washington, whose offices are in Rockville, Maryland. "They are looking to do something—anything—that will make them feel special and get them noticed."

Dr. Marvin Schwarz of Skokie, Illinois, a psychiatrist who runs similar hospitals (and has been dubbed Marvelous Marvin by grateful families), maintains that teenage problems in high-achieving households can also stem from the rage that erupts when those parents see their investment in the son or daughter going sour. "The anger toward the child is unbelievable," says Dr. Schwarz. "It crystallizes in adolescence because that is when those kids come home with poor SAT scores," he said. Those disappointing results may affect peer-group acceptance, too, he added. And this contributes to the cycle by encouraging the youngster to associate with those who support nonproductivity—usually the group that is into drugs, drinking, and casual sex.

Take, for example, the story of a sixteen-year-old we'll call Charles, who ended up at Four Winds. Charles had a father who was a scientist and a mother who was a lawyer. Neither could tolerate, it was later discovered, anyone or anything that was imperfect. Charles was a middle child with two brothers, both of whom were outstanding students and good-looking to boot. One was already in an Ivy League college. But Charles was different. He never did well in school. He was odd-looking. He was inarticulate.

Tagged the "black sheep" of the family, he began to be faithful to that image. (The film *The Breakfast Club* is especially useful in demonstrating the dangers of labeling a child a loser, because it shows how a child's behavior may become even more destructive as he or she starts to live up to that label.) He would yell at his parents in front of colleagues and friends in order to embarrass them—his way of getting back at his parents for their contempt for him. Since he could not gain respect through his academic or athletic achievements he would look for ways to make himself popular with friends by bragging about some outrageous feat or acquisition. No wonder he was soon pestering his parents for the finest car. Nothing less would satisfy him.

When the staff at Four Winds first heard about Charles he was already cutting classes. He had shaved off all his hair. He would talk about injuring and even killing himself. He had learned that only when his behavior and his threats were really outrageous could he get the attention of family and friends. He was very defensive. "He would tell us, 'You don't think anything I do is good enough,' " said Dr. Buccolo.

Eventually it became clear he might make good on his threats. "One night when his parents were abroad he drove here at ninety miles an hour to see a doctor," said Dr. Buccolo. Obviously he was out of control. He was admitted.

Then there was a thirteen-year-old we'll call Betsy, who was admitted to Four Winds after a suicide attempt. Betsy came from high-achieving parents, too, in this instance a corporate executive and a small-business owner. The father grumbled that his own father had never appreciated his accomplishments. He was determined that his children were going to be perfect people, to prove his own worth. He would sometimes make Betsy do homework several times over because he complained it was not good enough. Betsy became obsessive, a perfectionist.

So when she started to have minor problems in seventh grade she became panicky. "She could not tell anyone she had fallen down on the job," said Dr. Buccolo. She also told the staff later that she knew deep down that she was not meeting her parents' expectations and that it might get even worse later on. "Suddenly she became terrified of meeting life's challenges," said Dr. Buccolo. The only solution was to kill herself.

What kind of environment do the youngsters face at this type of hospital and what kind of therapeutic treatment do they receive? Initially such a hospital tries to offer them rehabilitation in an environment where they will feel most at home. For example, nestled within the fragrant pine trees of the Katonah campus of Four Winds are fifteen suburban-style houses that act as temporary group homes for sixty teenagers, the maximum the hospital can handle at any one time. There is even a small private school on campus. This type of care is proliferating, in part because mental health professionals often find that removing a child temporarily from the family is necessary. Cynics say, however, that it is also due to the way medical insurance is written— more plans cover in-patient care than out-patient treatment. And certain super-achieving parents find it easier to use hospitalization because they often do not have the time or energy needed to supervise and care for a troubled adolescent at home.

Four Winds, for example, now has a branch in Saratoga Springs, New York, and in suburban Chicago. Associates in Adolescent Psychiatry, a similar group headed by Dr. Schwarz of Skokie, Illinois, operates three such adolescent units in hospitals also in suburban Chicago. In 1987 Associates in Adolescent Psychiatry completed Meadow Wood Center—a brand-new hospital for such youngsters in New Castle, Delaware. Here again the appearance is deceptive. Meadow Wood looks like a resort hotel. In the center of the grounds stands a contemporary, single-story building replete with outdoor swimming pool, formal gardens for sunbathing, jumbo-sized gymnasium, and dorm-style twin bedrooms with matching chintz curtains and bedspreads.

Treatment is costly. However, the fees are covered by most comprehensive health insurance policies. At Four Winds the daily rate in 1987 stood at $790. But as a result of the cost, teenagers are able to benefit from the finest care, a small staff-to-patient ratio, and a pleasant environment that frequently includes a gym, music rooms, a swimming pool, and jogging and hiking areas. Four Winds is even euphemistically referred to as "the country club" by patients.

The pressure is lifted initially by separating the child from the family. Then the child is put into a surrogate family—a group house on campus where he or she encounters a consistent structure of rules and standards of behavior. It is also the place where the child has an opportunity to see himself or herself without the baggage from the past. "And these kids are often surprised to find that peers have some very positive things to say about them," said Dr. Buccolo. It may also be the first time such youngsters have been held accountable for their own behavior. This is achieved by establishing "levels." The youngsters gain more and more privileges by demonstrating increasing levels of responsibility. They must start by showing they are capable of following basic rules, such as going to the school each morning, tackling their studies, attending required meetings with peers. Moving ahead to the next level is prized because it permits more freedom, such as being allowed outdoors without an escort, obtaining a pass to go off the grounds, being able to vote in student affairs. But to move ahead one level the other kids must vote on that request. And during the debate the youngster who is making the request gets feedback on why the request should or should not be granted—in other words, peer evaluation.

The staff has found that the children develop deep insights into their own behavior this way. Some examples of those insights shine through in the poems patients write during their stay at Four Winds, eloquent testimony to the pain these children are clearly suffering.

The following verse is from a young woman who had become severely depressed and suicidal as a result of an extremely punitive childhood. Growing up in an environment in which the parents had placed great emphasis on doing everything correctly, the girl had never felt permitted to make even the smallest mistake. By the time she reached her late teens she had convinced herself she would never be adequate as an adult, no matter what she attempted.

> *So many times other people's needs*
> *came before mine.*
> *You brought me into this world*
> *but couldn't nurture me in*
> *loving and caring.*
>
> *All you knew how to give*
> *were sermons, rules, commandments.*

*I longed for strong arms to hold me,*
*lips to kiss away the hurts,*
*someone to tell me I was OK.*
*Instead, there were hands clenched*
        *to hurt and bruise,*
*lips to condemn and*
*voices to talk of my worthlessness.*

*You can never be the parents*
*I've wanted all my life.*
*Perhaps we can build a new relationship*
*based on mutual respect and concern.*

During hospitalization parents are brought in regularly for "cross-family group sessions"—workshops where parents can hear other youngsters and other parents talk about issues and problems in their own lives. The point, said Dr. Buccolo, is that parents can often "hear" the problems being discussed by other youngsters that they are unable to "hear" from their own child. The children also get to talk about a difficult issue, such as an abortion that was never revealed to the parent, with peer support in the room. In addition, everyone gets to meet everyone else's parents. This can help make the child see his or her own parents in a less jaundiced light. "Afterwards, if one kid still says his parents are awful the others will argue and say, 'Just wait a second . . . ,' " said Dr. Buccolo. The hope is that the youngster will return home with a more adult view of his or her behavior and a more objective idea of the parents. In turn, the parents may have had a chance to better understand their own actions and attitudes. "We have found that most kids go on to lead productive lives," said Dr. Buccolo.

Dr. Schwarz is equally emphatic about the need to involve the whole family—siblings, too—before he will accept a patient for treatment. Further, if the child has a drinking problem Dr. Schwarz will insist the parents stop drinking before he can treat that child. But he worries about fallout from hospitalization—the potential for that family to label that child a misfit or for the child to see himself as one. So Dr. Schwarz says he is increasingly trying to avoid hospitalization, even if the parents favor it.

A particular difficulty with some high-achieving families, according to his staff, occurs when the children are either told or intuitively know they must hide a parent's substance abuse from the professionals in order to help maintain the lofty public image that the parent has won over the years—a factor that frequently sabotages the efforts of the professionals. "The kid is in a double-bind," said Dr. Sharon Press, clinical director of Meadow Wood Center in Delaware. "He does not want to be disloyal, but he also wants to be able to tell." And she urges parents not to inhibit that revelation, especially as it will be made in the privacy of professional counseling.

For many parents the fear is that they will not recognize the danger signals in time, especially in an age when teen suicide, heavy drinking, and drug use are so common. To heighten awareness the team at Four Winds, together with other mental health professionals who have worked with troubled teens, helped me compile the following list of symptoms and situations that they have found most common among teens likely to encounter serious trouble:

> Any gesture, mention, or discussion of suicide; an action that is clearly self-destructive, like stealing money from a parent's wallet or taking off in the car after being told not to do so; an inexplicable decline in grades; a radical change of friends; a totally different style of dressing; perfect behavior of the sort that is too understanding, too pliant; becoming un-characteristically withdrawn; known substance abuse; behavioral problems at school; divorced or remarried parents.

A child who was adopted into a high-achieving family, even as a newborn, may also be more prone to emotional difficulties than a biological offspring, these experts have found. However, the evidence suggesting that such children may encounter more difficulties, despite the best efforts of the parents, is purely anecdotal at this point. There are no statistics.

## CHOOSING A THERAPIST

Even if a child is doing fine it is no longer unusual in high-achieving, affluent families for a therapist to be brought in for the child as a precautionary measure. Counseling sessions, under such circumstances, may be infrequent—perhaps a few times a year instead of the usual weekly meetings common among patients facing immediate problems. The reason expressed to me by the parents was that the child could benefit from the opportunity to talk candidly with someone who could help the youngster cope with even the ordinary frustrations of growing up *before* they became major problems. Seeing a therapist, they explained, no longer carried a stigma. And as they had the cash available, such counseling became yet another advantage an affluent parent could provide. But a word of caution. While we know that privileged children may be resented and unloved by those less fortunate than themselves, it can be troubling—even alarming—to learn that some of these youngsters may fare no better when it comes to a therapist.

Many therapists who have been heavily involved with well-to-do or prominent families—including Dr. Roy Grinker in Chicago, Dr. Frank Pittman in Atlanta, Dr. Michael Stone in Westchester County, New York, Dr. Roy Nisenson in Connecticut, and Dr. Burton Wixen in Los Angeles—have written in their medical papers or spoken out publicly about the danger of using a therapist who might envy the patient's wealth or family status. That envy, they note, can develop into full-scale resentment that may impede the progress of the therapy, since it becomes a barrier to genuine concern, cooperation, and communication.

Burton Wixen, in his book *Children of the Rich,* notes: "Envy is a basic human tendency and the psychotherapist is not immune . . . in addition there is another factor that may make treatment ineffective. This is the tendency to assume that what we know about middle-class patients applies to all patients."

Writes Roy Grinker in his paper "The Poor Rich," presented at the 1977 meeting of the American Psychiatric Association: "It is easy to become contemptuous . . . the therapist may envy the wealth, time, and freedom of the patient or feel injured when the bland, bored, and relatively uninvolved patient fails to make him feel important and effective."

How, then, to choose? An obvious solution would be to select a therapist who can identify comfortably with the patient either because that individual had a similar family background or is living and raising a family in the same type of community. Dr. Nisenson, for example, said he has been able to gain a far deeper empathy, compassion, and understanding for the problems of his privileged patients since he began raising his own three children in an affluent, fast-track community. He calls the therapist who actually lives and raises children in a fast-track environment "bilingual and bicultural"—someone who can act as an intermediary. This sort of person is more easily able to identify with the problems without prejudice and equally able to translate those difficulties into language the parent can understand and accept.

Dr. Stone suggests as an alternative someone who has already achieved a level of professional respect or has had an equally distinguished career—the sort whose accomplishments place him or her on an equal footing with the parents. This may be critical; otherwise the therapist may lose credibility in the eyes of the family. And that therapist *must* be respected as an equal, not a servant, by the parents. If not, the underlying contempt may make a mockery of the whole exercise.

## PRIVILEGED KIDS: SPECIAL HANDLING?

It is not easy to treat privileged youngsters. The therapists complain they tend not to be motivated to change because they know their needs will be met regardless. Bret Ellis has a powerful scene describing that arrogant attitude in his novel *Less Than Zero*. The psychiatrist threatens to tell the boy's mother that the boy is refusing to come to treatment. The boy scoffs at the threat, knowing full well no punishment of consequence will be levied.

These youngsters also have the resources to buy their way out of any unpleasant task. "My efforts to treat one highly narcissistic adolescent failed, for example, partly because of his capacity to dodge unpleasant topics in our sessions by taking off at a moment's notice to . . . go yachting off the Bahamas," writes Dr. Stone, the New York psychiatrist, in his 1979 article "Upbringing in the Super-Rich." Moreover, because the family owned several homes in faraway places, the shifting of the family base gave further excuses for the boy to break appointments.

A further problem is that there are usually no feelings of guilt about not showing up for appointments since their parents can afford to absorb the loss. Adds Dr. Stone, "Those from well-to-do homes may be particularly cavalier about their psychotherapy sessions since they realize that, from a strictly monetary viewpoint, having to pay for a skipped visit doesn't make much of a dent in the parents' resources."

A less apparent difficulty may be the faultless image that the child knows his parents enjoy in the community. Thus the child does not expect to be believed if he or she says anything critical about the parent. "They know their parents will charm you to death," said Sheldon Zablow, a psychiatrist in San Diego who treats many such youngsters. "And that scares them."

What, then, to do? Clearly, support for the therapist is as critical as a strict attitude toward attendance. Dr. Stone has even warned some parents that treatment will be terminated whenever two sessions in a row are canceled for frivolous reasons. He also insists, as do the staff at the psychiatric hospitals like Four Winds and Meadow Wood, that the parents must become involved, too. Otherwise the continued free-flowing of money and privileges or denial of difficulty by the parents may undermine any progress the therapist could make. These therapists further suggest that progress is impossible while the parent continues to "bail out" that youngster from trouble—putting in a good word with the judge, covering bad checks.

Dr. Pittman suggests that many of these youngsters might be helped by being allowed to take jobs that the parents consider inappropriate. "It is difficult for parents to let a son become a dishwasher when they had always expected him to be a senator like his grandfather," he noted in his 1985 article in *Family Process*. Yet there may be an important therapeutic lesson in learning to cope with the world as it really is. Helping such a child find a niche where he or she can feel purposeful and useful is also favored by these therapists. It helps the child keep a sense of balance through the rough moments. The involvement should also alleviate that "emptiness" so often associated with self-destructive behavior among the privileged.

The parents must allow their faults to show through so the child does not feel quite so inadequate by comparison. They may also need to encourage honesty from the therapist. "If someone has so much money or has achieved enough that everyone is in awe of him," writes Dr. Pittman, ". . . his inappropriate expectations of his children may go unquestioned."

Dr. Nisenson has found it helps both parents and children to place their difficulties in a sociological context, understanding that certain pressures, such as the focus on elevated standards or extreme competitiveness, stems as much from the kind of circles they are moving in as anything that occurs in the home. When he begins explaining what he has discovered about fast-track households and the peer pressures in these communities, "it helps lift that burden of self-contempt," he says, "and frees everybody to think of solutions rather than dwell on blame."

## KIDS' THOUGHTS ON THERAPY

The kids have their own views about the most helpful kind of intervention. Certainly the ability to start seeing their parents as ordinary rather than super-human beings is a big relief. "I always had an image of my parents as perfect," said an exceptionally beautiful sixteen-year-old girl. Her father is a self-made multimillionaire and her mother a respected artist. "They were flawless. And if they ever yelled at me I figured they must be right. But Ben [the therapist] explained they were *not* always right. And that if I felt I had done nothing to deserve their anger I should not be so quick to blame myself. He also showed me that some of my dad's rages were due to his moods, like if he had had a really bad day."

It was late on a cloudless fall afternoon. We were chatting in the privacy of my car, which I had parked at a quiet corner of a former private estate, since turned into a public park and museum. We were all staring out at the rust-, mustard-, and burgundy-colored leaves as they floated lazily down from the towering trees. As she spoke, her boyfriend, who was sitting next to her in the backseat, was playfully braiding the leather fringe on her jacket. After a pause he added his own idea about how a therapist had helped him. "It was the first time anyone explained to me why certain adults act the way they do," he said. "I was able to see things from my parents' perspective. It helped me understand what was going on."

Suddenly we all felt a chilly breeze floating on the autumn air. Blackened thunder clouds were racing across the sky. Winter was coming to the Garden of Eden. And I couldn't help but wonder what might happen to these kids if one day winter came to their paradise in an economic instead of a seasonal sense. Who would prosper and who would perish? Who would soar and who would sink? Come to think of it, were their generous parents concerned sufficiently about such a possibility as they acted like Santa Claus, frantically loading up their children's wagons with the best of everything?

# 15.

# Harvard or Bust

The stone mansion, evocative of English country elegance, stood majestically atop a pine-covered hill. It was reached from a twisting driveway that offered an approaching visitor every chance to savor the beauty of the rolling terrain and the grandeur of the setting. Four children had been raised in this rambling old house and now it was time for Josh, the youngest and only boy, to go on to college.

The father, an investment manager with a six-figure income, had been educated at a state university in the Midwest. And he had set his sights on Josh—the brightest of the bunch—getting the Ivy League degree he had never had the chance to gain for himself. "It's been a big pressure," said Josh, a slender, earnest young man with a freshly scrubbed face. His mother had just shown us into the ballroom-sized living room of the house, which had been decorated in gold leaf. Before Josh continued his discourse he whispered somewhat ruefully, "That's my dad you just passed in the family room, watching TV. He gets home so tired each night I hardly ever talk to him. He just collapses in front of that TV set."

We returned to the matter at hand. Typical of many stories I would hear, Josh continued: "I applied to eight colleges in all—not all Ivies. But good schools. My parents were very keen that I get into one of the best schools so I would get a good job and make the most money. I play saxophone and I knew I had a chance to get into Yale because one of their bandleaders had heard my tapes and told me so. But I found myself coming home after school and practicing for hours just to blow away the tension. Then I would lie on my bed and meditate for a while. You see, I was afraid I'd be in over my head if I did get in. I could picture myself studying constantly. So to get it over with I applied for 'early decision' at a small school in Pennsylvania. Not quite the Ivy League, but one where I had friends and I felt comfortable. At least it would end the tension quickly. It did. I was accepted before Christmas. Sure, my father was upset. We almost had a fight over it. I felt I had disappointed him. But I think his motives were based entirely on how much money I would make as soon as I got out and how much of a special privilege it would be. But I wouldn't have been happy. . . ."

Perhaps the initial question super-achieving parents may need to ask themselves about the college admissions process is "Why?" Why is it so easy to become so incredibly uptight about getting a child into an Ivy League college? Is it only because an Ivy-festooned degree can lead to better chances in life? Or is there a deeper, more narcissistic motive at work, too—the idea that admission to an Ivy League college will place the ultimate stamp of approval on one's own accomplishments as a parent? For whether a parent likes it or not, that rejection or acceptance letter becomes a scorecard. It is as if the parents as well as the child are being evaluated.

Is it any wonder that college counselors at the private and more select public schools I visited told me that when a student is rejected they have more trouble consoling the parents than the child? Some of them also believe that this may be why the euphemistic title "Public Ivies" has caught on so rapidly to describe some of the best state universities around the country—the University of Virginia and the University of California at Berkeley, for example.

The danger in all of this, of course, is that the child may end up feeling an awful sense of inadequacy if he or she does not make it—a feeling that it represents not only a personal failure but a humiliation for the family, too. And that is a pity because we all know that rejection by the Ivy League is not really a death sentence. There is life without Harvard. Nor is it necessarily the child's fault. Perhaps the serendipitous nature of the selection process needs to be stated over and over, as frequently to the parents as to their children. Harvard, for example, may have had more than the expected number of excellent applicants from the West Coast that year. Yale may have been overloaded with musicians. Indeed the Ivies are quite open and candid about telling everyone they are far more concerned these days about creating diversity—filling a class with students with a variety of talents and from broad socioeconomic, racial, and geographic backgrounds. This policy is even affecting "legacies"—children of alumni who used to be certain of a place irrespective of academic achievement. Not so anymore.

Despite the hurdles, the obsession to win that coveted place remains, in part because the United States is a meritocracy rather than an oligarchy. The best law firms and the top corporations *do* favor Ivy graduates. Moreover, the social cachet is enormous. There is no doubt that a degree from an Ivy League college is the closest Americans can come to conferring a peerage on somebody. It is an honored badge. So there is justification for the ambitions such parents do have for their children.

## SAVING A PARENT'S SANITY

Under the circumstances how can a parent negotiate the college-entrance maze with a minimum of tension? How do you avoid turning it into an obsessional quest that can tear a family apart?

First, the pursuit needs to be put into its rightful perspective. There is strong evidence to suggest that the most prestigious schools are becoming even more selective as the years progress. Observers have attributed that strength to increased demand for an Ivy education from segments of the population that rarely applied two or three decades ago—Asian-Americans, blacks, Hispanics. In addition, an increasing number of foreign students are flocking to these shores, and it doesn't take foreign families any longer than Americans to learn what's hot.

So youngsters should be aware that rejection is far from a disgrace. "We have found that SAT scores of the students who are accepted at the most selective schools are increasing far more rapidly than the national average," I was told by Sally Reed, editor of a specialized insider newsletter for educators called *College Bound,* which regularly polls admissions officers. "It's making kids very scared." The top schools can do this because applications are pouring in, in ever-increasing numbers, despite the late 1980s demographic lull in college-age students.

Thus, unless a son or daughter is a straight-A student or has a really outstanding talent, a parent may need to be more realistic about that youngster's chances (even though it may still be a good idea to "reach" for the Ivy League, as the college counselors put it when they talk about making the submissions). Frank H. T. Rhodes, president of Cornell University, advised students in an October 1987 *Newsweek* article: "Think realistically about your own likes and dislikes and about your academic ability as measured by such things as class rank and grade-point average." Having lived through the process four times with his own children and listened to countless parents over the years, he said he has also come to the conclusion that families and youngsters often cling to a far-too-parochial view, given the wide range of excellent colleges available in this country outside the Ivy League.

Next, the parents may need to be more sensitive to the feelings and fears of their children. After watching dozens of families struggle through the process year after year, Margaret Addis, chairman of the guidance department at Newton South High School in Newton, Massachusetts, has reached the conclusion that too often the dialogue in the household centers on the parents' expectations rather than the students' feelings. "Keep the conversation going," she urges. "Listen to what they are trying to tell you. Be supportive of their anguish as well as their joy." If that exchange does not take place in an honest, open fashion, the result, she said, is that the youngster may try to push aside the pressure by refusing to cooperate—by not showing up for tests, by not writing essays, or by becoming "sick" whenever an interview is scheduled.

Another fact to bear in mind is that though an Ivy League degree may improve career opportunities, it is not the only ticket to success. On the contrary, the United States is still sufficiently wide open so that someone from any background can do well. Indeed, one only needs to look at how rare it has been for a twentieth-century American President to have gained his academic credentials at an Ivy League school to realize that a lot of roads lead to the top. On the other hand, admission to an Ivy League school does not necessarily guarantee success. College admissions counselors have a stockpile of stories of students who actually wither under the intense pressure and academic arrogance, and feel second-rate in such a rarefied atmosphere, occasionally even dropping out.

Incidentally, having a child assume at least partial responsibility for his college costs, regardless of the parents' financial resources, can be an effective means of encouraging him to mature. I found a number of parents who told me they could have easily paid the full tab, but insisted their youngsters contribute to the tuition with money the child had earned during vacations or by taking out a student loan. Taking out such a loan may even improve a child's academic performance. The rationale is the same as that of the parents who insisted that their teenager contribute to the cost of a car. The theory is that by requiring a child to assume some of the financial responsibility for his or her education that child is being treated more like an adult. And a child who is treated like an adult is more likely to behave in a responsible manner—and feel more pride and "ownership" in the endeavor.

## KIDS' REACTIONS

When making out that short list it is worthwhile noting that placing too much emphasis on the Ivy League could backfire, even if the child's chances are good. A cautionary tale lies in the behavior and experience of Sharon, an articulate, charming seventeen-year-old from the Northeast. Sharon was an outstanding student at a top-flight private day school. She told me: "My father went to Yale and when we were little we always had Yale paraphernalia in the house. Somehow it was ingrained in me that I had to go to Yale, too. It was a family tradition. But a few years ago I decided no, they have no right to force me, to run my life. It used to bug me that they would say things like 'We are applying to Yale.' It was like it had turned into a private goal for them. What about me? What about my goals? What about what I wanted to do and what I wanted to be? So I guess I really didn't try very hard. I stopped caring. It was horrible in the house. I had always wanted to go to the University of Chicago. And that's exactly where I got in. But it hurt a lot. It hurt me to see my parents disappointed. It would have been so much nicer if they had supported me. Am I bitter? I am."

The idea that a youngster may purposely sabotage his or her chances to avoid facing the challenge is not farfetched. Educators and guidance counselors increasingly insist it is unquestionably the reason why the grades of so many stable, good students suddenly start to sink like the Titanic in tenth or eleventh grade—otherwise called Sophomore Slump. And they suggest that such a seemingly inexplicable behavior should be viewed as a warning signal—perhaps the student is not feeling good about the plans the family has for college. Perhaps he or she needs to articulate fears and obtain some reassurance about the future. Another difficulty therapists have noticed is that these youngsters are not comfortable when they do self-destruct academically. Many have absorbed their parents' ambitions and they do not really want to flunk out. They just feel caught in a no-win situation. So, in effect, they run and hide. It is the best way out they can devise.

Parents might also wish to consider the alternatives offered by Howard Greene, the private-college counselor and author of *Scaling the Ivy Wall: 12 Winning Steps to College Admission* (one of a number of books for the college-bound now available to help a youngster understand the dynamics of the admissions process and prosper in a competitive marketplace). He suggests to parents that a fine, competitive school with an excellent reputation—even though it may not be the Ivy League—may actually be more suitable for certain children at the undergraduate level. Many of these schools are becoming known for getting their students into top graduate schools and thus are equally likely to propel their students on to successful careers. Among those he cites: the University of Richmond, Denison University in Ohio, St. Lawrence University in upper New York State, and the University of Vermont.

Two other excellent sources of up-to-the-minute facts are *College Bound,* mentioned earlier, a monthly (except summer) newsletter for college advisers that contains information on the admissions game not necessarily found in the popular press; and *U.S. News & World Report,* which regularly polls college presidents for a list of the best colleges in various categories—region, size, areas of special strength. It also tells about the latest strategies and requirements of admissions officers—information that postdates much that is contained in many of the how-to-get-into-college books. That survey is conducted biennially.

## TAKING THE LONG VIEW

Certainly it helps to take that longer view. "We try to put families in contact with students who have graduated from some of the colleges that are not in the Ivy League," said Virginia Vogel, director of the Educational Guidance Service, a private center in Chevy Chase, Maryland, "so they can see that you can still go on to an Ivy League graduate school or receive a very good offer from a company." She mentioned, by example, the experiences of a boy whose mother and father were both college professors. The parents had set their sights on the Ivy League. Their son clearly did not have the grades or the scores to make it. The family was devastated. However, the boy was an avid physics student and was perfectly happy when he was accepted at a small college in the Midwest known for its physics program. Though the parents were still fretting months later he gained such self-confidence in the smaller, less competitive setting that his grades flourished. He became a student leader. And he had no trouble getting into Harvard Law School—to pursue the graduate degree he then had the confidence and the grades to seek upon graduation.

College counselors repeatedly told me stories of students who had won Ivy League graduate school degrees in the end, suggesting that the graduate degree from an Ivy League institution can be even more valuable than an undergraduate one. One told me, for instance, about a boy who was a fourth-generation legacy at Dartmouth. Even so, he failed to get in and went to Kenyon College instead, ending up in a Ph.D. program in diplomatic history at one of the Ivies.

## SEEKING AN INTERMEDIARY

A fee-based, independent college counselor can be enormously helpful as an intermediary between parent and child, especially when communication does break down. Typically, Ms. Vogel said she often finds parents calling her to say they cannot get their child to fill out an application or write an essay. "We talk to that student and try to find out the real reason why. We don't accept the idea that they are 'too busy.' Sometimes it's because they are afraid of leaving home to go to college. Or maybe it's the first time they are being evaluated by an outsider. Just being there to enable these kids to talk to someone outside the family or school sometimes removes the block." If they are still resisting, she said, she occasionally recommends a therapist.

These counselors find that to create the kind of climate that will encourage that youngster to reach for the best possible college, it helps to start by allowing that child to talk about his or her feelings about risk-taking. The adviser or parent then needs to underscore the fact that in order to get ahead it is often necessary to take risks, such as applying to a few places that may seem beyond reach. But part of that risk is facing the fact that "you may have to face rejection." If the parents can reassure their child that a possible rejection will not be greeted in the family as a major catastrophe, so much the better, and the student will feel more confident to try. Counselors have also found that students who are more likely to feel good about aiming high are those who have chosen a "safety" school they are really enthusiastic about attending. This way they know there is a welcome fall-back position if the risky reach fails. "I've had a lot of unexpected successes that way," added Ms. Vogel. Moreover, feeling good about that non–Ivy League choice right from the start also seems to have a beneficial effect upon the student's adjustment and future success at the safety school once he or she gets there.

What about the use of tutors as well as business or family contacts to help open the Ivy door? The consensus among the kids is that this is okay and even welcome—provided it is for a college of *their* choice, not simply to bolster a parent's ego. As a freckled, eighteen-year-old boy in the Midwest put it: "When my dad offered to call someone at Yale for me I said, 'Great!' I wanted to go to Yale. I really wanted to. And I saw it was a chance to maximize the opportunity. I believe if someone can hand you a chance like that in life you grab it. You would be stupid not to take advantage of all that you can. I know I can handle Yale, provided I get the chance." He said he felt the same way about tutoring help. He had resented it in grade school, he said. But when he saw his algebra grades slipping in high school and he wanted to go to an Ivy League college, he was eager to accept the offer from his parents.

Above all, do not dwell on the failure if it happens. Switch to a positive approach. Begin finding reasons why the other school might work—a chance to shine among less competitive peers, a more relaxed atmosphere, greater opportunities for personal attention from faculty members. But try not to narrow the alternative for geographic reasons. Many of the finest colleges appear to be a great distance from home. But the speed of modern air travel can often make these locations quicker and simpler to get to than a school in a nearby state that can be reached only by car.

## ALTERNATIVES TO COLLEGE

What about the child who is not motivated to go directly to college? Or the one whose grades have slipped so badly that getting into a good college might be impossible at this point? Not to despair. Much is now being done to address this problem.

The solutions come in two flavors, so to speak. One is called the PG year, otherwise known as the postgraduate year of study, or thirteenth year. This particular concept is geared toward the youngster whose grades and motivation are not up to selective-college caliber. Burgeoning primarily among the private boarding schools, it normally takes the form of a curriculum designed specifically for students seeking an extra year of academic experience—a second chance, as it were—before applying to college. Many of the PG year programs were initiated because a growing number of high school athletic stars were in need of an additional boost in order to fulfill the tougher academic requirements established by the National Collegiate Athletic Association. For these individuals or anyone else, actually going away also removed the stigma of being left behind in the neighborhood once friends took off for the various college campuses. "But I do warn parents that this is not necessarily access to the Ivy League," noted Phyllis Steinbrecher, an educational consultant who serves the New York metropolitan region. "You are putting yourself in competition with the regular students who have had four years of solid records."

Diane, a sixteen-year-old daughter of a senior executive at a *Fortune* 500 company, was one such girl. She came to Mrs. Steinbrecher vainly searching for some way out. She had an older brother and sister who had both been excellent students and had made it into Ivy League colleges. By contrast, Diane had combined SAT scores that barely reached 900, which is slightly below average. So rather than slip shamefully off to a less prestigious college, feeling like a failure, she eagerly embraced the idea of a PG year, opting for one of the newer college preparatory study programs for affluent young Americans that are being established abroad—in this instance in Greece. Having studied hard in Greece and improved her grades and her scores significantly, by the following spring she was able to gain admission to a small, fashionable college that preserved both her pride and self-confidence.

She was able to do this because schools like the one in Greece are small, select institutions that limit their enrollment to the precollege American student or the child of Americans living and working overseas. But as a result they are expensive. In 1988 the average cost was about $20,000 for tuition, room, and board, and virtually none of them offer scholarships. But they certainly do a good job. Indeed, their success is underscored by the fact that many foreign families, eager to prepare their own youngsters for admission to the better American colleges, are now using them as a preparatory vehicle, too.

The other alternative is known simply as "taking a year off." This does not mean that the youngster just tosses hamburgers at McDonald's or (God forbid) loafs around the house. It is much more likely to be a structured plan, worked out by an academic or educational adviser, that includes community service or travel that is tied to an internship or maybe even a job abroad. That option is normally chosen by youngsters whose grades are good but who feel the need for a breathing space to find out more about themselves and what they are seeking from life and a career. In these instances the counselors normally encourage the student to apply to the usual range of colleges and then opt for deferred admissions from the school of choice (readily granted by virtually all colleges). This way the future is not being jeopardized but simply put on hold.

Mike was one of those kids. Son of a wealthy businessman and a TV production coordinator, Mike had been the sort of student who admitted to me that he had been able to maintain a B-plus–A-minus average without doing very much work at all. "My study habits and motivation were so lacking that it looked like my dad might be spending $16,000 a year for me to party," he conceded.

"So I guess the idea first came from my dad," he continued. "He offered me the chance to go into a program that provides five different types of internships during the year. This way you can try out a lot of jobs and meet a lot of different sorts of people. They also put you on a strict budget—forty-five dollars a week for spending money from your parents—so it's not play.

"I grew up fast," continued Mike. "I worked in a music store, for a preservation society, at a radio station, with gifted children, and finally at an outdoor environmental education center as a counselor. You see, kids like us are very sheltered. We really don't know what the world's all about. Even summer jobs never make you feel you are part of the working world. But that winter I started to meet all types. I even had to live much more simply and with people from very different backgrounds from myself—something you don't do even at college. I began to feel really independent and proud of it. One job paid me enough so I could say to my dad, 'No, I don't need your money this month.' I liked the feeling of responsibility, too. I'd never had that before. I learned something else about well-off kids like us. We are much less serious and committed compared to kids from homes without a lot of money. Maybe it's because you grow up feeling that everything's always going to be there for you." Eventually Mike went on to a small but highly respected midwestern college. And based upon what he learned about himself in one of those internships, he is now considering teaching as a career.

In 1988, the cost of tuition plus accommodations (youngsters pay for their own food) for this type of program was running around $8,000 for the year. Dynamy in Worcester, Massachusetts, is one of the better-known programs of this type. College counselors are usually an excellent source of information and guidance for these programs. The National Association of Independent Schools in Boston can also make referrals.

Though the concept was considered almost shameful only a few short years ago—the kids looked upon as dropouts—these alternatives are becoming increasingly trendy, even favored by some parents and advisers who have discovered that a more mature college student often becomes a more serious student. Such parents are in good company. Queen Elizabeth had several of her sons engage in such programs in order to help make them more self-confident and self-reliant before sending them on to higher education.

Well-known examples are Outward Bound and the National Outdoor Leadership School in Wyoming (NOLS). Both teach survival skills by taking groups of kids into various wilderness and unfamiliar settings for weeks at a time. These can be incorporated into a year that also allows time for a youngster to hold a job and take courses that will help provide a stronger academic foundation for college. Because it is assumed that these youngsters do accomplish something of value, even the colleges are beginning to look upon them with new respect, treating them like courageous pioneers. "It can turn someone with a lackluster academic record into an exceptionally interesting candidate," one admissions director told me. In addition, "Colleges find that students who do [take a year off] generally outperform those who start directly after high school," noted Herbert F. Dalton, Jr., director of enrollment planning at Middlebury College in Vermont, in a 1988 *New York Times* article on the topic of college admissions.

Few know better than Cornelius H. Bull, a feisty, former private school administrator who had the foresight to see the trend emerging as early as the end of the 1970s. It was then that Mr. Bull, a snowy-haired, blue-eyed gentleman who bears a striking resemblance to Peter O'Toole, started "Interim," an agency in Princeton, New Jersey, that helps kids and their parents choose alternatives to college. He maintains files on hundreds of options.

In sum: there is never only one route to a successful future. Nor do certain children necessarily mature as fast or as easily as others. Some may fare better during the undergraduate period in a less pressured environment, while others will flourish in an Ivy League setting right from the start. Still others might do better if they first have the opportunity to assume the level of personal responsibility expected of them in the workplace. Fortunately, these differences are increasingly being acknowledged as such—differences rather than deficiencies.

# 16.

# A Word on Teenagers

Every teenager is at risk to some degree these days, whether from suicide, drug and alcohol abuse, sexually transmitted diseases, or the impact of divorce and remarriage. And I think it is clear from all that has been mentioned in this section that teenagers from high-achieving households are not immune to these perils, even though they may seem from outward appearances to be so very fortunate. Attending a good school and having money and a family that commands a great deal of respect are no insurance policy against the turmoil that accompanies adolescence.

The danger among this group is that normal adolescent pressures may be too easily dismissed by a parent because the child's life seems so pleasant. True, these youngsters do not have to worry about paying for college. They do not have to worry about having to work during the teenage years because the family can afford to—and probably will—give them a generous allowance that will allow them to purchase a car, fine clothes, great vacations.

But this cannot make up for the perils facing them within—in their own peer group or even dealing with the academic expectations of their parents. Or, for that matter, the anguish and mixed emotions that may be generated by a parent's remarriage or any personal upheaval that spans economic and social lines.

In fast-track circles I think it is clear that parents need to be especially vigilant during adolescence when dealing with the self-labeled loser—the youngster who feels academically or socially inadequate compared to peers and parents. These are the ones who may need special care and affection to offset that sense of having let everyone down, and the likelihood that they may act out those fears by getting involved with the "wrong" friends, which is a common response during this time.

High-achieving parents should also be prepared for unusually sharp criticism of themselves and their lives from their teenager during adolescence. These youngsters really do have a strong need to unhinge their "perfect" parents as they search for pride in their own identity. For it may be one of the only ways they can bolster their own emerging egos in light of their parents' exceptional achievements. Try not to take it personally.

Be alert to the temptation of using gifts of cash to relieve guilt feelings over unavoidable absences. Being showered with too much money is no panacea. Rather, it may set up unrealistic levels of entitlement in the child's mind. And understand that some of the most meaningful ways to help a youngster cope may be to place what is happening in sociological terms, explaining that many of the pressures emanate from the demands of the subculture in which that child lives.

To help maintain a modicum of emotional equilibrium during this period it may be necessary to place less emphasis on some of those loftly academic aspirations. This is particularly true when looking at potential colleges, bearing in mind how competitive the entrance game has become. And watch for warning signs of buckling under the pressure, such as a sudden drop in grades at tenth or eleventh grade. Obtain outside help if necessary.

Ultimately it may help to take the long view. Eventually most adolescents—including those from high-achieving households—do settle down in a responsible way and find a niche for themselves. They even prosper.

# V

# Young
# Adults

# 17.

# Growing Up May Take a Little Longer

It is hardly a secret that it is taking youngsters a lot longer to "grow up" these days. One only has to look around at neighbors, colleagues, and friends to see and hear the stories about "children" well into their twenties who are still being supported financially, still calling home whenever a crisis occurs in their lives, still in class full-time, even though it may be at the graduate level, and sometimes even returning home to live for a short (or not-so-short) period of time.

The syndrome seems to be particularly acute among well-to-do parents who are high-achievers. And rather than feel guilty and blame themselves, such parents should realize—as with so many issues raised in this book—that if one looks at what is going on in the broader sociological context of our day one sees a valid reason for what is happening. It is so prevalent, by the way, that someone has come up with a name for the phenomenon—"The Postponed Generation"—coined by author Susan Littwin for a book of that name, published in 1986, which offers a series of profiles of such youngsters. Her sampling is predominantly among California young adults, since that is where she lives and works. But it seems to be an accurate reflection of the nation at large.

Several factors are converging to prolong growing up. Our highly specialized, highly skilled society demands a far longer period of schooling. Thus the old idea that a child can be launched at eighteen or even twenty-one is hardly possible in this day when anyone-who-wants-to-be-someone needs an advanced degree. And since children of high-achievers tend to be the sort who are encouraged, or have the ambition, to make the most of this opportunity they go for the most they can get. Further, they are bound to play a somewhat dependent role until they achieve a financial level comparable to their parents, which can take a very long time or may never indeed happen. And this, of course, is the antithesis of the way things used to work in prior generations.

Children of high-achievers also have parents who are used to being managers and in control. Thus these adults-who-would-remain-children feel—again with valid reason—that their parents continue to be the resource they might just as well turn to when trouble strikes, rather than solve their own problems. Why not? Those parents have the contacts, the know-how, the desire to help. They are not sick, over the hill, or even long since passed away like their own parents might have been at such an age—thanks to the miracles of contemporary medicine. Moreover, I sense that the parents get an ego boost and a great deal of joy from remaining a valued source of counsel and assistance. This, in turn, appears to have a catalytic effect, further delaying true emancipation. And that sort of help, Littwin found, ranges from emotional to financial. It even includes housing. Many of these parents have large homes that can accommodate an adult child anxious to return to the nest. Where that is not feasible they frequently help out by contributing to the rent on the young person's apartment.

Littwin also found that many of these youngsters take a lot longer to make a commitment to a career, caught between the promise of their golden childhood and the crude realities of a far less sympathetic work world. It is a world, she discovered, that may seem so much of a disappointment that these young adults continue to change plans again and again in a sort of desperate search to find what was promised but perhaps cannot always be delivered.

Thus it is apparent that many different pressures, needs, and difficulties conspire to lengthen the childhood of children of fast-track parents. With that in mind it seemed inappropriate to end a book like this, which attempts to outline the many issues facing these children, at the customary finish line of childhood—the twenties. It had to be continued into the young-adult years. Let us look at the issues that can come to the forefront during that period.

# 18.

# Careers: Redefining Success

*I must study politics and war so that my sons may have liberty—liberty to study mathematics and philosophy, geography, natural history, naval architecture, navigation, commerce and agriculture, in order to give their children a right to study painting, poetry, music, architecture.*

— John Adams, second President of the
United States, in a letter to his wife, Abigail

One of the bonuses that come from being a child of fast-track parents is that you normally have the financial backing to become almost anything you could possibly dream of being—from a ballerina to a biochemist, from an author to an astronaut. Yet it is an elusive advantage. For such children are equally likely to feel constrained by the need to do something, become something, that guarantees them the same status and income as their parents. Even more terrifying is the implied expectation, born of the old American dream of continued upward mobility, that at some point they will exceed those achievements.

Though this can become a superb motivator for the truly ambitious, it can be daunting for anyone else; exhausting just to think about. Dr. Nisenson, the New Canaan psychologist, has noticed that every time he mentions careers to the teenagers he counsels they suddenly grow weary. Said he: "They start to yawn. They can't seem to concentrate. They give excuses like 'I went to bed late last night,' or 'I was up late studying for a test.'" But Dr. Nisenson thinks there's more to it. "It's upsetting because it seems so insoluble," he observed.

## LIVING AS WELL

Another constraint is lifestyle. Accustomed to an extremely high standard of living, these youngsters are quite candid about their addiction to luxuries like fine cars, designer clothes, mountain homes, foreign travel. And they admit it puts a crimp in their career plans.

"When you have everything, you are less likely to take risks," a member of a Girl Scout troop told me. We were sitting with nineteen other girls in a circle on gray-metal folding chairs discussing the dilemma in the basement of a venerable Congregational church. All around us the rest of the girls nodded knowingly. "Look at my dad," continued the fifteen-year-old who had been speaking. "He took a lot of risks to get where he is today. But he had nothing to lose. So he could try anything. But when you have a lot to lose you don't want to take those risks."

"So you wouldn't choose a career where you couldn't make it," added the girl a few chairs to her left. "Like trying to be a successful artist . . ."

"Or trying to be a newscaster on TV . . ."

"Or starting a business instead of becoming a lawyer."

From other groups I heard similar tales of constriction. A high school sophomore told me: "I love photography. But I know I will have to make it a hobby, not a career, because it doesn't bring in much money." She thought for a moment and then added softly: "People expect us to make a lot of money, just like our parents. They just expect it. That's a lot to carry."

Income seemed less of an issue among those whose parents had accumulated sufficient capital, or money had been in the family for a sufficiently long time, so that there would clearly be a substantial sum to pass on. With these youngsters the presence of a financial safety net seemed to free them to take some of those chances. "We know we will have our parents to fall back upon," said a boy at a prestigious private day school.

But that advantage has to be handled with great sophistication and caution. In her book, Susan Littwin points out that parents who are too eager to provide the resources to keep an adult child afloat may actually retard practical and serious commitment to a career (more on this in the following section).

## YOUR WAY MAY NOT BE THEIR WAY

The youngsters whose parents clearly loved their chosen careers seemed far more eager to follow in their footsteps than the ones whose parents came across as jaded, tired, and cynical—which says a lot for the unintended way parents often communicate the nature of their careers to their children. If the parents do not appear fulfilled from the way they discuss their work they should not therefore be surprised if their children positively hate the idea of becoming like them, or seem poorly motivated even if they do agree to go along. Take, for instance, the girl at a private school in the South who observed, "The future is no longer intriguing when you know you are not going to end up doing what you want to do." She continued, "My father expects me to be a lawyer just like him." She did not particularly like the idea of spending her days as a lawyer, she said. But she hated the thought of letting her father down.

The youngsters dub such a narrow view The Three Options, law, medicine, or business, as though nothing else counts or has value. One dark-haired, twenty-two-year-old girl, whose father is with a multinational corporation in Asia, told me, "When I told my father I was looking for a job as a junior high school teacher, he said, 'When are you going to think about getting a job-job, a real job?"

The same dilemma is described in *Money and Class in America*. "The boy had a talent for painting," comments the author, Lewis Lapham, talking about an old school friend. "But his parents had made a mockery of his ambition to study art, and he had learned at St. Paul's to suppress any sudden or suspicious movement of his imagination."

Not all success-oriented parents behave this way, of course. But quite a significant number do have that approach, judging by the remarks of the children I met. And there are valid reasons. "They see the success and all the good things they have gained from what they became," as one sixteen-year-old girl put it, "and they want the same for you. I can understand that. But it may not be what I want from my life."

Counselors working with these families have noticed the same syndrome. "The first thing I always ask is 'How do your parents feel about your choice?'" said Barbara-Jan Wilson, associate dean at Wesleyan University and director of its Career Planning Center. "I know that many are under pressure to go to law school or sign up with an investment banking firm. And it's better to discuss these things in advance." If the interest clearly comes from the child then there is no problem. If it comes more from a desire to please a parent then some further dialogue may be needed.

Peer pressure also plays a major role. Even youngsters with the most broad-minded parents must be prepared to face the ridicule of their peers if they favor the helping professions rather than those that offer fame and fortune. "When I said I wanted to be a nursery school teacher because I love young kids, all my friends laughed," said a shy sixteen-year-old girl. "They said, 'But you'll never make any money at that!' "

Added another: "You can't just do your own thing among this crowd. You're supposed to become a professional or an executive."

These youngsters do not therefore have it as easy as it looks. For these contraints come as much from the social climate of our times as from the family, which make them even more difficult to resist.

## STARTING OUT
## IN AN OVERCROWDED WORLD

Yet a further fear expressed by these youngsters was a feeling that the world had become so overcrowded that getting to the top was now only possible for the truly shining stars among them. In this context they talked of feeling cheated, as though the Land of Boundless Opportunities had slammed its gates just as they are about to enter. They also seemed deeply affected by the longevity of adults today, sensing that opportunities that might have opened up for prior generations would not be made available to them until late in their lives because everyone lived for so much longer. An interesting portent of possible things to come came from a sixteen-year-old Brooke Shields look-alike who worried that she would be held back by the financial drain and time demands of aging parents who would just "live on and on and on."

With success defined in such narrow terms and opportunities appearing to be limited, it is little wonder that many of these children are not rushing out to change the world as their parents may have done (or tried to do) in the 1960s. Others just seem to grind doggedly forward in an almost joyless way, more out of fear of slipping than the excitement of reaching. And the mavericks who are determined to follow their dreams, irrespective of parents or peers, do not get much sympathy or support from peers.

## REDEFINING SUCCESS

Is there a way parents can help?

First, as the title of this section implies, it may help to start by having the parents redefine success in their minds as well as those of their children, thinking through the idea that self-worth does not have to equal net worth. It has certainly not been that way throughout history. Many people have enriched society and been recognized as highly accomplished without necessarily enriching themselves. Was Freud honored because he amassed a vault filled with cash? Was Pasteur lauded for building a pharmaceutical empire? Was Christ a wealthy man? Would Gandhi have commanded as much respect had he been rolling in rupees? Is Mother Teresa revered because she works twelve hours a day trying to crack the glass ceiling in order to make it onto the board of a major corporation? Of course not. Success can also be:

- achieving recognition for outstanding talent or service
- having a positive impact upon society

It might also be liberating to remember that nothing in the world is ever static. The pendulum is always in motion. Thus a career that today may appear to be on the express track to Nowhere might be among the shining stars of tomorrow.

Few understand this as well as Dennis Flavin, founder and former publisher of *Careers* magazine. He maintains that the late 1980s may be the final hurrah for the idea that status and success have to be defined primarily in terms of income and title, and that anything less classifies you as a failure. "When I would go around the country talking to the kids I would tease them," says Mr. Flavin. "I would tell them that pretty soon I would have to publish a magazine called *Burnout* because of the unrelenting punishment they are giving themselves by putting all that emphasis on success and materialism."

Already, he said, investment banking is losing its panache as a result of the crash of 1987. Lack of ethics and shabby behavior are placing a cloud over the heads of certain business tycoons. Even law is losing its earnings potential now that so many people have law degrees. The glittering future, he maintains, may be won by those who find a way to lead a more balanced life—a life that clearly does have redeeming social value as well as time for personal pursuits, even if this must be achieved at the expense of an extra dollar, or membership in the executive suite.

Indeed the desire for a less pressured, less frantic work life was already visible among the younger children of certain high-achievers that I met. Many mentioned, time and again, how they did not want to spend their adult years as frazzled as their parents, especially if they could find ways to live well on less. Even at that tender age they were astute enough to see that so many of these adults might have been living *The* Good Life while not necessarily enjoying *a* good life. Moreover, many of them seemed really anxious to find a way to "help others" as they frequently put it, if this could be done in a financially viable way. They felt that their privileged childhoods somehow put them in an obligatory position, as Old Money families have long believed it does.

## 2001 AND BEYOND

Flavin has some intriguing thoughts on how the meshing of altruism and financial independence might come about. Consider his notions about the likely picture of the career world, circa 2001 and beyond, which I have woven into a potpourri of ideas gained from others in the career-planning fields, too:

*The elderly.* The number of people over sixty-five years old is growing at an accelerated pace. By the year 2000 demographers expect about 35 million individuals to be in that category, almost 40 percent more than during the late twentieth century. And those numbers will continue to swell. This will create an explosive growth in health-related fields as well as other services that cater to older people. And these older folks will not necessarily be poor and housebound. They will be better educated and have more disposable income than ever in the past. They will be an affluent population willing to pay for services they want and desire. Those services will include pharmaceutical products, special housing and the development of interiors and furnishings that cater to the elderly, sales and development of medical implements or aids, nursing (which in general is in a renaissance), entertainment or travel opportunities for their increased leisure time, fitness classes or fitness centers, and psychological support. "There's going to be a lot of discretionary dollars out there," predicts Flavin. "So helping them does not necessarily mean giving up a good income."

*Teaching*. No longer a lowly field with no status and bargain-basement income, it may become increasingly well compensated with higher status as the need for instructors of all kinds grows more acute. For instance, our modern, rapidly changing business and technical world requires most adults to constantly update their skills irrespective of their field of endeavor. Such continuing education is already being taken over by entrepreneurs offering immersion courses or high-intensity sessions for busy executives or professionals who have no time to go back to school. The organizers and teachers offering such courses are extremely well paid by the business world for this service. The rebirth and new popularity of the Dale Carnegie courses are but one example. That concept should grow. So will courses designed for all those older people.

In addition, we are entering a period where there will suddenly be a dearth of college professors, bringing a new market demand (which frequently translates into heightened respect) for the person who has earned a Ph.D. in such subjects as medieval history or anthropology. The lack of academic positions that characterized the 1970s and 1980s is due to give way to an acute period of faculty shortages. By 1995 about 40 percent of 108,000 people who currently hold positions as tenured faculty in American colleges will have reached retirement age, according to research on the topic conducted by *Time* magazine. Where will the new ones come from? Will there be a frantic rush to lure people into these fields with better pay, as there has already been among teachers willing to go into the public schools? Logic suggests this might very well happen.

*Childcare*. This is perhaps the biggest sleeper of them all. Childcare is likely to become a hot product as private and public funds are channeled increasingly into this underdeveloped field. Families will demand it. And families with the income to pay what it takes will be willing to compensate really top-notch people to care for their kids or organize that care. That girl who yearned to be a nursery school teacher may be the most farsighted of them all—and one of the happiest if she does retain the inner strength to sign up for the needed training. In fact, the entire childcare industry is ripe for a major overhaul that may improve both the quality of care and the income it generates. This change is also likely to include improvement in the image and income of the early-childcare professional who is willing to live in.

*Public service.* Long in eclipse in terms of status or income, elected or appointed jobs in federal, state, and local government—as well as the nonprofit sector—may take on a new luster as the country and even the world becomes increasingly focused on issues of survival and social concerns that tended to get brushed under the (fancy new) rug during the get-rich-quick era of the 1980s. These include the Third World debt and the federal deficit, clean energy, atmospheric and environmental decay, the homeless and the chronically poor, population control. President John Kennedy's 1961 rallying cry, "Ask not what your country can do for you, ask what you can do for your country," may seem as out of place today as a bonnet at a rock concert. But for that very reason its time may just be coming around again. Moreover, it would be fulfilling the destiny established for us decades ago by the patrician families of this nation who have made an honorable practice of favoring public service among their second and third generations.

*Manufacturing and craft skills.* We are already so deeply into a service rather than a manufacturing economy that the pendulum may be about to swing back, but with a slightly different twist. The demand for hand-made or hand-built items is getting more pronounced, especially as there is a lot more affluence around to pay for such luxuries. Skilled craftsmen likely to command substantial incomes include stonemasons, restoration carpenters, fabric weavers, glass blowers, and ceramic artists. Organic or specialized farmers providing exotic foods will also be in demand.

*Social organizers and personal support.* For those who are natural "people persons," there could be a bright professional future riding on those skills. Take, for example, the rise of the specialist adviser. We have already seen the burgeoning use of counselors of every hue—family therapists, educational consultants. In addition, with the continued growth of technical jobs that subject so many more people to isolation as they interact with machines rather than people all day, there is likely to be an even greater need for people adept in organizing social or fitness clubs as an antidote to that daily grind. Again, these services are likely to become so much a fundamental part of everyday life they will be better compensated. Think of the money already being made by entrepreneurs operating businesses in the fitness field. A number of corporations are also incorporating fitness facilities into their office buildings and have hired fitness managers.

*A less, not more, crowded job market.* Demographers say we are headed into a period of labor shortages at many levels. A controversial book, *The Birth Dearth,* about falling fertility rates in the United States and other advanced nations, has come to the same conclusion. Catalyst, a nonprofit business research organization focusing on executive women in the workplace, points out the same fact in demonstrating how opportunities for women managers should increase in the 1990s, irrespective of attitudes. And when you take that point one step further, the logical conclusion from the Catalyst assumption is that the shortages must create greater opportunities for both sexes. Thus the children of the baby boomers may actually face the *reverse* of the job marketplace of their parents.

And finally, it is probably not even necessary to add that young people with advanced technical or scientific talents and expertise will be able to write their own ticket—whether in business for themselves or in the employment of others.

## LIVING WELL ON LESS

And what about a way to live well without necessarily making as much money? It could be found by seeking a job in a community that is not as expensive as the fashionable enclaves where these golden children might have grown up, particularly in more rural areas that offer extensive outdoor advantages. Small college towns are one place where some are already migrating. Admittedly status and income may be compromised, but as the associate dean of Columbia Graduate School of Journalism wrote in a *Newsweek* article, some young people really do "scorn overbearing competition and what it does to human relations . . . and that simply and gently [they are telling us] enough is enough." Living abroad—especially in developing countries where the drop in the value of the dollar has not had as great an impact on the cost of living—is another possibility as commerce becomes increasingly internationalized.

Alternatives could be found in a job that offers appealing perks rather than dollars, such as the chance to meet people from all walks of life or travel to unusual places. I found this to be true during my many years in journalism. (Nobody ever became rich going into journalism, I often remind my higher-income friends. But in what other calling would I have had the chance to go to the White House, the prison house, and Paul Newman's house all in the same lifetime, and the personal fulfillment of being able to raise awareness of social issues or inequities?)

A college administrator I met offered some similar thoughts from her own life. When we spoke she had just been offered a job at three times her present salary by a major New York City investment banking firm. And she had turned it down. Why? Because she realized she had the life she felt she wanted without the need for so much more money or a fancier title or even a fancier address. She had a magnificent, carpeted office (with working fireplace) in a converted Victorian house that overlooked a charming old village green. Along with the job she and her family had been given free living quarters—the right to live in one of the school's lovely old houses which was only a half block from her office (no commuting, no expensive home to buy). Moreover, it was on a street brimming with interesting and talented people that included two Pulitzer Prize–winning authors. She had extended vacations during school holidays that gave her as well as her husband a chance to enjoy their retreat in New Hampshire, a second home they could never have afforded if they had been paying for their primary residence. Free daycare was provided on campus for her four-year-old daughter. The 1,800-member student body offered her access to baby-sitters galore. She had an unusually generous retirement and medical package. How could she beat that!

"I think many of these young people have an unrealistic idea of what it takes to be happy and fulfilled in life," noted Barbara-Jan Wilson, the Wesleyan University Career Center director. "And how badly you can feel if you do not do what you really like."

## HOW TO "TRY OUT" CAREERS

Of course, not everyone knows what he or she wants to be. And for this reason career counselors increasingly favor a series of internships for anyone in that predicament. There are now several organizations that package these so that someone can sample a variety of endeavors in a relatively short space of time. Career counseling offices at the various schools or even private educational counselors can normally make these referrals. And one of the advantages of being a child of super-achievers is that there is usually the money to afford such programs.

Judith Stern Peck, a family therapist in Manhattan who has worked with many children of successful adults, has found that it is often difficult for a super-achiever to accept a child with humble or out-of-the-mainstream ambitions. Yet it is far better to encourage the child's soul-searching and experimentation early in life, she noted, than it is to have that person wake up at forty realizing that he or she may have spent a life fulfilling someone else's ambitions or ego needs. By then it could trigger a personal crisis that could hurt a lot more people.

Greater flexibility concerning options may also be warranted since it is not uncommon these days for people to have several different careers in a lifetime, so that even if something does not work out it is hardly a calamity. Nor does it usually mean scrapping an expensive education. It may just require taking a slightly different route using the same skills.

Take the story of Greg. When we spoke he had been doing what all his peers were favoring and their parents applauding: he had gone on to law school and was now working for a small law firm with a general practice. For some youngsters it may have been a perfect choice and a great beginning. But not for Greg. "Right from the start I absolutely hated it," he said. "I hated having to fight all the time. And you couldn't always tell the truth because you had to put your client's needs first. That was tough because I've always thought of myself as someone with a very high level of integrity. Anyway, it just didn't excite me. I expected deep insights. But all it turned out to be was learning a set of rules. And I didn't even believe in the system. The more I learned the more it seemed to be a very poor form of conflict resolution."

So Greg quit and took a temporary summer job at a children's camp where he had spent his youth. Slowly he came to realize that teaching was his calling, and his preference was for elementary school. "But I still held back because it offered such low status and was so poorly paid." Ultimately, he said, he dealt with the "status issue" by enrolling in the Harvard Graduate School of Education ("in case I want to become an administrator or policymaker later on"). The limited income still bothers him. "But I'll figure something out," he shrugs. "At least I won't be miserable eight hours a day. And in my mind teachers are more valuable to this world than lawyers. Well, most lawyers."

Ultimately I think it is important to let these young people know that they are not being looked upon as failures, or that they have let anyone down, if they do choose to march to a different drummer. For I sensed that this was indeed the way they often saw it. As a result the parent may need to express that fact openly and discuss those plans with the child in a nonjudgmental way. If this indeed does happen, try to be positive and offer ideas of ways to make the career work, rather than all the reasons why it might turn out to be a disaster. Express support and encouragement, even if the road may be totally different from your road. If the youngster's choice turns out to be a dead end—for any number of reasons—he or she will start exploring other options soon enough without the parent having to say or do anything at all.

Finally, if things do not work out, try to avoid the I-told-you-so mode. That youngster is probably feeling bad enough. Some supportive and compassionate words on the topic of learning from one's mistake may be more appropriate. This kind of conversation is especially needed in the sort of family where failure may appear to carry a stigma.

# 19.

# Handling Inherited Wealth and Financial Support

"I'm afraid I was the reverse of the American Dream. Both my father and grandfather were businessmen who reached the top of the money pyramid. But have you ever wondered what happened to their children? The inheritors?" She gave a mocking laugh, then reached for a gold box, took a pill, swallowed it with some water. . . . "I was glutted with privilege, softened by luxury, weakened by indulgent nannies . . . when you inherit as much money as I did, it destroys whatever incentive or goal you might have. . . ."

The woman talking is Barbara Hutton, granddaughter of the founder of the great Woolworth chain of retail stores and arguably the most sensational heiress of the twentieth century. The conversation took place one rainy afternoon in her suite of rooms at the Ritz Hotel on the Place Vendome in Paris and was recounted by her longtime friend Philip Van Rensselaer in his biography of Barbara, *Million Dollar Baby*. It is a cautionary tale. And though hardly anyone has $250 million to leave to a child, the pages of that glitzy book offer a poignant case study of the difficulties a privileged young woman can encounter when she is "lucky" enough to become the recipient of inherited wealth, among them the dread that nobody would ever love her purely for herself.

"Tough," you might be saying in a cynical manner. "I'll take those kinds of problems any day." But that *is* the problem. Too few people recognize it as a real issue that has a profound effect upon the recipient's personality and actions. The idea that someone who inherits money is so lucky that he or she could not possibly have problems obscures the fact that indeed pain can walk hand in hand with privilege.

It may be time for everyone—benefactors, inheritors, and outsiders looking in—to cast aside the fantasy that money provides the solution to all ills. Instead, it may be more realistic and helpful to acknowledge that it simply juggles the deck, substituting one kind of difficulty for another. Moreover, working to mitigate those difficulties is not to appear ungrateful or even paranoid in the face of "good fortune."

Thus to plan intelligently—even if the parents may be able to leave a child only a small amount of money—it is necessary to first acknowledge that these young adults will be struggling with mixed emotions and a host of self-doubts while outwardly, possibly even in an arrogant manner, acting like jackpot winners.

Among the uncertainties I heard repeatedly expressed by young people who had inherited a sizable sum:

- Could I have ever lived this way had I had to make it on my own?
- What might happen if the spending power of that capital evaporates as it could in a period of accelerated inflation or economic chaos?
- Is my friend/lover jealous of my money?
- Dare I tell him or her just how much I really have?
- Who should be managing this money for me?

In short: it can be very, very scary. Indeed that very sensation is noted in the book *The Fords*. It includes an insightful anecdote about the day Henry Ford handed his twenty-one-year-old son, Edsel, a million dollars as part of an upcoming inheritance. Edsel apparently panicked and, wrote the authors, "later said he made more errors on the job that day than ever before or again."

Three types of situations are likely to face the children of super-achievers. First, the parents probably have the excess capital or high income to be able to support their children financially, or "help" them, as it is euphemistically called, well into adult life. The statistics confirm this. The Federal Reserve Board reported that by the late eighties some 1.3 million U.S. households had a net worth of at least $1 million, a sum we formerly associated only with the gilt-edged fringe of society. In addition, the Conference Board, a business analysis group, has suggested that today's young adults in general will inherit more than any other generation—an estimated $1 trillion in assets. So it is not surprising that we are already seeing part of that bounty trickling down. Some of these young people need that help far more than others, and for longer. But most can count on some form of Golden Sendoff unless there has been a major setback in the fortunes of the family, through divorce, illness, layoffs, or business failures.

Some parents set aside capital amounts for their children early on in the child's life, frequently through a trust. A trust is a way of transferring assets to a child without giving that child control of the money for many years to come. There are an almost infinite number of ways a trust document can be set up (more on that later in the chapter). Most commonly the trust fund is placed in safekeeping using a bank as trustee. The bank appoints a trust officer to administer the funds and make all the discretionary decisions, according to the terms established by the donor.

Most parents start by discussing the various trust options with a family lawyer and a financial planner. Often the family's accountant will also be consulted since that initial phase normally focuses on ways to avoid incurring large taxes upon the death of the parent, rather than dealing with the impact of the inheritance on the child. When the family lawyer, the parents, and financial planner have made a decision on what to do, a trust document is written up and handed to the trust officer at the bank.

A parent doesn't need millions of dollars to set up a trust. It can be established with no money at all. For instance, a life insurance trust is specifically designed not to have any money in it while the parent lives. Its aim is to automatically receive the proceeds of a life insurance policy upon the death of a parent. This way there will be some safeguards on the way that money is used. Another vehicle that needs little startup money is a living trust—the parents placing a certain amount each year into the trust. Income from the money can continue to be used by the parents during their lifetime with the assets and income reverting to the children automatically upon the death of either parent.

While all this may seem applicable only to the very wealthy, it really applies to thousands of parents these days, even those who may only have that life insurance policy and a family home to leave their children. Introductory reading might include *Finance and Estate Planning,* which is written in lay English and offers some good ideas; for further information see the Appendix.

In other instances the inheritance may be handed out simply as a supplementary income—so many dollars being given to that youngster each month—rather than arranging for a specific capital sum to be set aside for the purpose. Whatever option is chosen, the effect is similar. The young person, in a somewhat childlike manner, may seem incredibly fortunate. Yet in truth he or she is still tied to an older adult by financial apron strings. And this can make these young adults feel (and even act) like eternal children, always at the mercy of a parent; or in the case of a trust, the trust officer who has jurisdiction over the disposition of funds.

Finally, there are situations—through the premature death of a parent or as a result of philosophical attitudes—where capital amounts (frequently the proceeds of a generous corporate life insurance policy, executive stock options, or even proceeds from the sale of the parents' former home) are handed over, free of restrictions.

In all instances the same question arises: how do you help the young person anticipate that windfall so it will be a ladder and not an impediment to maturity, responsibility, and a rewarding life? Fortunately we are learning quite a bit about the behavior of the recipients of inherited wealth and strategic ways to hand it on, now that the issue is affecting a growing number of people.

Two individuals who are making a concerted effort to analyze these problems and come up with helpful ways to cope are Tracy Gary, creator and driving force behind The Women's Foundation, the San Francisco support group that provides counsel and programs for women of inheritance, and John Levy, the executive director of the C. G. Jung Institute, also located in San Francisco.

Levy, a jovial white-haired gentleman, began his study of the subject in 1980 at the urging of an aging tycoon who suspected his generosity to his children had somehow not helped them to develop into responsible and happy adults. He paid Levy $20,000 to study the wider implications of inherited wealth. To accomplish that goal Levy interviewed money managers, psychologists, and more than thirty Bay area inheritors. It ended with Levy writing a privately published twenty-four-page booklet called "Coping with Inherited Wealth." The booklet is so filled with compassion, insights, and good sense that I think it should be required reading for anyone who has a substantial sum to leave a child.

According to Levy, individuals who have not been adequately primed are in danger of losing the longer-term benefits of that windfall because they may fall victim to the spendthrift or miserly modes of behavior common among the ill-prepared:

1. they may squander it all on poor investments or have themselves a ball while the money lasts because it seems such a novelty and such a fun way to behave, becoming in effect the irrepressible kids in the candy store who never know when to stop;

2. or they may hang on too tightly, never spending, never enjoying its possible benefits, because they do not have the self-confidence to believe they can ever make it back; and to lose it would be a betrayal of their parents' legacy. That type of behavior, says Levy, is the reason we see so much seemingly inexplicable stinginess among recipients of inherited wealth.

"Give them tools," Levy likes to say with almost missionary zeal, "along with the toys."

What are those tools?

*Tell them early.* Levy has found that a lot of irresponsible mishandling of money in subsequent generations arises because parents find that talking candidly about family money is even more difficult than explaining sexual conduct. And that reluctance can be as great even if the family has a few hundred thousand rather than millions of dollars to bequeath. The Great Inhibitor, he says, is the fear that once those children find out the truth the annals of that family will resemble a Greek or Shakespearean tragedy; the youngsters will secretly yearn for the early death of those parents in order to get their eager fingers on all that loot.

Therein, argues Levy, lies the real tragedy: that this terrible fear born of legend, tabloid news items, and literature will result in inaction by perfectly normal, loving families. Not only can these fears be avoided through sensitive trust planning but if there is an effort to hush up the family's assets, "The children are apt to see the money as something dark and shameful," says Levy, even if there was nothing sinister involved in how it was made. Instead he maintains that parents should talk about how it was earned. The young people are also entitled to some candid answers about what they might get and when, such as whether there will be enough for graduate school or if they will be required to seek loans. It may help them plan their lives more intelligently, says he.

For instance, Bret Ellis told me that if he had not known he had his father's money to fall back upon he might have never spent his college career majoring in creative writing, a move that allowed him to concentrate totally on developing his talent. Other young adults may favor public or political service and could become extremely valuable to society if they knew for certain, early enough, that they would have the financial freedom to follow that dream.

Leaving them in the dark also maintains them in a childlike state that can linger well into adult life. That dilemma is also mentioned in *The Rockefellers*. "In some ways they were a collection of timorous souls," write the authors, talking about the fourth generation of Rockefellers, "permanently juvenilized by their relations with their fathers and their dependence on Room 5600 [where the Rockefeller family money and trusts are controlled]."

Obviously careful preplanning is not possible when the bulk of the money is acquired late in life by the parent. In other households there may be the fear that too-early knowledge could foster lack of commitment if the young person has no idea what he or she wants from life. Therefore, it may be prudent to also:

*Teach sound money management along with a sense of purpose and social obligation.* Once the (financial) cat is out of the bag it enables a family to start some preparatory work on asset management, as described in the previous chapter. This need is underscored by a shocking statistic from the insurance industry showing that, on average, any lump sum that is paid out as term insurance is frittered away by the beneficiary within six months. Ditto for lottery winners. Gary favors the idea of making up a comprehensive financial plan for a child as early as possible—starting with banking, budgeting, spending and saving strategies, and attitudes and plans for financial assistance from parents in the early adult years. It is even useful, says Gary, to talk to the children about how they might handle *your* financial affairs if you become old and incapacitated. "Take time to teach," she urges. "Make a conscious commitment to it." Gary attributes her own self-confidence in handling large sums of money to a mother who was keenly aware of the need for this sort of education.

But that schooling, say Levy and others, should ideally be accompanied by a sense of social obligation—a lesson that explains that privilege has been bestowed at a price. And that price is the understanding that a recipient of such bounty becomes something of a custodian, obligated to use part of it, or some of the personal freedom it generates, for the benefit of others. Old-line European families have been heavily steeped in that idea for centuries. They call it *noblesse oblige*. Gary, for instance, firmly believes that anyone who has been endowed with this sense of obligation becomes a far happier and more responsible person because that money is accompanied by a sense of purpose that develops maturity and direction.

Left undirected and unprepared, the result can be a self-indulgent, drifting sort of existence as troubling and unsatisfying as that led by

Barbara Hutton. Words are even being developed to describe the syndrome. Wixen, in his book *Children of the Rich,* calls it "dysgradia"—
the lack of need to make any commitment or strive for any goal because
the income is already there. Others, as previously mentioned, have
labeled that aimlessness "affluenza"—a combination of low self-esteem,
lack of motivation, a perverse questing after kicks accompanied by no
sense of accountability to anyone.

One young millionaire who collaborated with others in a similar
situation to write a book, *Robin Hood Was Right,* about their dilemmas
with inherited wealth explains the feeling: "I remember at one of these
meetings of this group . . . where people with inherited wealth talk
about how they deal with it, one guy set everyone in the room nodding.
He said, 'Sometimes I feel as if everything I've done in my life has
been a hobby.' I think that's the crux right there . . . money takes away
a certain drive . . . if you look closely you see those people tend to
work part-time . . . or flit from one job to another, or go to school for
years. I think our whole society is geared so totally around trying to
make money that it really takes someone who has their head totally
together to be able to work absolutely full-time when they don't need
the money."

Perhaps that is why, if one looks at the lives of the *successful* rich,
says psychiatrist Wixen, "one notes a tendency toward activities in three
areas: philanthropy, public service, and creative business"—areas
where success is not measured by the dollars made. Creative business
is the hybrid that derives its rewards from more than just the bottom
line: in developing far-sighted labor relations or a product that might
be highly worthwhile but too much of a gamble for anyone only concerned with profits.

Other successful rich find fulfillment in devoting their lives and
their energies to a cause, notes Wixen. Creative talents are also appropriate to foster, argues Levy, since success is again not necessarily
measured in financial terms. And the accolades handed out are rarely
a direct result of the family's fortune, name, or status.

Writes Wixen, "The essential fact in the successful transition from
middle class to upper class involves the establishment of a new system
for maintaining self-esteem." All the above endeavors promote self-
esteem, he suggests, but in an alternative mode. Yet, he concludes, the
need to foster such alternatives is rarely found among parents who
have actually made the money themselves—the first generation, as it
were. These people overlook the fact that, in many instances, their
children may not have the same drive because they will not have the

same needs and thus may be better off in other fields. And the mis-understandings that can ensue create a generation gap peculiar to the top end of society.

Levy, meanwhile, has noticed several other personality traits likely to emerge in beneficiaries: denied struggle, they are also denied pure joy. "In limiting pain," he writes, "we almost inevitably cut off some of the delight at the other end of the spectrum." They may show decreased frustration tolerance unless such perseverance has been purposely nurtured early in life. "The difference between those who have made fortunes and those who inherit them," writes Levy, "is that the builders have both the willingness and the ability to keep their hand in when the going gets tough. Inheritors often haven't had much experience of slogging through difficult and frustrating times, and it's hard for them to recognize the value of enduring such pain when it can be avoided." Others may become workaholics, obsessive about making a mark of their own "to prove they are not just inheritors," says Levy.

*Fully include girls in all preparatory planning.* Gary has found that women feel especially inadequate—and thus may have a harder time—unless they are most carefully prepared and primed. There is still a chauvinistic tendency, she finds, to leave them out of much of the family's financial decision-making (while including sons) or any needed financial schooling. And trust officers often have the same irritating manner. "We're sort of kept in this 'You needn't worry about this, dear,' posture," she says.

*Consider how your own actions may affect the way your children handle money.* "The ways in which parents manage their own money inevitably serve to teach their children about ethical and psychological values, for better or worse, even more than what their parents tell them," wrote Levy after studying those thirty Bay area families. Gary further suggests making a conscious effort, as her mother did, to explain why you are doing what you are doing while you are doing it. It could be anything from a system of bill-paying to making and keeping within a monthly budget.

*Make every effort to ensure that your children are self-supporting.* The most comfortable beneficiaries are the non-needy beneficiaries. They are the ones who have the self-assurance and self-reliance to know that whatever happens to that money their lives should only be marginally affected. So through graduate training, summer jobs, talent development, and even experience in a relatively humble job (which should not be treated with contempt), try to give them every opportunity to savor that strength.

*Have the courage of your convictions.* A 1986 *Fortune* article that examined the attitudes of some of the country's wealthiest men found that they were not rushing to hand over their self-made millions, standing fast against resentful young adults who criticized them as Scrooge-like (although later on many of these children conceded the wisdom of the strategy). A man who built a fortune of over $50 million founding a technology corporation is reported in the article as saying that after he paid for their college education he handed each of his three children just "a nominal sum" but plenty of encouragement. And he insisted they all became productive people—one is a lawyer, another an actor, and the third an investment analyst. "I wanted to give my kids the tremendous satisfaction of making it on their own," said he. Others said they thought that enough for the down payment on a house and sufficient capital "to allow them to do anything but not nothing" was a good balance. Many planned to leave the remainder of their estates to charity.

## TRUSTS THAT CONSIDER
## EMOTIONAL AS WELL AS FINANCIAL GOALS

*Set up a trust that shows trust.* Most wealthy people will be leaving money in the form of a trust. It is virtually impossible not to do so, given today's inheritance taxes and other estate planning needs. However, while conceding they are necessary, a handful of lawyers, bankers, and trust officers, speaking to me confidentially and off the record, suggested certain precautions.

First, if you do not want any of your children to have the money, or even much of an income, until they are thirty or thirty-five years old, explain your reasons, preferably in an accompanying letter in case you are not there to deliver that message in person. "It's impressive how important these messages can be to the beneficiaries, particularly since they're usually received at such critical and vulnerable times," Levy told a lunchtime gathering of members of the Santa Clara Bar Association, having been invited to address them on the issue in the summer of 1987. It is critical that the trust does not imply that you consider your child profligate or a fool (which I am sure you don't).

Also consider an informal meeting with a trust officer before sitting down with a lawyer to draw up a trust. You may get a more balanced idea of likely future problems, since a trust officer is used to dealing with beneficiaries; your lawyer may be more focused on current tax or liability protection issues.

Second, understand that the trust officer has his own agenda. Money managers explain that the trust officer frequently becomes the arch-enemy of the beneficiary because that·officer and the institution have needs that are at odds with the beneficiary. The trust officer has a fiduciary responsibility to protect the "remainder interest"—the money due to help the next generation, the grandchildren. Any mistakes or poorly judged discretionary moves could damage the reputation of the institution as well as the trust officer's personal future. The trust officer could even be sued for mismanagement by the grandchildren. More-over, the institution itself earns a substantial annual custodial fee. Thus it is in its interest to see that the trust is sustained and not disbanded.

Weigh these realities when setting up that trust and consider es-tablishing written guidelines so your original intent is not undermined. Also try to be sensitive, says Gary, in the way you introduce your child to the trust officer. It can be a terrifying moment. Make it into a pleasant occasion with some ceremony, she suggests. One trust officer I met has found it helps even more to hold that initial encounter in the home, since this is the least intimidating atmosphere (unlike many of today's physicians, trust officers will make house calls). "I tell parents I'm just like Palladin," said another trust officer. "Have briefcase, will travel." It is an honored tradition. Remember how Babcock, the buffoonlike trust officer in that classic play *Auntie Mame,* was constantly making house calls? In addition, foster a rapport between the trust officer and the beneficiary. Encourage regular periodic meetings, just as you would a medical or dental checkup. If that youngster begins to view the trust officer as a "trusted" intermediary, he or she is more likely to feel comfortable about discussing fears and plans—something that could be beneficial for both the future use of capital and the financial edu-cation of the youngster.

Think also about providing your child with a copy of the trust document. Gary found that dozens of the women she counsels have never seen the actual wording of their trust, nor do they know what is in store for them down the road—something that undermines their confidence and perpetuates that childlike behavior. And is that what you really want?

Third, consider appointing a co-trustee who is a member of the family or a close family friend, who would have equal discretionary powers with the trust officer. This would make the arrangement less impersonal and allow for compromise solutions if called for. It would also give the young person another trusted counselor if he or she has problems or concerns that are not easily discussed with the bank's trust officer.

Fourth, consider a "stepped-in" trust (sometimes called a pilot trust). This normally allows a child to obtain that money in increments free of strings—a percentage say, at twenty-five, then more at thirty, and the remainder at thirty-five or forty. Gary had a stepped-in trust and is a firm believer in the method. "It let me feel my wings," she said. "It let me experiment without worrying I would blow it all. I learned slowly how to choose financial advisers, how to invest." Since all the money is eventually handed over, it also avoids the idea that you distrust your children's ability to provide for their own children. As Ross Perot, the Texas billionaire who founded Electronic Data Systems, told *Fortune,* "Let your children decide how much to give their children." And how they want to do it.

Fifth, consider an incentive trust. This works well with a lay co-trustee and is usually designed to match or double the income to the beneficiary at the achievement of certain objectives—obtaining an advanced degree, a salary of a certain size, a career position of certain standing, holding a job for a preagreed period of time. An incentive trust might also be used to help the child start a business, a use of the money strongly favored by Wixen—provided, of course, that there is a solid business plan and the needed expertise. Donald Trump, the real estate magnate, got his start that way.

Sixth, make sure your trust is sufficiently flexible to allow for unseen problems that might occur, like the need for some capital to be freed up to pay unexpected school or medical bills. And be careful to avoid situations that could benefit one child while harming another. One estate planner told me the story of a man, earlier in this century, who invented a well-known household device that made millions. The man set up a trust that would provide income for his three children with the principal paid out to his grandchildren upon the death of both of their parents.

Child number one, a boy, became a millionaire and is living abroad. Child number two, a girl, married a successful investment adviser. Child number three, also a girl, married a ne'er-do-well. Number one wanted the trust invested in highest-income corporate bonds since he lived abroad and did not have to worry too much about income tax. Child number two wanted the trust to favor tax-exempt bonds since her husband was in a high tax bracket. Child number three, worried about inflation, needed growth stocks or growth real estate to ensure that there would be plenty of money available for her children's college educations and their future. In hindsight, say the experts, not knowing what their lives might hold, it might have been better to separate the inheritance into three parts. As it turned out, the trust officer could never please all three. He could only do his best by balancing the portfolio. Nobody could look forward to a lump sum at any point in their lives, which also limited options.

Finally, whatever strategy you decide to pursue, there is probably no finer book you could give a young person about to inherit serious money than that book, previously mentioned, *Robin Hood Was Right,* a wonderfully light-hearted yet vitally important guide on ways to handle that money. You do not even have to agree with its politics to appreciate its wisdom. Written by a group of counterculture young rich folk during the mid-1970s, it covers all bases—from personal feelings of panic and shame to investment and philanthropic options likely to be meaningful to the fledgling beneficiary struggling to feel good (and not make a fool of himself or herself) in contemporary society.

## FINANCIAL SUPPORT

Before rushing in with that helping hand it might be worth considering what is really going to help those youngsters get a head start. I got the impression that the loss of the Good Life, at least temporarily, was less important to many of them in their early twenties than the resolution of other issues (although most eventually wanted to be able to afford the kind of life they had enjoyed as children). Those issues included the following:

*Guilt.* Having been given so much for so long, many seemed anxious to be given the freedom to get out of their systems the sense that they still needed to draw from their parents, even if the money was available. For some of them this guilt seemed to translate into a need to pursue a helping profession rather than a more lucrative field—at least at the start. And I think it would be a pity to deny them the emotional support for that idea or denigrate such a need.

*Self-reliance and self-worth.* "It's such a good feeling to be independent," said a twenty-one-year-old boy from Southern California. "It's good to know you can pay the rent. I need to believe that if I was thrown into a city with just a suitcase of clothes I could survive. It's a very secure feeling." A few of the more cynical youngsters questioned whether that urge to provide ongoing financial help came more from the parents' own psychological needs than from the youngster's real problems—such as personal peace of mind, a desire to continue controlling their lives, a lack of faith in their abilities, or even an inability to cope with the thought that a child of theirs might be "suffering." One young woman suggested that those of her friends who regularly received checks seemed to have the lowest self-esteem of any in her crowd—even though they would brag about a fancy co-op or condo a parent had purchased for them outright (eliminating even mortgage responsibilities) or the furniture in it.

How, then, to tackle these early adult years? There is a case to be made for getting that child off the family payroll at least for a while or unless genuine disaster strikes, and for refusing to feel like a wicked parent if that child is temporarily forced to pinch pennies. Susan Littwin suggests that a financial safety net too eagerly given—whether as monthly income or payment of rent—may actually foster the very indecision and lack of fiber the parents complain about. "There was always Dad's money to tide her over, and Dad's connections to get her another job, and the house in Larchmont when all else failed," she writes of one young woman she met who could not make up her mind what she really wanted to be or do. Of another, "Nick doesn't get it together because he doesn't need to. . . . His parents help out."

Further, the danger is that these young adults may again find themselves stuck with the sort of pejorative label that somehow gets attached to the rich, rubbing away at self-esteem like an abrasive. "Kept Kids" is one such title, bestowed on them by *New York* magazine when commenting on the increasing numbers of such youngsters, especially noticeable in recent years in and around an expensive area like New York City.

Cutting that financial cord has actually been a therapeutic technique that Dr. Schwarz, the Chicago psychiatrist, has developed for young adults who seem unable to grow up. For he has become increasingly convinced that many times it is the environment, rather than the patient, that is unhealthy. So he likes to pluck such Peter Pans out of the posh suburb or city where they may have been living (and working for parents or friends of parents) and move them to Chicago where they are expected to find a job, an apartment, friends, and support themselves on what they can make for at least two years. Armed with that sense of being able to survive independently, and even prosper, they frequently return to the family with a far more mature approach to life—and a vastly improved self-image.

Again, the book *The Rockefellers,* particularly the final section called "The Cousins," is replete with examples of the need and value of a totally self-reliant and anonymous rite of passage. Marion, second daughter of Laurence, retreated for a while into a caboose parked in a field in California where she grew organic food and lived only on the money she and her husband earned from their various endeavors. Larry, her brother, lived in an East Harlem tenement for three years while working as a VISTA volunteer. Peggy, David's daughter, lived in a shack among the poor of Brazil while doing social work. Hope, the daughter of John III, lived incognito in Nairobi. Michael, son of Nelson, was believed by his cousins to have been obsessed by the same need when he disappeared while on an anthropological expedition in New Guinea. Michael Reagan talks of the same inner need in *On the Outside Looking In* when explaining why Patti Reagan changed her name to Patti Davis.

Clearly some financial or even career help is warranted. Advanced degrees may have to be financed, or partially financed, if only to give these youngsters the needed tools for today's society. However, loans or fellowships should be required at this stage. For as we pointed out earlier, it fosters independence and a sense of pride as well as more adult behavior. A sizable down payment on a house or condo is not unreasonable, given the sky-high prices of today's real estate (so long as it is not offered too early or given away without mortgage or other responsibilities). It is not easy to watch a child struggle, especially if you have the ability to make life more comfortable. It is not easy to sit idly by and watch a child yearn for a certain job when you could so easily pick up the phone and put in the good word that would immediately tip the balance. But unless there is a clear reason for behaving otherwise, these most privileged of young adults may be better served in the end if they know they must negotiate life head-on, without the security of that protective bubble, at least for a little while.

# 20.

# Private Lives

One of the most uplifting realities that seemed to emerge from conversations with the youngsters and their high-achieving parents was the way in which both were continually striving to do the very best they could under the circumstances, and usually with the most noble of intent. Far from trying to hurt one another, each was usually making extraordinary efforts to please or help the other. Yet, because each one was operating from a totally different perspective, and with a totally different set of pressures, those actions were frequently misunderstood or caused more aggravation than assistance.

I have selected one set of interviews I had with a mother and her young adult daughter to illustrate just how easy it is for a parent and child to misread each other, placing each of their versions of a just-completed childhood side by side to illustrate just how different it all looks depending upon which side of the adult line you may be standing. In this case divorce intervened to disrupt the childhood, but I do not think it changes the basic pattern we are trying to understand.

If there is any lesson to this twice-told tale it is surely to show us how important it is to continually try to walk in the shoes of the person with whom we are dealing. And I believe this can help a child equally as much as a parent, assuming the child has reached an age where such transference is possible.

| DAUGHTER'S STORY | MOTHER'S STORY |
| --- | --- |
| "I was born in a suburb in Ohio," began the daughter, a dimin- | "Even as a small child I never wanted someone else to rule over |

utive dark-haired girl of twenty-one. We had met by the swimming pool of a resort hotel in Southern California. "Not the fancy kind. It was sort of ordinary. I had a brother three years older than myself. My mother always worked, even when my dad was still with us. She worked at a TV station. I don't know quite what she did in those days but eventually she became a producer. My very first memories of her were how tired she would be when she got home at night. It would make me mad because it was like she was never there even when she was. It was hard because my brother was often left to look after me. And sometimes he would say I would do things that I didn't.

"My mom wanted me so much to get good grades and be a success. But she never explained why it was important. It always seemed to me it was only important because this way she could tell her friends that her children did this or that . . . like she was trying so hard to have the right image. Even when I wanted my hair cut a certain way she would tell me to do something else. She would say, 'How can I take you to my friends looking like that?' I didn't want to do these things just for her life. And that's what it seemed. I think she expected more from me than I could manage. It was like I was always letting her down. So I sort of gave up. I began to really get into trouble. I flushed a book down the toilet. I got suspended. . . .

"So my mom decided to send me to boarding school. That didn't work either. I was unhappy there. I

my life," began the mother, a warm and gracious woman with more of a maternal than an executive air about her. Slender and well-groomed, she spoke softly and slowly and evidently with a great deal of pain when facing the memories of her child's growing-up years. "That's maybe why I wanted to work, even when the children were small. I was in a bad marriage and I wanted to feel some control. It was so important for me to be able to earn my own living that I wanted it for my daugher, too. It was also part of the way we all felt back then, at the beginning of the women's movement. So I kept trying to tell her she could do anything, if only she set her mind to it. I did not want her to ever have to depend solely on a man. That meant being smarter, harder-working, and even more perfect than anybody else.

"At that early time I was struggling. I had no child support. I had absolutely no help. I felt I had to work harder than everyone else. At first it was because I was worried about making ends meet but at heart I am very, very ambitious, so that even now I have a tendency to think I haven't accomplished enough. But then there were the children. And I was terrified that if they did something wrong—stole something, or got into drugs—it would hurt that dream. Besides, I could not cope with the idea that perhaps I would not make it as a mother or a professional. I could not fail at both.

"Perhaps that is why I had such a need (back then) to make a suc-

came home. And when I got home they—my mother had remarried by then and had also got this fabulous new job—decided to put me in a Catholic day school. We had a lot more money. We lived in a great house. Had new cars. Lots to spend.

"Then one day I was on my way out with a bunch of girls. We were all about fifteen. I had put on a pair of jeans, a black trench coat, and a torn T-shirt that was very tight. I had fixed one of those punk hairstyles where you get your hair to stand straight up. My mom saw me just as I was leaving, and she refused to let me out of the house until I had changed my clothes and put my hair down. She screamed, 'You look like a tramp!' She was afraid people would look at her funny because of the way I looked. That's what she said. The way I took it was that she wanted me to change for her sake, not mine. I felt like an extension of her ambitions. . . . Then we had a car accident. They called my mother. She came over. The first thing she said was, 'You look terrible. How can I take you home like that?' She never once said, 'Are you okay?' It hurt.

"But she wanted to do so much for me. I could see that. Even when I moved away—I didn't go on to college—I remember I would come home and when I would want to go out for the evening I would find $100 on my bed. I had probably said I needed $20. But she left $100. And when I look back I know it started to make me lazy because it was like the money was always there. Even with a car. She gave me

cess of myself as a mother. It was so important to me that they be good kids that I tried to bully them into it. I never stopped to ask myself: 'Why is my daughter resisting?' or 'Why is my son choosing the wrong friends?' At other times I would go exactly the other way and overlook transgressions, like I couldn't face it. It just made me sick to feel unsuccessful. I couldn't even ask my parents for help because they were so judgmental. Nothing would have been good enough for them either.

"I remember the night my daughter got dressed up in those terrible clothes—the safety pins in the T-shirt, that jacket with the vulgar sayings plastered all over; I felt so embarrassed. I had had this dream about the perfect child and suddenly it hit me that she was exactly the opposite and I had failed. All I could think about was my failure, not her problems. Later a therapist explained this all to me. He said I should try to separate what she was from my own life. She was a separate person, not an extension of me. It was a real step forward. . . . I was able to begin to see my daughter as a person, what she was and what she was fighting. Because I wanted so much for her to be perfect she never felt good enough and hated herself for it. I see that now. . . .

"Why did I start to give her so much money when I started to have it myself? Guilt, maybe. Whatever I had done wrong to make her so rebellious and so unhappy as a kid I wanted to make up for. . . . I wanted to make amends. Even though she

a car and whenever it broke down she would always send me a check to fix it, or even get me a new one when it was necessary. My friends would say, 'Oh, you're so lucky.'

"Now I sometimes wonder if my mom isn't doing too much for me, like she feels guilty or something for the past. She sends me money each month, so I'm really not too worried if I quit a job. . . . Whenever my friends see the check I find myself making excuses, like, 'I need it to pay bills or fix the car.' I hate to say I get it for no reason because it feels sort of like I had stolen it. . . .

"The other day my mom called and said, 'It doesn't pay to waste the money in rent. Would you like a condo?' A condo! At twenty-one! I said, 'Can I have one with two bedrooms?' I had a friend in the room when she phoned and the friend looked at me afterwards and said, 'I can't believe what a spoiled brat you are!' I think she was jealous, but I do feel awkward sometimes having all of this. But I love my mom and I know why she does it. She went through hell to earn the money and be what she is today. And she feels so proud of what she can do for me, like she wants to make up for all the difficulties I went through as a child. . . . I'm going back to school in the fall and I'm going to try to keep a part-time job, too, so I can earn enough money so I don't have to call my mom."

did not go to college I felt I should help her get on. She needed money for rent. She couldn't earn much. She had no skills. It is also a question of passing the torch. What I have accomplished I want to pass on to her, so her life will be a little easier. I never want to see her have to struggle like I did. I don't know how much is too much. I want to be helpful, that's all. I never want her to feel she has no money in her pocket. And her expenses are tremendous."

# 21.

# Returning Home

It may seem inexplicable to members of an older generation that young adults would actually *want* to come back and live at home after college or at any time during their twenties. Looking back at their own youth, these older folk remember the family home as being the Dwelling Place of Last Resort. Anything, truly anything, was preferable to one's parents' house. Besides, by that time most had wearied of being treated like a child and didn't want a parent hovering over daily comings and goings.

How times have changed. Take any street in any neighborhood and the chances are you will find an adult child in residence. Statistics bear this out. By the mid-eighties the Census Bureau reported that 54 percent of all Americans between the ages of eighteen and twenty-four were still living at home, up from 47 percent in 1970. Further, a startling 10.4 percent (more than one in ten) of those between twenty-five and thirty-four were also still at home, compared to 8 percent in 1970. Social scientists became aware of the trend and started to write about it in scholarly journals. Jean Davies Okimoto and Phyllis Jackson Stegall, psychotherapists in Seattle, found the practice to be so common that in 1987 they came out with a helpful book for parents about the phenomenon called *Boomerang Kids.* Moreover, though there is no way to prove it statistically, the impressions I gained from my interviews are that fast-track, affluent parents are even more likely than others to end up with one or more children using that highly polished door knocker—and staying for longer than just the weekend.

Why is it happening and what should parents do about it? First, it may again help to place some of the actions in the sociological context of our times. Otherwise the knee-jerk reaction is to see this as yet another failure—the direct result of parental inadequacies or something going terribly "wrong" with that particular child. Indeed, that is exactly how many parents do react, according to Leland J. Axelson, a professor of family studies and sociology at the Virginia Polytechnic Institute and State University. Dr. Axelson came to that conclusion after conducting a pilot study of such families. "These parents feel like failures," he told me, "and guilty, too, that perhaps they did not get that child launched properly." Yet think about it for a second: if so many more children are cluttering the nest, surely there must be some fundamental changes occurring in the outside world, too.

There are. Dr. Paul C. Glick, formerly senior demographer with the Bureau of the Census, studied the phenomenon for a 1986 article in the *Journal of Marriage and the Family,* a publication of the American Association for Marriage and Family Therapy, and discussed its implications in *The New York Times.* He attributes much of the trend to availability. For most of the postwar period, he explained, homes were filled to the brim with baby boomers growing up. There was literally no room at the family inn. Prior to that era other sociologists had observed that people were normally packed into far more crowded quarters than is commonplace today. Children frequently grew up sharing a room with siblings or cousins. And as each set of parents tended to have a sizeable number of children the whole cycle continued for a longer period of time. So the opportunities for coming home were more limited.

In addition, in prior generations, the parents aged much faster and were often burned out and ailing by the time their children were young adults. So unless they were all part of an extended family farm business, *à la* the Waltons, there was no way those parents could accept their youngsters back. Moreover, if you grew up on the wrong side of the tracks, what would be the attraction of going back? You would rather go forward. Today there is less likelihood of outpacing one's parents, at least among a fast-track crowd, and not usually until much later in life. So the best thing in the world to many of these young people is the opportunity to go back—to that picture-perfect neighborhood where nothing ever goes wrong that can't be fixed with a phone call, the sea washes the sand, and the bed is still made by the housekeeper.

A further attraction is that today's parents are still probably brimming with energy, bursting with life, and living in a big house that in itself is seductively comfortable. "You can get very attached to having your own pool," said one twenty-six-year-old woman who came back to her parents' massive Colonial home after living in a dilapidated room at the tip of Long Island. "My footprints—from when I was small—are still embedded in the cement around the edges of our pool." Further, that home is probably in a community or a neighborhood that is exceptionally appealing—say, by the shore or in the middle of an exciting cultural center. And because it is so well situated the cost of anything similar in an equally appealing location would be out of reach. "I couldn't think of anywhere I would like to live more than Southern California," one young man who had grown up in that part of the country told me. "And if that means living with my parents for a while, well, okay. They're always traveling anyway. And they don't mind what I do."

The new sexual freedom is also a significant factor. Dr. Glick notes that the sexual revolution has made it socially acceptable for parents to adopt a far more liberal attitude toward their children's relationships, allowing them freedom within the family house that would have been unthinkable prior to the 1970s. In turn, the young people themselves can indulge in those relationships without making a commitment to anything as permanent as marriage.

There is yet another inducement. Accustomed to having a pocketful of spending money, many of these young people do not relish the idea of having to use all their earnings—which are often still relatively meager—on the exorbitant cost of shelter these days. They would rather make the trade-off and live at home. "It really takes the financial pressure off," said a twenty-seven-year-old insurance executive who has been living at home since college. "I can have a nice car. I can travel. Go out. Save a little."

The divorce rate has also had an impact. For the single mother living alone, the presence of an adult child can provide companionship and practical help. One single mother with a rambling house explained how both she and her thirty-year-old son benefited from the arrangement. He was able to live in a style that his income alone could not yet provide. She had someone around who gave her a sense of security and was also of invaluable help with the small repairs that constantly face any homeowner. Moreover, there was such a surplus of rooms in their neo-Tudor house that neither was tripping over the other or intruding upon personal privacy. It became, in effect, a *quid pro quo* arrangement, an even exchange that made sense for both parent and child. "You feel you are really doing a service," said a twenty-nine-year-old woman who works in public relations. "My mother's become a hermit since her divorce and anyway, I think older people enjoy having younger people around."

Susan Littwin, the chronicler of these young adults, takes the cynical view. She believes that many of them have been so pampered during childhood and given such unrealistic expectations about what they could accomplish that they are now ill-equipped to deal with the harsh realities of the real world. So the very first time they face a serious setback—an irritating roommate, a job that doesn't pay so well, a cold-water flat in a run-down neighborhood—they come running back to the womb. "They tried independence, it didn't work, and that sapped their confidence and sent them home crying," she writes.

Then there is the wide social acceptance of the arrangement. As more and more of their peers go home the idea takes on greater social acceptability, even among the peer group, adding even more bodies to those statistics. The youngsters themselves told me it also had a lot to do with being part of a generation that puts a lot of emphasis on success and living well even at a tender age and on a starting salary. Among their lot, they said, it is no longer acceptable to live in a run-down apartment or neighborhood, even temporarily. So home becomes the only alternative.

In sum: the inviting physical setup, the laissez-faire attitude of the parents, the divorce rate, the growing social stamp of approval on the idea, the high price of alternative shelter, and the unrealistic expectations of what it takes to live well may have all conspired to seduce many more youths back into the nest—at least until something better comes their way.

## HOW PARENTS REACT

How then to react? First, it may be a comfort to learn that there seems to be a predictable pattern in the way a great number of parents respond to that homecoming. If it sounds vaguely familiar, at least you know you are not alone. My own interviews for this book and prior articles I have written on the topic suggest that:

- The initial reaction is probably one of concern and caring: the young adult is in temporary trouble—without a job, without shelter, low on funds. So it seems only natural to suggest coming home, "until you get more settled or find a new job."
- The second stage is likely to be growing resentment: dirty dishes are left on the kitchen counter, clothes are dumped on the living room furniture, the phone is constantly ringing (at annoyingly late hours), cigarette butts show up in the ashtrays, you get into

arguments reminiscent of the battles that raged during the teen-age years. All of a sudden that peace and quiet you have grown to love are shattered and your life feels like a rerun of adoles-cence. The difference this time is that you have rearranged your life to include other ventures or activities that clash with all that commotion. You no longer have the patience. Besides, you feel it is no longer your job or your responsibility.

Indeed, you may also feel it is a difficult or draining intrusion. Or you may mumble to yourself that it is high time the middle-aged adolescent learned to live an independent life (and you may have begun to tell yourself, "I'm not going to be around for ever").

- The third stage is likely to be self-recrimination again: how did I get myself into this mess? And finally, how can I get out? Not all want their children out, to be sure. But many do.

## MAKING IT WORK

Those who have dealt with the experience as professionals and parents, like the two psychotherapists in Seattle, suggest it helps to lay strict (even written) ground rules the moment the child comes back home—and not wait until some months have gone by and the tension is unbearable.

The most common and ultimately satisfying to both sides—is to expect some weekly or monthly financial compensation. Normally the young adult is working, albeit perhaps at a low-paying job. Most young-sters know from talking to their peers that some payment will be expected. So they understand. Payment also helps retain those crucial elements of self-esteem and self-confidence that will probably be needed to relaunch the youngster into the adult world.

If there is sufficient space, set aside a room other than the young adult's bedroom as a place where that youngster can retreat in the evening, or entertain friends. A former family room, a basement room, an empty guest room would all be suitable. For example, a young woman from New Jersey who came back home told me she was given the old basement playroom to redecorate as an art studio for herself. She had been an art major and was now working as an illustrator. She also liked the idea that she would have a place to bring home friends in a way that would not impinge on the needs of her parents.

Renegotiate the terms of living in the same house. There should be different responsibilities and privileges compared to the days when you were living as parent and child. A professor at a well-known north-eastern medical school told me he did this when his thirty-year-old daughter suddenly arrived on his doorstep. Among recommended provisions: an agreement that you will not ask questions about friends or late-hour homecomings like you might have done during the teenage years. As a trade-off you might suggest that the young adult limit entertaining to reasonable hours (no heavy music after 11:00 P.M.) as a way of respecting *your* needs. You may also want to insist upon an adult level of self-care such as being responsible for one's own laundry, grocery shopping, or meals (unless you all happen to be around at a particular mealtime and want to get together).

The young adult should also be made responsible for some jobs that keep that household operating, like handyman chores if that is suitable. In return, you may be asked to respect privacy to a greater extent than before. "My mom could never understand that I wanted to be left alone after work," one young woman told me. "Even if I would shut the door to my room she would keep coming in asking if I liked her new dress or whether I would remember to take the dog for a walk. And she would still love to rearrange my things, just like when I was small." Understanding these needs and responsibilities, say our experts, makes that youngster retain pride in his or her capabilities while accepting the help. It also lessens the resentment that can build up on the part of the parent.

Make sure that the young adult continues to know it is only a temporary arrangement—"I kept giving her the 'little needle,'" as one mother put it to me. Her daughter had come home after college because she had no job and no friends who might serve as suitable roommates. When the daughter found a job and made some friends, the mother started to recommend moving out again, suggesting that the daughter was fully capable of maintaining her own place—and would probably enjoy the independence again. Being told it is only temporary right from the start, say the youngsters, helps motivate them to get out. A few youngsters actually admitted to me that as time went along it became harder and harder to muster the will to make the move.

More desperate parents told me of stronger medicine, such as moving to a smaller house or apartment, or offering to pay part or all of the rent on another place. That may be fine. But again, it would probably be wise to make sure that this is not done in a way that makes the youngster feel like a discard, which could further undermine that young adult's self-esteem. In one focus group of young adults I had gathered to discuss this issue, the consensus was that it helps if the parent builds in some transition time—at least two or three months to find an apartment and save up for the security deposit. It also helps to articulate the reason in a nondemeaning way, such as a desire to see that young person become more self-reliant since you will not always be around to help. That is why (as recommended in an earlier chapter) it may be best to make sure that any financial assistance offered is seen as a temporary gesture. For instance, help in paying the rent on that outside apartment might last only until the first pay raise, or other mutually agreed upon reason or termination date.

## THE CAUTIONS

Finally, remember that even in the most well-balanced families an adult child at home can set the stage for delayed maturity. Therapists who have seen many such stay-at-homes and their anguished parents maintain that it is not easy to foster independence and personal growth while that arrangement persists. One of them told me of a twenty-seven-year-old young man who was still "asking his mother's advice about appropriate clothing and whether he should go to a certain concert or out with a particular girl." Even the young adults themselves admit to an inner discomfort, on occasion, and some guilt at freeloading. "You are still living in someone else's house, by someone else's rules. And you know you are even dependent financially," observed the twenty-nine-year-old public relations specialist.

Staying on too long at home can make the young person feel inadequate to deal with the world in any capacity. As Okimoto and Stegall repeatedly remind parents in *Boomerang Kids,* the goal is not to foster dependence but "to send this young adult forth again as a more capable and competent human being."

# VI

# Special
Situations

# 22.

# High-Achieving Families with Differences

Perhaps more than ever before in this century there is a sense that family life no longer has a "normal" pattern. The era of the Norman Rockwell type of stay-at-home wife, breadwinning husband, and two or three children (plus the obligatory dog, cat, and fishing rod) is past. Today, that structure fails to represent the vast majority of the nation's families. Factors such as a high divorce rate, remarriage, the increased number of women in the work force, and a more enlightened attitude toward the handling of a child with any form of disability are forcing everyone to accept a whole array of diverse situations as equally legitimate. Fortunately, the result has been a lessening of the old stigmas attached to being "different" and a greater willingness to discuss the special issues that arise in each case.

I found fast-track families as much a part of these changes as anyone else. But again, there appeared to be issues within each of these situations that seem to affect affluent, high-achievers more acutely. These issues need to be articulated, if only to try to bring some deeper insights into the difficulties that can face such families irrespective of their overlay of good fortune.

I have not tried to cover all the special situations that can occur, for that would certainly be beyond the scope of this or any other book. For instance, I have not talked about children with serious physical disabilities, as that is a vast and very specialized topic. I have concentrated instead upon the more subtle complexities of dealing with a child who may be learning-impaired. This is because such a problem immediately puts that child at odds with parents who are likely to be more accustomed to dealing with nimble minds. Similarly, anorexia and bulimia need to be addressed, as these ailments are statistically proven to develop more readily in a high-achieving, affluent environment.

I purposely avoided talking about parents who are alcoholics since that is an equally vast subject that has been heavily researched and written about elsewhere, as have teenage alcoholics and drug addicts (with the exception of the brief discussion in Part IV, "The Teen Years").

I looked into the experience of divorced families on the fast track because the affluence and professional achievements of the parents clearly made their story different from the customary tales we hear about divorce and single parents. Similarly, the experience of the high-achieving mother who makes the decision to stay home—if only for a few years—to raise her children differs so markedly from that of the full-time mother who has no interest in a career outside the home that she definitely has a place in a book of this type. A fuller understanding and acknowledgment of those differences, I felt, could help both parent and child.

The special issues facing the children of high-achieving minority parents were another topic that seemed to need some exploration, if only because these families rarely get much attention from the academics or in the popular press. Perhaps these families are overlooked because the minority parent is still stereotyped as economically disadvantaged and poorly educated. That is no longer necessarily so. Nor, in fact, was it ever accurate. Certain black, Asian, and Hispanic families have belonged to the professional classes for generations; others are moving rapidly forward now. I hope a lot more will be written about these families in the future.

# 23.

# When the Children Have
# Learning Disabilities

It had never been easy for Rosemary . . . but when she returned from England she became aggressively unhappy, irritable, and frustrated at not
being able to do all the things her siblings could do. . . . All through her
childhood she had fought against her limitations by never giving up and by
retaining the sweetest nature you could ever imagine. . . . But now she
seemed to realize that no matter how hard she tried she would never even
come within sight of her Harvard-educated brothers and her glamorous
journalist sister. And once she recognized this, her level of frustration grew
so high that she became almost impossible to handle. Every day there
would be one terrifying incident after another: physical fights where Rosemary would use her fists to hit and bruise people, long absences at night
where she'd be out wandering the streets and violent verbal exchanges. . . .
in a family of such strong characters and high ambitions it must have been
terribly wearisome for Rosemary to keep on striving. . . .

The agony of Rosemary Kennedy, the retarded daughter of Joe and
Rose Kennedy, has been recounted many times, as in this passage
from *The Fitzgeralds and the Kennedys,* by Doris Kearns Goodwin. But
the story of Rosemary and the desperation of her highly ambitious,
high-achieving parents in trying to cope and come to terms with her
disability—a desperation that eventually led to a prefrontal lobotomy—
is perhaps the clearest picture we have of the searing anguish that can
envelop a family that prides itself on producing super-achievers.

Dr. Stephen P. Hersh, the psychiatrist from Chevy Chase, Maryland,
who has dealt with dozens of high-achieving parents, believes these
sorts of parents suffer acutely because their identity is so closely tied
to their children. "Since for [such] parents their children represent
extensions of their social and physical self-images," he writes in his

book, *The Executive Parent,* "the [disabled] child at first stimulates feelings in the parents of being imperfect. These feelings usually are rapidly followed by self-questioning, 'Why me? Why my child?' and then by anger, bitterness, shame."

Unfortunately the presence of a child with a learning disability in such circles is no longer a rare occurrence. Perhaps one of the more surprising findings of the many months I spent talking to high-achieving parents and those who help, teach, and advise their children was the frequency with which I would be told—maybe halfway into an interview and with a certain heaviness of heart—that one of the children was learning-impaired in some way.

## WHY DISABILITIES SHOW UP
## SO OFTEN AMONG THIS GROUP

But is it so surprising? Not in the least, suggest medical experts. First, many of today's high-achievers are older parents. The women are frequently in their thirties before giving birth. And we know that by that age the statistical likelihood of bearing a child with a disorder such as Down's Syndrome is above average.

Second, such parents normally have access to the medical resources to bring to full term an embryo that might otherwise not have made it. "In a less affluent setting that pregnancy might well have ended with a spontaneous abortion or a stillborn infant," observes Dr. Sirgay Sanger, the Manhattan psychiatrist and early-childhood specialist. This is also true, he notes, of such a couple's ability to marshal every technical support as well as the highly skilled expertise needed to sustain life in a high-risk premature infant. And it is not uncommon for a premature infant to be at risk for learning disabilities. He further warns that by striving for perfection—or because of their otherwise busy schedules—many high-achieving parents may inadvertently overlook the hypersensitivities and weaknesses in these infants which could increase the likelihood of trouble later on.

Third, superior testing methods have enabled specialists to diagnose more readily many more types of learning disabilities—subtle differences that might have slipped by unnoticed as recently as a generation ago. Even more of these disorders came out of the closet after Congress passed the Education for All Handicapped Children Act in 1976, a law that defined the term "handicapped" in such broad language that almost any child who did not perform at grade level could be included. As the law required a school district to make provision for such youngsters, many parents began seeking such a designation since it permitted a low-achieving child to be placed in a more intensive, personalized setting where remedial help could be given.

Fourth on the list—and perhaps the most controversial finding to emerge and one that so far has only anecdotal confirmation—is that some of these learning disabilities may be the hidden legacy of the drug culture of the 1960s. These are the children of the children of the sixties, remember? And the potential for genetic damage among drug users has not been overlooked. However, since this group was the first generation to use drugs on such a massive scale the implications for future generations are now only beginning to surface—as *they* become parents themselves. Thus it is still a largely untested theory. But a number of physicians and psychologists I interviewed noted that the probability is regularly discussed during informal conversations between colleagues. However, no studies confirming or denying the connection could be cited.

## PREVENTION AND COPING MECHANISMS

What has been the response among the parents? Prevention is very strong among these families. Genetic-testing clinics find success-oriented career couples heavily represented among their clients, according to a 1987 *New York* magazine article. This is undoubtedly because price is normally no object (amniocentesis alone, which tests for Down's Syndrome and other defects, costs about $1,000, with slight variations depending upon the area of the country). Moreover, high-achievers tend to be can-do people, eager to control a situation rather than passively accept what seems to be their fate. Thus embracing the notion of prevention is a natural extension of their regular outlook on life. As one of the women in the article explained, "I am sure that there are women out there whose opinion is 'It is God's will.' That's not my opinion. I can change it. And I don't think you get struck down for changing it." Such couples are therefore unlikely even to be restrained by the fear of social or religious stigma for opting for an abortion if they discover something amiss. Moreover, the opportunity becomes increasingly tantalizing as tests proliferate and all sorts of disabilities are included. Doctors are now able to test for cystic fibrosis, hemophilia, muscular dystrophy, spina bifida, and Tay-Sachs disease, among others.

If the disability is more subtle—as many learning disabilities are—and only shows up later, high-achieving parents may need to be more sensitive than most to the wide gap such children will feel between their performance and that of the rest of the household, not to mention the achievement-oriented circles in which they all move. It is the slower-sibling syndrome, magnified a thousandfold. These parents may therefore need to do all they can to foster any talent or ability that can make that youngster shine. A music teacher told me how many learning-disabled children she had taught gained enormous pride at being able to excel at the piano, and how the contact with a nurturing adult outside of the competitive atmosphere of school or family circles seemed to have a strong therapeutic effect. "One of them just liked to come to my house to cry," she said softly.

Language used to describe such children should also be handled with extreme care. "I won't even use the expression 'learning-disabled,' " one mother told me. "I say 'differently abled.' It may be just words. But words change perceptions."

Indeed, those who have dealt with these families warn that the LD (learning-disabled) label, although often a face-saver for the parents, should not be awarded without a great deal of careful testing and counseling because the child may use it as a crutch. One counselor explained the thought process this way: "They will say, 'I won't push myself because there is no point. I am stupid. People say that. So why try something I might never be able to accomplish.' "

Those warnings are increasing. Dr. Thomas Armstrong, a learning-disabilities specialist from Santa Rosa, California, who spent five years teaching classes for the learning-disabled, talks about the eagerness with which parents and teachers now use this designation. In his book *In Their Own Way*, he says that some of the children had extraordinary abilities that did not show up on the tests. He told the story of one boy with an exceptional facility at doing mental calculations in his head who could not duplicate that calculation on paper. Thus he suggests that testing methods may actually be flawed since they do not allow for the enormous variations in the way children process information. Gerald Coles, an associate professor of clinical psychiatry at the Robert Wood Johnson Medical School in New Jersey, raises similar questions in *The Learning Mystique: A Critical Look at "Learning Disabilities."*

In addition, many children with learning disabilities devise such excellent ways to compensate that they become successful despite their handicaps. Famous dyslexics, for example, have included Thomas Edison, Isaac Newton, Hans Christian Andersen, Auguste Rodin, Nelson Rockefeller, Woodrow Wilson, and George C. Patton.

Dr. Sara Sparrow, director of research at the Yale Child Study Center, is equally concerned that assumptions are too frequently made on too little data. And she urges parents to have the child tested at the highest level of expertise before taking any remedial action—preferably at a clinic attached to a major medical center or university.

The impact upon the rest of the family should not be underestimated. Considerable work is now being done on the effect of disabled children upon their "normal" siblings. Dr. Selma Miller, a family therapist in Manhattan who has been conducting an ongoing study of what happens to siblings of the disabled, maintains it is vital for parents to encourage those siblings to discuss their fears, frustrations, and concerns openly, without being chastised or made to feel ashamed of their reactions (such as embarrassment when inviting a friend to the house). I heard similar stories. One such sibling, now a highly successful physician, told me how when she was eight years old she remembers growing so irritated with her mentally retarded younger brother that one afternoon she screamed at him, calling him an "idiot." Her anguish was compounded, she said, when her parents scolded her for the outburst. That same woman also remembers feeling resentful at the amount of parental attention her brother constantly received. Eventually she became so hungry for that attention that she started flunking school. Her immature rationale was that difficulties with school work were clearly the way to get that attention. Hadn't her brother proven it to be so?

Some high-achieving parents have found they can help alleviate their frustrations about what they can do for their own child by using their financial resources, their abilities, and their connections to work for various causes related to the disabled, as the Kennedy family did— turning, in effect, a troubling situation into one that enhances their own feelings of pride, purpose, and accomplishment. Certainly they are in a special position to make such a contribution.

Such parents should be extremely cautious about how any trust is set up for a child with any kind of disability. Even youngsters who also have serious physical impairments now live far longer than anyone with these problems did in the past, so sibling involvement in future plans may therefore be needed. Further, the form in which assets are passed on may disqualify the child from receiving certain state and federal benefits. And the estate could rapidly be dissipated—unless that trust is very carefully structured or the money placed in the hands of another family member on behalf of that child.

## ONE BOY'S TALE

How does it feel from the child's viewpoint? Clearly there are as wide a range of experiences as there are disabilities. However, to be most helpful, I chose a story with a happy ending—the tale of a young man able to recall what he went through and what helped him the most.

When I first met Scott Bedrick he was twenty-nine years old. It was a day of record low temperatures in New York City. Scott's tall and bony body was bundled up against the cold with a heavy woollen coat whose collar was turned up. He had just dashed across midtown for this meeting from his job at Pfizer, Inc., where he was employed as a computer technical data analyst. That week he had received a promotion to its international division. He was also renting a one-bedroom apartment in a fashionable section of Brooklyn after having grown up in Simsbury, a suburb of Hartford, Connecticut.

All of these were major accomplishments, for Scott suffers from dyslexia, and to take his rightful place in a family accustomed to substantial achievements had not been easy. Scott's father is a highly successful corporate engineer and real estate investor. His mother, a homemaker and teacher, is also used to high standards. Scott has two sisters who are achievers, too.

Nobody really knew something was seriously wrong with him, he said, "until I was in first grade . . . I was doing so poorly that the teacher told my mother she thought I was mentally retarded. My mother, perhaps sensing there might be another explanation, said, 'No son of mine is mentally retarded.' So I started being taken for a battery of tests, ending up at Massachusetts General Hospital where I tested positive for dyslexia."

He stopped for a moment, explaining it was not easy to recall these days, suggesting he might have blocked out many memories because of the pain. Even now, he said, he had only just begun to be comfortable talking about his childhood. He continued: "The next few years were disastrous. My mother, being the fast-track sort of person she was, started lobbying for a law that would pay school districts to provide special instruction—we had none of the programs we have today. All I had was some rudimentary help. So it was very, very embarrassing. I would get ridiculed by the other kids, and by some of the teachers, too—badgered and belittled. I remember one teacher kept saying, 'Step on the gas, Scott. Step on the gas.' But the tank was empty. I think a lot of adults really thought I was just lazy. I remember sitting reading with my mother. I used to dread those times because I was forced to sit with a book in my hand and read. And I could not sit still. I had to fidget. Now I know my mother was just trying to help, trying to push me to keep up as best I could. She did not belittle me. But it was hard. I think she must have seen what I was going through because she never compared me to my sisters or let them say anything to me.

"The turning point came when I was twelve years old and my parents sent me off to a special boarding school. What a relief! I think I was only homesick for a week or two and after that I started to enjoy myself for the first time. Everyone else had learning problems. Everyone else was in the same boat. So the competitiveness of everything was taken away. And all you had was positive reinforcement. You were led at your own pace. It took the pressure right off. No more ridicule at school. No more remarks by other kids in the neighborhood. No family pressure. And at that school I seemed even a little ahead because I was much more emotionally stable. Some of the others would lie and steal and act out their frustrations. They would tell stories just like mine of having been ridiculed and called dumb or stupid by teachers and peers. Boarding school also gave me the idea I might go further and that I was not an outcast. I also began to hear about famous dyslexics like Einstein and found out that dyslexics even have higher IQs than most. It meant a lot. I remember also my mother would not give up on me. That helped, too. She would say, 'You are going to go to college,' which was unheard of for someone with dyslexia in those days. I was still so uncoordinated, still so bad at reading and math."

After managing combined scores of around 1100 on the SATs (he took them untimed, which the learning-disabled are permitted to do), Scott went on to Hartwick College in Oneonta, New York, and then obtained a master's degree in computer science from Pratt Institute in Brooklyn. "I was pushed. But in a positive way," he added reflectively. "I don't think I would be where I am today if it hadn't been for the pushing. But it was not the sort where my parents complained if I got a D. They would just say, 'Well, you will do better next time. . . . Just so long as you did the best you could possibly do' . . . or, 'We are proud of you because you gave it your all.' It was more that they were thrilled every time I did do well. And the family was so strong. There was always so much love. And I have been taught how to compensate. I still have to read things two and three times. I still need to use the Spellchecker on my computer when I write even a small memo. But I am looked up to by my peers at the office. I am good at what I do."

There is no question that the increased level of understanding about these learning disabilities, coupled with an educated, affluent parent's ability to tap the best medical and educational resources, means that far more can be done for such a child than ever before. Facing these situations is never easy. But it is uplifting to realize that the problems can be mitigated to a point where these children can find a place for themselves in the world.

# 24.

# Bulimia and
# Anorexia

Some disorders appear to be a direct consequence of the type of environment in which a child is raised. Bulimia and anorexia fit that category. No wonder. In success-oriented circles where a tanned, lithe body is one of the ultimate success symbols, it is hardly any wonder that attempts to attain that symbol lead to all sorts of desperate moves. Bulimia and anorexia are two of the most extreme results.

According to a summary of recent findings published in *Family Therapy Today,* nine out of ten anorexic or bulimic individuals are young women who belong mostly to middle- and upper-middle-class families. These families are further characterized as setting unusually high standards. The parents are often overprotective and rigid and have difficulty resolving family disagreements. Occasionally, those parents are also insecure, frustrated, and unhappy.

What exactly is anorexia? And what type of child is likely to slip into that category? Anorexic individuals are known to have an intense fear of becoming fat and may starve themselves to death in an effort to be thin enough to satisfy their own notion of what constitutes a perfect body. They are also likely to have felt depressed for a long time and may be suicidal. They accomplish weight loss through dieting or a combination of dieting and purging.

Bulimic girls are usually a little older than anorexic girls, possibly already past their teens. Also obsessed with body image, they control weight through repeated episodes of binging and purging. The purging is done through self-induced vomiting or excessive use of diet pills, laxatives, or diuretics. A bulimic woman usually has normal or above-normal weight. Typically she is someone who has faced repeated failures in her school work or with boys and is more likely to have been involved with drugs and alcohol than the anorexic girl.

Often hospitalization is needed in both instances as the eating disturbances may have led to serious medical problems. The usual treatment is to involve medical, psychological, and nutritional specialists who work as a team to help the youngsters understand what is occurring and the misguidedness of the self-imposed solution. The goal is to break the pattern permanently. Increasingly, the entire family is involved in treatment as changes in the entire family's behavior are now considered necessary before the patient can improve over the long haul.

Because so much has been written on these subjects, a more detailed discussion will not be included here. See the Appendix for books that can help put these illnesses into perspective.

# 25.

# The Single Parent on
# the Fast Track

About fifty rather formally attired men and women are gathered in the carpeted library of a neighborhood community center for one of the monthly meetings of their local singles group. The difference this particular evening is that the organizers have invited me to lead them in a discussion on the impact of divorce on single parents in fast-track communities. Clearly there were different economic issues to confront and different problems facing their children, compared to the bulk of the population who must cope with the same prospect. And I am here to learn about them as part of my probe into fast-track single-parent family life.

The meeting had been arranged for parents only rather than parents and their children, so there will be no inhibitions. The men and women are lively, enthusiastic, and can hardly stop talking about their experiences. Many chat in a most animated fashion, jumping up from their metal folding chairs, waving arms aloft. And it is not to complain of their plight or garner sympathy. No way. After all that we now know about the pain and distress caused by divorce, I am totally unprepared for the positive manner in which so many of these parents and children on the fast track describe the impact of divorce upon their lives.

Once the initial trauma and disruption of the divorce had subsided, the parents spoke of an unexpected calm, a cleansing, as though it had actually helped rather than hurt many of their children—whom they conceded may have been overprotected and dominated to an extent that perhaps had not always been too healthy. Expressions like "My daughter began to blossom as soon as we were less in control" or "He began to feel a sense of accomplishment by being able to do so much more for me" were commonplace in describing welcome changes that were taking place in a child.

A few parents also admitted they were secretly thrilled that they no longer had to struggle to keep up with the CEO next door, or the senior partner down the hall. Realizing that the cost of fast-track life was now way beyond the single-parent purse (true in many cases, although certainly not all), or that they had an ideal excuse for shifting to a slower lane, it also gave them the freedom to reevaluate their outlook on life. Some even began to wonder if their former values and goals had really ever made sense. "Can you believe that I woke up one morning and decided that my driving ambition had actually been an addiction, not something to be proud of?" said one dark-haired woman. "Now I knew I could stop and smell those roses without feeling guilty. Even my neighbors expected less of me and seemed more compassionate."

For those whose careers continued to be an abiding passion it lessened the strain that had gone into maintaining the demanding trinity of marriage, parenting, and work. Now, at least, though it sometimes seemed to be an embarrassing admission, they had the freedom to devote more time to pursuing the goals they had originally carved out for themselves.

Elsewhere I heard similar stories. Barry Farber, the well-known talk-show host, was divorced when his two daughters were still very young. "It was easier in a way because visitation times were clean-cut," he told me. "You could make plans." During marriage, he noted, the danger was that you assumed you were spending enough time with your children simply because you lived in the same house. But if you had an extremely heavy schedule this could turn into an illusion— *being* there both physically and emotionally is very different from *living* there. "I would look forward to those visits," he continued. "But I wouldn't try to duplicate home." Instead, he said, he made the most of his own interesting career environment by taking them on interviews and involving them in broadcasting. "I gave them what I could give best," he said.

This is not to suggest that any of these people were unrealistic about the difficulties they faced. Indeed, seeing themselves as success-oriented role models created a special concern. One divorced father, owner of a thriving advertising and public relations agency, told me he feared that he would no longer be able to share his "thought process" with his two teenage sons—how he had handled situations from his daily business rounds that he had hoped would help his sons when they went forth on their own. And keeping up the same material standards, even though money was much tighter, became so important to his sense of dignity that, he said, "I would wrap up things I had around the house to take to them. I remember giving away my stereo, a portable radio, and even a car radio I had been meaning to install in my own car." He also admitted he opted to fall behind in his taxes rather than give up the ski vacations he had always taken with his two sons.

Certainly many suffered terrible pangs of guilt and anguish over the fact that they now felt hampered by a major handicap as parents. Understandably, at the top of the Items Most Missed list was no longer being able to so easily afford private school or prestigious college fees along with a feeling of stigma at not having enough to make sure their teenager had a fine car or the right clothes. Yet, in the end, what surprised so many of them was that their children did not feel deprived. In fact, some of those youngsters began to feel a lot better about themselves.

I conclude that the good feelings emanated in large measure from the parents' own strong abilities, enabling them to cope with adversity in ways that might have overwhelmed less take-charge types. It clearly helped that each partner's financial underpinnings tended to be solid, if no longer gold-plated. Individually, many had strong earnings potential or assets to fall back upon—all of which meant that even if they had to reef those sails just a little bit they soon realized they were so much better off than the average single-parent household.

I came across the same attitudes when I talked about divorce with a group of thirteen-year-olds, one of a number of group and individual interview sessions I was to have on the topic with young people, too. The youngsters also insisted that in some ways they were now *better* off than peers from intact families.

Said one boy, "My friend is actually jealous of me because my dad will spend a whole day just taking me places or talking, whereas his dad is always too busy or too tired."

Added a girl, "When my dad was here he kept expecting more and more of me. Now that he's gone my mom is pretty lenient. We do more things together."

Little wonder that when I started to organize the most salient points from all these interviews into a Plus and Minus table the former outweighed the latter. Originally intended for the purpose of sorting out my personal notes, it was so striking a list that I decided to include it here. Certainly this list, along with the following personal stories and comments, gives pause to anybody who may still be under the misapprehension that little good can ever come out of divorce. Among certain high-achieving families this certainly does not seem to be so.

| UNANTICIPATED ADVANTAGES THAT SEEMED TO FLOW FROM THE DIVORCE | DRAWBACKS THAT CAUSED PAIN TO PARENT OR CHILD |
| --- | --- |
| Greater closeness between each parent and child | Fear of less money available for private school or top-rated university |
| Far less tension | Fear of less money to maintain former lifestyle |
| Children mature as they come to terms more quickly with the idea that you cannot always get whatever you want | Even more difficulty finding enough time and attention for a child |
| Vulnerable parents help make child feel more useful and valuable—and needed | Threat of moving to less acceptable neighborhood |
| Less academic pressure placed on child to achieve because parents are more preoccupied with own problems | Feeling you still had to keep up the old standards like vacations in Europe or having a second house; it seemed cruel to take these perks away after having brought up a child to expect them |
| Greater chance for self-assertion at all ages as though a welcome vacuum had just been created | Conflicts over which parent would have control of child and with whom that child would live |
| Need of child to assume greater responsibilities at home and in personal life—again fostering maturity | Worry over how that child might fit into a remarriage |
| Chance to develop more compassion and empathy for others because of own family problems | |
| A less arrogant attitude in the teen and post-teen years | |
| More one-on-one occasions mean more real listening taking place between parent and child | |

Greater emphasis placed upon
needs of child because so many
studies suggest children of divorce
may get into difficulties; thus less
cavalier attitude that everything at
home is probably okay

Learning to get by on a lot less
money—and being just as happy

Perhaps these general observations are most easily understood by
following the progress of two families: one where we hear in a reflective
manner from the mother, and the other where we look at a similar
experience from the perspectives of both mother and daughter.

The first woman was from the Midwest. When I met her she was
slightly overweight, on the far side of forty, and living with her two
teenage daughters in a suburb north of Boston. Both her former husband and herself, like the vast majority of fast-track couples, had not
stayed in the communities where they had been raised but had hopped
from city to city to further their respective careers. She began, "Both
my husband and I were ambitious, striving people. He was a clinical
psychologist and I was busy getting an advanced degree in counseling
and then setting up a consulting service. We loved to live well. We
were always living on the edge of our means. Looking back, I think it
added to the stress we all felt. . . .

"When my husband and I separated I was left in the big house and
I was dedicated to the idea that we were not going to cut back. I wanted
my daughters to have the same as all their peers—the clothes, the
vacations. I didn't want to see them embarrassed. I didn't want to say
no. I also couldn't cope at first with the idea of failure. If you are a
striver, a perfectionist, it's hard to admit you might have made a major
mistake. Every little setback starts to seem like a catastrophe. So I
pushed even more for a while. But maybe I was trying too hard for
the wrong reasons. I remember when we had to give up the horse my
daughter wasn't shattered. Instead she confessed she had always felt
scared around horses. And all the time I was worried I was letting her
down!

"But it was still chaos for a while. Perhaps the only really helpful
thing I did was to bring someone in to rent one of the rooms. It gave
us extra money. But it also gave us another adult, a buffer person, who
cut the tension and made us more respectful around each other. But

even that didn't work for too long. So I put the house on the market and said to the girls, 'We are in for serious downward mobility. It's not going to be easy.'

"We sold the house. We moved into a rented house about ten miles away in a town that was nice but not as expensive. It was a big relief. Without a big house to worry about I had more time for the girls. No lawn to mow. No repairs to panic over. But I did go through a resentful period. Why me? Why should I suffer and the kids suffer after we had worked so hard to get where we were going? But then I found myself changing my mind. I saw my children becoming far more relaxed. Being in a fast-track town had never been easy for them. Their grades weren't the greatest. Their self-esteem had never been good around all those kids who seemed to be able to do everything well. It became a respite for us all. I learned to question my own strivings and think about other things in life besides winning—a sort of less-is-more formula. I found myself able to say 'no' if someone called to ask me to serve on a board or join a group. Before I was always afraid I would miss out on something special. It was like I was telling myself, 'a clever, smart person is always busy doing.' I remember my girls would always complain I had lived my life in a rush, always doing three things at the same time. Suddenly it didn't seem to matter that much anymore. And I was actually happier. I had more time to relax. More time for the children, too, more time to listen. And when I gave up my expectations for them I suddenly started to see what extraordinary creatures they were."

The mother-daughter story offers some similar observations. But I could not help wondering, after hearing such views repeated far more often than I have mentioned here, whether the changing outlook had more to do with the manner in which we help ourselves come to terms with crisis and loss than with any real change in philosophy.

| DAUGHTER'S STORY | MOTHER'S STORY |
|---|---|
| The daughter was an attractive eighteen-year-old with hoop earrings, blue jeans, and a cheeky smile. She was refreshingly modest although she seemed to know where she was going and what sort of person she wanted to be. "I was thirteen when they sat me down one night and said they were going to get a di- | The mother was a vivacious, well-dressed woman who was wearing stiletto-heeled boots, a long flowing paisley skirt, and an oversized turtleneck sweater the day we met. She was working at the time as a marketing and public relations consultant and was doing exceedingly well. "The main reason I had stayed in |

vorce," she said. "I knew it had been coming. But it was still a shock. It was a hard time at school, too, which did not help . . . I had never really thought about financial problems before. I had assumed there would always be enough. Now it started to hit me, especially when my mom said I might have to transfer out to public school. I had all my friends at private school. I fitted in. And I had been brought up where everyone seemed to have a tennis court and a swimming pool. It seemed like the norm. So not to have these sorts of things was being different. And I also felt bad about being told I might have to go to a state university instead of a good, Ivy League school.

"Then my mom said we might move into a little condo. And I thought it might be kind of nice, just her and me together looking after the thing. And helping out sounded so grown up. But my dad also wanted me to live with him. So they gave me the choice. But I think that is wrong because you know that the one you don't choose will be upset. So I would not make the choice. I felt very self-conscious back then. I remember walking into a classroom one day and when one of the seniors, a great guy who was real cute, said 'Hi!' and started talking to me I was sure it was because he felt sorry for me, not because he wanted to make friends. The same thing happened with one of my girlfriends. I was sure she had dropped me because of the divorce and the fact that we did not live in the nice house with the pool any-

the marriage for so long was because I did not want my daughter to suffer," she began as she smoothed her skirt with her hands. "I had planned to stay in until my daughter was eighteen but I couldn't wait any longer. So she was still only thirteen when we separated. We had everything then. My husband was a very successful lawyer. We had a beautiful Colonial house with a tennis court, a swimming pool, five acres, live-in housekeeper, a gardener, a Mercedes. I never went to work in those days. My husband did not want me to. He liked to be totally in control. He even had to make all the decisions and get his own way or there would be terrible fights. That's what made me want to get out, in part. . . .

"But I was afraid that my daughter was so used to living the affluent life she might not be able to adjust to counting pennies. If her friends were all going off to Aspen, what would I say? I hated the idea of her feeling like the poor relative who is left out. I was not sure I could even do it. I was particularly worried about school. She was at private school. Having her go to a good school and good college meant a lot to me. Eventually, when we did separate, I even chose to move into a little house in a good neighborhood rather than a better home in a place where she might feel awkward. It was an old beach cottage. But we're fixing it up. . . .

"As it was, my husband paid for private school in the end. So she stayed there. Even so, my daughter started to change a lot. You could

more. I think I must have been very depressed for a while.

"Then when I was sixteen everyone was being given cars. But I had to use my own money and settle for a six-year-old blue Chevette. But I was kind of proud in a way because I had bought it myself. . . .

"I also got to manage my own life more. If they'd still been married I know there would have been more curfews, less trust. As it was, my mom had to trust me and I found myself trying to be more responsible. I got a job selling magazine subscriptions one summer, I'll never forget that. I had to go door-to-door and call on people. When my dad heard he was really concerned and said it was not right for his daughter to be doing something like that. But I was glad for the chance. It made me feel independent, self-motivated. I learned a lot about how to talk to a whole lot of different people and see the way they lived. I saw that only a handful of people ever lived the way we did. And that we had been lucky. I think I have become far more realistic. Even today I see my cousins who still live that way. And they are so spoiled. . . ." She looked into the distance and added with a shrug, "So maybe it was good . . . in a way."

see the difference. My husband had always made decisions for her, too. Now she had to make some for herself. . . . And I changed. The value I had put on having a lot of money, the right vacations, clothes, keeping up with status things now didn't seem to matter so much. It was like I was cured of a disease. I realized these things had not made me happy. I even changed my thinking about my daughter. Before the divorce I felt there was no end to the education she would get and how she would soon be on a success track of her own. But that got less and less important. Instead, I felt it was very important that she come out of undergraduate school with a skill that could get her a job—a more practical approach. Graduate school could wait. I started seeing that all that striving after success did not necessarily lead to much in the end. It may sound stupid but other things like helping others, feeling good about what you do, peace of mind—all those clichés—have a lot to offer, too. I think I have turned from being a fast-track parent to being a laid-back parent      ."

## RECENT FINDINGS ON DIVORCE

Not all families successfully negotiate the transition as well as these two. Indeed, one of the consistent facts that regularly appear in newspaper accounts of murder, drugs, and mayhem among rich young folk is that their parents are divorced. There is no question that these children have a bumpy ride, on balance, regardless of the advantages outlined in the list above.

However, having spent nearly a decade writing articles on divorce issues and keeping up with the literature on the subject, I am aware that society is far more knowledgeable now about strategies that can help mitigate the pain and upheaval. Many are equally applicable to success-oriented families. Among these findings:

- Virtually all recent studies indicate that there is frequently a substantial period of emotional and practical child neglect following parental separation. Much of that neglect appears to come from the personal and economic stress faced by divorcing parents rather than any lack of concern for their youngsters. Children who fare best are those whose parents make specific plans to ensure the continuation of their normal routine, including supervision and discipline. It also helps if there is a cooperative attitude concerning the child, and both parents stay actively involved in the child's life.

- Boys seem to be more severely affected than girls at elementary school age with the opposite true by adolescence. Adult children may feel equally as distressed as young children with common reactions being anger, mourning (for the passing of such cornerstones as family holidays at home), disillusionment, and even outrage at being unfairly burdened when they feel they have more than enough of their own problems to handle. They also do not take kindly to suggestions that the parents may have made "sacrifices" by staying together until they were grown.

- Children should be allowed to help an overburdened single parent, but never to the point where they become overwhelmed by being cast in the multiple role of emotional confidant, family babysitter, and housekeeper. This can lead to resentment and even an unexpected outburst of fury if the parent remarries and that child loses the favored position.

- Children may not take kindly to any "date" that the parent brings into the house because that person automatically represents a threat. He or she violates the "sacred spot" the child may have maintained for the missing parent and erases the fantasy that the parents may one day reunite. Any sign of sexual contact with the date may also trouble or unsettle a child (especially a teenager) and might be best handled away from the house until a more permanent relationship has been established.

- Grandparents can be a wonderful source of support for both parents and child at such a moment—but may need to be told quite specifically what type of help is needed and what is actually harmful.
- Keeping close to the divorced spouse's larger family may seem difficult. But kinship is extremely valuable to a child in maintaining the sort of emotional stability that comes from belonging to a cluster of close-knit relatives and knowing that some bonds are truly there for life.
- If you remarry be very sensitive to the child's feelings about participating in that wedding. He or she does not necessarily share your joy and may worry that an active role in the ceremonies could be construed as an act of treason toward the other parent. Remain open-minded about the way the youngster might (or might not) be included.
- Blended or stepfamilies are not easy on either parent or child despite the media's glamorous treatment of such households. The emotional tug-of-war is frequently so acute that participation in a support and counseling organization like the Stepfamily Foundation or the Stepfamily Association of America may be wise.
- Forget about trying to be perfect. How about human?

(See the Appendix for a sampling of books on divorce and remarriage that seem particularly appropriate for the highly educated, more sophisticated fast-track family.)

# 26.

# When Mother Stays Home

Colby Caron, a chubby, blue-eyed girl who had just turned ten months old, was snoozing on the beige corduroy couch in the living room, snug under a rose-colored shawl. A few feet away her mother, thirty-four-year-old Nancy Caron, was busy with the usual end-of-day chores—picking up stray toys from around the base of the grandfather clock in a corner of the living room and preparing food in the adjacent blue-and-white kitchen.

The scene, set in the quaint Colonial home on a quiet street of similar two-story frame houses, was truly a celebration of family in the traditional sense: rosy-cheeked baby, at-home mother fussing around a neat-as-a-nest house, daddy (a banker) on the way back from the office. There was even a just-completed igloo the parents had built on the front lawn in whimsical tribute to the freshly fallen snow. Only a handful of telltale items suggested something different: a copy of *The Wall Street Journal* lay on the coffee table in place of the expected stack of glossy magazines. And on an antique sideboard sat two plastic-jacketed library books: *Raising a Confident Child* and *Growing Up Smart and Happy*.

Nancy Caron, a thin, no-nonsense sort of woman, looked contented as she went about her errands with quick, energetic movements. She wore faded jeans, an oversized white woolly sweater, sported no makeup, and allowed her short, unkempt brown hair to remain disheveled as she pattered about. Few would have ever suspected that for ten years this wispy woman had been a highly respected member of a senior management team, most recently an assistant vice president at a division of a *Fortune* 500 company.

Now, however, she was an at home mother, prey to all the nonsensical joys, gnawing doubts, culture shock, insecurities, and ambiguities that so often overtake former executive women. Neither totally domesticated nor totally committed to a lifelong career, such women become hybrid people, inhabiting—for the period of their lives they choose to stay home—a kind of no-woman's land, one foot here and one foot there, members in good standing of both camps yet totally fulfilled by neither.

## THOSE A-PLUS TRAITS
## ARE NOT LEFT ON THE DOORSTEP

To believe they are instantly transformed into laid-back Type B's just because they have decided to temporarily forgo the business world is a tempting but erroneous notion. The homespun façade is deceptive. Underneath they have not changed one whit. Rather, there is increasing evidence that many end up turning those hard-driving A-plus traits inward toward the project at hand—child-raising—becoming even more compulsive about their children's activities and achievements than the working mother. Child replaces business venture as goal. Moreover, faced with the prospect that they may be giving up five to ten of the most critically important years of their careers for their children, it becomes unbearable to think they could end up with nothing more than a ho-hum child—even worse, one with *problems*. Besides, their goal-oriented training is already too deeply ingrained. They have to produce results to prosper. Isn't that what the business world has taught them?

## NANCY'S STORY

Listen, for a moment, to Nancy tell how it feels firsthand. Settling into a wing-back chair she begins her story, a tale not dissimilar to that of hundreds of other professional women in their thirties and forties who are choosing to put their careers on hold to face a different kind of bottom line each morning. Like so many of her peers, Nancy's original intent had been to take a brief maternity leave. But somehow when the day came to return to the office the idea of wrenching herself away from her firstborn child became too difficult. She explains earnestly: "When they had originally asked me if I would come back I had said, 'Absolutely!' I couldn't think what else I might do. I had even arranged for all the memos to be sent to me while I was out. But," she adds thoughtfully and with a shrug, "something happened."

She pauses for a moment to pick up Colby, who has woken up from her nap. Returning to the chair Nancy places her baby tenderly on her knee, caressing one of Colby's doll-sized feet. Then she continues: "When I first started staying home full-time I had torn feelings. I felt I had sold out the feminists. That haunted me. I also found that my corporate identity had been my identity for so long I felt nothing without it. . . . I wanted to stay involved so badly that I found myself calling my old friends from the office and arranging to meet them for lunch. But I found it took nearly all day just to get ready. And when I saw them in their business suits—it was a business crowd—I started to cry because I was so exhausted and it seemed that their lives were so exciting compared to mine. That does not mean I am sorry for what I did. I still know it was the right decision. . . .

"You see, it's a real problem going from a highly structured, goal-oriented environment to one where absolutely nothing seems to get accomplished. I am a very structured person. And when you stay home you start to think that everything is passing you by. My friends were getting promotions, raises. Even the commuter train ride started to look good. . . .

"I don't think I was prepared for that terrible feeling of worthlessness. So I would try to *do* a whole lot. I would take Colby down to the library, more for me than for her. I tried to arrange a play group to make sure she developed her social skills. I began reading everything I could on child-rearing. I felt that since I was at home I should be offering her as many experiences as I could. I felt I had to come up with new and exciting things all the time. If I had one day where I took it easy I felt guilty. From my days at work I think I was all keyed up. Unless I had something to tell my husband at the end of the day I felt I had failed. I also began to feel isolated and was afraid that I would have nothing to show for my time. So I would find myself insisting Colby do this or that. I became so embarrassed about saying I was a housewife that when my professional women's group called to ask how they should describe me in their membership book I said, 'professional musician.' " She grins sheepishly and then explains, "I'm the choir director for our church and I play the organ and piano."

Others talk of similar feelings, of the danger of being caught up in a goal-oriented approach to child-raising that can distort the nurturing role of motherhood. Take, for instance, another former corporate woman that I met—a thirty-seven-year-old M.B.A. in finance who was formerly in corporate development at a major photographic corporation. The woman's husband was a structural engineer, also with an M.B.A. After her most recent baby was born she said she did not want to miss this baby's early years, so she decided to stay home. She explained: "Right now my kids are my project. I have no other area of accomplishment. And the danger is that I will push them too hard. I am always doing something with them, maybe because I'm used to being on the go. Sometimes I have to pull back and ask myself, 'Is this good?' Almost every day each child has some lesson or class or we are going to a museum or a play."

## WHAT WE KNOW ABOUT
## STAY-AT-HOME EXECUTIVE WOMEN

Bettie Youngs, the child development specialist from California, has found that such parents are indeed in danger of going overboard, in part because they feel a tremendous social pressure to look as accomplished and as involved as the working mother. "We find these kids in every single activity you can imagine," says Youngs. "It's often because these mothers have more time to arrange those activities and get them back and forth. I even found myself doing the same thing when I gave up work. I started us both [her daughter and herself] on horseback-riding lessons. I would put 'riding' on my calendar for Mondays, Wednesdays, and Fridays. And because it was there we had to go."

Youngs continued: "The child becomes the achievement—the job, the career, the status symbol. What is the difference from the fifties? Back then nobody expected us to raise super-children just because we stayed home. Nobody was raising super-children. Today the standards have become elevated. 'Ordinary' is no longer enough."

Dr. Kenneth Howard, head of clinical psychology at Northwestern University, tells the story of one woman who was so used to being managerial she started supervising her child's after-school group by sitting in on the sessions. He also recalls another at-home mother whose sense of accomplishment was so wrapped up in her children that she would subconsciously set up situations where they would continue to need her; because to be no longer needed would have been like being fired from a job she felt she had been doing extremely well.

Some mothers who stay home do so because they have married exceedingly successful, high-profile men. Many such men *demand* a stay-at-home wife. They want a full-time person to tend to their social life and complement their image. In these cases, the professionals have found, the danger lies in the likelihood that instead of the child receiving opportunities for added nurturing, that youngster may become ancillary to the demands of the marriage. Compounding that danger is the chance that because this sort of woman has made the commitment to be at home she will lull herself into a false sense of complacency. In fact, her overflowing social calendar leaves her even less time or energy for motherhood. "What worries me is that they get so involved in their volunteer activity, in their husband's lives, in rushing to this meeting and that club that they don't have any time for the children," the director of a nursery school told me. "Yet they still tell me, 'I'm staying home for my kids.' And they really believe that is what they are doing.

"But the children see it differently," she continued. "They get the message that those activities are more important than they are. So we are back to the problem of low self-esteem. Only the other morning I saw a mother who had no time to look at her child's art work because she said she had to make a lunch appointment. So she just rolled up the painting and shoved it under her arm. The little girl looked crestfallen. She had spent most of the morning on that painting. And all it would have taken would have been a few moments. . . ."

The message that comes across is clear: if you are planning to stay home be prepared for social stigma and little social sanction to convince you that what you are doing is genuinely worthwhile; accept the fact that this is a period in history when full-time motherhood (however valuable) has been devalued by your peers; don't overcompensate; instead sit back and relax and take time to enjoy that child.

And if you still feel a compelling need to prove yourself, go back to work, or spend some of that energy on developing a latent talent, as Nancy Caron is doing with her music. Or take some old-fashioned pride in "nesting," as former *New York Times* columnist Anna Quindlen admits she secretly loves to do (like picking out slipcovers, gardening, making quilts or brownies, restoring furniture: the activities that really do make a house a home). Don't shift the burden of your personal frustrations or societal pressures onto a child.

What is left? Plenty. The reward of simply knowing that what you are doing feels right to you. And that you now have time to hear those First Words and see that First Step—magical moments that are all profit and no loss. So stick around if that is what you have chosen. Toss aside the datebook. Stop counting and comparing. And instead, consider the period to be a magnificent interlude and one of growth of a different kind.

# 27.

# Minority Parents on the Fast Track

Eighteen-year-old Francesca was leaning delicately against a wall in an office building in midtown Manhattan on the day we first met. A ballerina-in-training, she was truly the artist even in her choice of clothing. She was wearing a man's tuxedo jacket over an oversized purple-and-black-striped sweater and baggy black pants.

Francesca is a black teenager. She comes from a family of physicians, lawyers, writers—superbly talented, one and all. She was educated at the Nightingale-Bamford school—an all-girls private school in New York City that could have catapulted her into almost any degree program she wished. But a few months before we met she had eschewed college—put her acceptance at Hunter College in New York City on hold—to throw herself totally into the rigorous training needed to become a classical ballerina.

Not going on to college had been a particularly difficult decision for a fast-track black family to accept, she conceded, mindful as such families are that privilege among minorities is still sufficiently rare that it cannot be tossed lightly aside. This was so even though she had recently been accepted as a full-time trainee in the workshop ensemble of the highly rated Dance Theatre of Harlem. For being black frequently means less room for experimentation, less room for error, she explained. And recognizing this she felt caught in a bind. "But, then, how do you postpone a dancing career?" she questioned, rhetorically, adding that the decision not to enter college had been especially tough on her grandmother, who knew well the struggles the family had faced in previous generations to gain admission into the professions.

I had a number of conversations with minority young people like Francesca as well as their parents. I spoke to counselors familiar with minorities either because they themselves belonged to a minority group or because their work had brought them in close touch with minorities. And I read whatever written material I could gather on this minority within minorities. It certainly helped confirm what we all might have guessed—that black, Asian, or Hispanic families on the fast track are in most ways no different from anybody else moving in similar circles. Their children face exactly the same issues as all other children from families with a heritage of high achievement. The differences that *are* apparent are in relative terms—the degree to which certain pressures may be accentuated or lessened due to the differences in cultural, racial, and ethnic backgrounds as well as the ever-present specter of prejudice and stereotyping.

It is unsafe to generalize because there are obviously as many differences of style, attitude, attainment, and experience within these minority circles as there are anywhere else. But a few basic observations can perhaps be offered, if only to increase awareness of the dangers, difficulties, and dreams that do seem to accompany and affect the parenting styles of high-achievers among these groups.

## FEARS ABOUT DOWNWARD MOBILITY

First, it appears to be common for many of the parents to be even more worried than their white counterparts that their children could be headed for downward mobility at the mere whiff of trouble. Counselors attributed this to the fact that a lot of them achieved a lot very fast without feeling that a great many of their group had been able to do the same. Thus they often felt highly insecure in their professional status. "The thinking is that if you fall, you will fall farther back. And if it happens it will happen very quickly," explained Priscilla L. Vail, a learning specialist at the Rippowan-Cisqua School in Bedford, New York, and author of *Smart Kids with School Problems: Things to Know and Ways to Help*. Other teachers used the word "desperation" to describe the intensity of fear among certain minority parents they have counseled. Clearly there is a valid rationale. For such parents explain that even if they are the second or third generation of professionals in the family, they are afraid that continuing prejudice could make it even tougher to climb back up again, once a child has slipped back down.

Francesca, for example, says she is well aware that as a black adult without a college degree she could face a far rougher time after her dancing years are over than would be the case if she had been a white dancer. So she is already talking about a way she might go on to college later on. Carlotta Miles, a black woman who is a child psychiatrist in Washington, underscored that feeling in a 1982 speech she made at Exeter, one of the country's top boarding schools. "Every black person," she explained to the crowd, "regardless of economic status, has to develop a survival kit which will enable them to deal effectively with a white world that constantly projects for them a picture of inferiority, a mood of indifference, and an environment of exclusion."

In such a climate the quest for an Ivy League degree could loom even more crucial. "One of the reasons I knew I needed to go somewhere like Dartmouth or Yale," said Pete, a black boy who was raised in the West and attended private schools, "was because in the long run it will open up more opportunities for me. It does put a strain on the family because of the costs. But it will help me get on the right track, give me the needed boost."

Stereotyping certainly creates added problems of self esteem for many of these youngsters. Esther Lee Yao, professor of education at the University of Houston–Clear Lake and a noted authority on cross-cultural family issues, said Asian students complain that they are automatically expected by their peers to be smarter than anyone else, and get taunted if they are and ridiculed if they are not. "A sort of 'damned if you do, damned if you don't' dilemma," she said.

Similarly, certain black youngsters find themselves struggling to overcome inaccurate assumptions that can also undermine self-confidence. In that same speech at Exeter, Dr. Miles told the story of a black girl in Washington whose mother and father were both physicians. The girl had graduated from a leading private school in that city with the top prize in journalism. She was therefore perplexed when she was given a C− on her first English essay in college—a leading New England institution. When she asked the professor to explain why she had done so poorly, he said, "You black students must understand you can't come into these schools expecting to excel—it will take some time for you to reach the level of the rest of the class."

The extreme emphasis many Asian families place on truly exceptional academic performance can become an added source of pressure if not kept carefully in check, said Dr. Yao. It should not be lightly dismissed; it is very real. It emanates, she explained, from the distinguished status Asians have always awarded their outstanding scholars compared to merchants or other people in the community, even political leaders.

Teachers confirmed that this quest is sometimes so strong among certain Asian parents that it leads to requests to place a child into a grade well beyond what is appropriate for his or her chronological years. The belief is that this will provide those children with a greater competitive edge. Many Asian parents "do not seem to worry as much about social or emotional development," said Ms. Vail. "The aim is to get going and get going early." But this does not necessarily lead to better grades or a competitive edge, as Dr. Elkind points out in his book *Miseducation*—citing in particular the findings of that Hawaiian study about the negative impact of grade acceleration, as mentioned earlier.

Dr. Yao, aware of these attitudes, is worried, too. As early as 1979 she published an article in the professional journal *Reading Improvement* warning fellow Asian parents and American educators of the dangers facing an Asian child who is under too much pressure to perform academically. The article tells a cautionary, true-life tale—the story of Min-Ming (a pseudonym), the daughter of highly educated immigrant parents from Taiwan. Both parents had doctoral degrees. So naturally Min-Ming's parents were exceedingly anxious for her to be outstanding in school, too. And indeed she began to show great promise even in preschool activities. But rather than applaud her for her achievements the parents began piling on even greater demands. "Since Min-Ming demonstrated excellent motor skills in gymnastic and rhythmic movements in dancing class," wrote Dr. Yao, "and since her performance with her peers in the Christmas recital was truly outstanding [the parents] requested, with the approval of the dance teacher, that she be promoted to an advanced dancing class. Unfortunately, Min-Ming was terrified at the prospect of dancing with children who were older and taller than she. She cried and refused to participate by claiming that she was shy and insecure. Her unexpected behavior irritated her parents to such a degree that, as a punishment, she was not allowed to attend dancing class." The mother later came to Dr. Yao for advice when Min-Ming seemed emotionally distraught.

The danger in acceleration is that it can also exacerbate the social difficulty that many minority children face, she said. Friendships, these professionals have found, tend to be more difficult whenever any child is considerably younger and less mature than the rest of the class. When friendships become more strained, due to the minority status, such acceleration can place even greater social hurdles in front of these youngsters. Dr. Yao noted in her article that these youngsters are constantly struggling with different "physical characteristics and value conflicts" even when they are among their chronological peer group. Dr. Yao concluded her article by observing that this heightened level of anxiety has even been known to lead to poorer school performance and emotional difficulties. Min-Ming ended up as a highly anxious child.

Asian parents—particularly first-generation immigrants who are less familiar with American culture—need to be reminded, said Dr. Yao, that fitting in socially may be as important to their children's future as academic success. And opportunities for feeling part of the larger social group should not be denied or inhibited.

## TAKING AN UPDATED LOOK AT ATTITUDES

The fact that the needs of upscale minority youngsters and their families are perhaps not always being as candidly addressed or even as fully acknowledged as one would hope led Sidwell Friends School in Washington to conduct a study in 1986. It called for certain changes in the way teachers and students handled minority students. Among the findings were a greater need to help faculty and students overcome that "stereotyping"—expecting certain behavior because of race or color. For instance, black students were indeed often being prejudged as likely to have more learning or behavioral problems, or to have come from more disadvantaged backgrounds, just because they were black. Not enough had apparently been done to regularly remind the other students and teachers that many such families were not always on scholarship, or that the child had fulfilled all the normal academic entrance requirements.

Recommendations included folding into the curriculum the history of a wider array of peoples to help make students more aware of the richness of various cultures (rather than assuming a white American heritage is the ideal), training faculty on appropriate responses to outbreaks of prejudice, and encouraging students to discuss the nature and consequences of racial attitudes.

## BENEFITS OF STRONG FAMILY TRADITIONS

When it comes to self-esteem fostered in the home, many minority youngsters may have an edge over their white counterparts. This is because inside many of the homes they are still made to feel very special. I found the old immigrant American idea that one's children will go on to fulfill a destiny higher than one's own is still alive and thriving among such families. "My parents always gave me the feeling that I was a fine person, a great human being," said Wanda Hill, a black educational counselor in McLean, Virginia, who acts as an informal intermediary on behalf of minority students and their parents within private boarding schools. "Certainly there were incidents at school. But I was able to smile through a lot of adversity as a result."

Bettie Youngs, the child development specialist from Southern California, has found the same inner strength among the children of high-achieving Hispanic families. Other educators have found it among black families. "The warmth, the love, the good communication we would see between a small Haitian boy and his parents became a lesson to us all," added a teacher at a Connecticut private school. "He could take anything with that kind of support." And among the new Asian immigrants Dr. Yao adds that the children still see their parents making heavy financial sacrifices for them in much the same way as European immigrants behaved toward their children when they first came over. And this becomes a great source of personal pride.

## SOME IDEAS FROM PARENTS AND KIDS

Even so, the minority parent and child must still tackle the problem of dealing with the day-to-day difficulties of growing up in circles that are still predominantly white. Many of them have thus had to learn to cope on an individual level. Recounting these personal experiences might be helpful to others.

Take, for example, the child-raising tenets of Jewel Lafontant. Mrs. Lafontant is arguably one of the best-known black women in the United States. Her listing in *Who's Who* is daunting by anybody's standards. She is a lawyer. She serves on a multitude of corporate boards. She has been active in politics and on civil rights issues, including spending time as a delegate to the United Nations. Her former husband is John W. Rogers, a Chicago juvenile court judge who is also active in politics. They have one son, John Rogers, Jr. At twenty-nine, John is already distinguishing himself as president of his own asset management company, Ariel Capital Management, Inc., and as a community leader.

Looking back on those child-raising years, Mrs. Lafontant recalls that she was fully aware that John might face social difficulties attending any one of Chicago's private schools. Thus she believed that being comfortable in his environment was as important as a stellar academic record. So she decided to select a school that had a greater racial diversity even if it did not have the finest academic reputation in Chicago. "I felt it was important for John to like where he was," she said, adding that she also accepted an offer to go on the board of trustees of the school. "This way I could bring any problems right to the top and keep in closer touch with what was going on."

Mrs. Lafontant said she found it was important for her son never to be permitted to use race as an excuse for a failure, but to look instead for other ways he might need to change. Later on she found it vital to reassure John regularly that his personal accomplishments were the reason he got ahead—not the fact that he might have been the ideal guy to fill a quota. "I remember the day he was accepted at Princeton," she said. "He came home and said that a girl in his class had told him, 'Well, the only reason you got in is because you are black.' He believed it and it hurt. I had to help him understand it wasn't true. I had to explain that the school had been looking for a lot of different things. He had a fine academic record. He had shown leadership skill as captain of his basketball team. And the girl was probably just looking for a way to excuse her own failings. Even after a year at Princeton—when he made practically all A's—I felt I had to reassure him that he could now see for himself that he wasn't just there because he was black, that he was getting by on his own merits. It was important to continue to build up his ego."

She added thoughtfully: "I think we have to remain more aware than most of what is happening on the outside. And that our children may constantly be bombarded with slings and arrows from their peers."

Young John credits his father with also helping him by continually reassuring him that he was just a regular guy. Even so, he admits he always felt he did stand out. "There are still so few of us in these positions that the spotlight is always there," he said. "Your successes and your failures will feel like they are magnified because everybody knows who you are. There is no way you can blend in totally with the white community or the minority community. And you just have to learn to live with that fact. I was even wealthier than some of the white kids in my school and there were jealousies and resentments. In seventh grade I was always getting into fights. But later I learned to get by through compromise."

A black educational administrator in the Midwest, the mother of two girls and a boy, agrees. She told me she advises minority youngsters and parents to learn to tackle the problems in a nonconfrontational way. "These children need to learn how to deal with different kinds of kids and make an effort to understand others. You aren't going to change the world overnight. And the best way to make even small changes is to be the best role model you can. Your behavior, I tell kids, can teach others more than anything you can say."

Hill, the counselor from McLean, Virginia, insists that it is vital that the parents not bad-mouth the white establishment, as this can set up terrible conflicts in the mind of the child. "Do not give them mixed signals," she urges. "If they hear all the time how wicked white people are it can be confusing. It becomes difficult to make friends at school."

The sting of social isolation or racial incidents can be lessened, said Pete, the black student who felt it was important to attend an Ivy League school, if "your parents can tell you what it was like for them, as my parents did. Those stories were more helpful than anything I could read or see on TV."

Barbara Jan-Wilson, the career specialist from Wesleyan University, urges minority parents not to downgrade less prestigious professions, or the creative arts, if that is the route their children choose. Too often, she said, those parental fears and hopes for that child translate into a legacy of guilt and even resentment. "The child feels compelled to become a lawyer, a doctor, or run a business just because those parents have worked so hard and spent so much money to give them the best possible start." This sense of obligation seems particularly acute, she has found, when the minority parent has built a business that the child is supposed to take over.

The best way to blend in and still retain those ethnic traditions appears to come from a heavy emphasis on ethnicity in the home. Joining various ethnic clubs also seems to help these children—much in the way that upwardly mobile Jewish and Italian families dealt with the same dichotomy in the past, and still do today. This appears to work better than insisting the children start or join a support group in a school, which may only accentuate the differences. The black single parent from the Midwest remembers how her daughter refused to join a black support group at college, suggesting it was demeaning to be ranked as different, and even needy emotionally. Francesa came to the same conclusion. "I remember a few kids started a minority awareness group once at my school," she said. "There were about fifteen of us, blacks and Hispanics mostly. But it wasn't successful. It tagged us as a violent, disturbed minority. I much preferred the idea of getting together with other black children outside school."

Francesca maintains that a minority child probably has a better chance to fit in and be more easily accepted at a single-sex school since the dating pressures are not there. "When you are growing up," she continued, "all you want to do is fit in and be like everyone else. I remember straightening my hair, wearing Lacoste shirts. It becomes very important to be accepted. Maybe parents sometimes forget this."

\* \* \*

Though the intent here has been only to provide a sampling of different ideas, there was wide agreement on one point: minority parents need to help children feel comfortable in both the white and the ethnic worlds, since they will probably spend their lives operating as a part of both. "You learn you have to do that to get on and succeed," as one boy put it. This could mean that the parents may need to actually articulate the fact that they do not consider it an affront to their heritage if the child adopts some of the mores of the white world while among schoolmates. But at the same time they might explain the value of taking personal pride in continuing to honor family and ethnic traditions.

Such youngsters may also wish to consider playing the role of intermediary between the power structure of both worlds as they become adults or take a leadership role among their own groups—as John Rogers has chosen to do. It is an opportunity that could provide built-in purpose and meaning to their lives, and is an exciting niche that is not as readily available to white youngsters.

# VII

# For Children Only:
# An Open Letter

**D**ear Paul and Susan and Steve and Ruth and Jennie and Sarah and Nick and all the wonderful young people who poured out their hopes and dreams and worries to me during my research for this book:

I could not complete my work without writing an open letter to all of you, the purpose of which is to help you better understand how to communicate with your parents. All we ever hear is how parents can communicate with their children; nobody ever seems to put the challenge in the other court. Well, communication is a two-way street. And I kept on hearing how you were having trouble "getting through," as you would put it. You continually tossed out remarks like "But they never *hear*" or "They are always too tired or never around" or "They have one idea and won't even *listen* to anything else."

I know you are speaking the truth because my own son always complained about the same thing. He still does. He even devised a formula—"Earth to Mom!" he would cry out to me in desperation in his Space Age vernacular. "Earth to Mom!" I would know instantly he was referring to the fact that I had clearly not heard a single word he had been saying, even though I might have been looking straight into his eyes, nodding in all the right places. I plead guilty.

But let's look at why it happens and what you might do to "get through" when the line seems incessantly busy. First of all, before you even make the overture, it may help to pause for a moment to gain some insights into why you are like you are and why your parents behave the way they do.

I mean, why are they so anxious for you to get into a particular college? Why are they so hung up on grades? Why can't they seem to take any career seriously that does not fit into their idea of the Right

Idea? And why do you get the feeling that nothing you do is ever good enough?

Your parents are as much the victims of peer pressure as you are. In your world peer pressure usually means wearing the right clothes, listing to a certain type of music, or whatever. For them it means making sure their children follow a certain path and achieve at a certain level. It helps them hold their heads up high with *their* friends.

You may also be hearing that for the first time in the history of this nation you may not be able to live as well as your parents or even continue to enjoy the luxuries you have had for all these years growing up. It is known as downward mobility. It may also make you feel like a failure before you have even begun since it is an intrinsic part of our culture to assume that you will match and even surpass your parents in achievement and income.

Moreover, your parents are worried about downward mobility because they probably feel that unless you do achieve academically, the struggle they went through to get to where they are will be for naught. But, you may say, it doesn't matter so much to you. You don't think you will necessarily be unhappy if you do live a little more modestly. In fact, you think it might be better to trade off some of those material possessions for a little more time to yourself—something your tension-filled, overextended parents do not seem to have. Well, that may be one thought that needs to be articulated. They may automatically assume you want to live just the way they do and may be making their judgments about your future based upon that assumption. But having grown up with wealth and privilege, you may no longer feel the same need to prove yourself to others through material acquisitions. You are more confident of your place in the upper classes. You can afford to take a detour and move on to other things that may be more meaningful to you—in other words, you may be redefining success.

You should also know that many of your insecurities about being "good enough" may come from the circles in which you move rather than any lack of competence on your part. You are part of the gilded upper crust of society whose standards and expectations are so high they are not representative of the world at large. And that means your school population, too.

Now, how to "get through." First, try to make sure you get your parents' full attention before you even start. This may mean being attentive to their schedule and not trying to unload whatever is on your mind at just the moment when they really must leave the house or take a telephone call. You are always asking them to respect your busy schedule; you may need to respect theirs, too. This could mean making an appointment to talk, maybe even asking your mother or father if you could go out to dinner one night for this purpose. This way they become a captive audience. But when you are setting up that meeting don't get drawn into the why of it. Just say, "I want to talk about a few things." And "No, I can't go into it all now."

If that does not work verbally, try leaving a note. One school administrator admitted to me there is nothing that gets her attention faster than a written note from her teenage son. "It really jolts me," she conceded. "If I find a note on the table I will go out of my way to find time—in a hurry!" Probably this is because we rarely communicate to friends and family in writing these days, so the novelty of it makes a strong impact.

When you do start talking, try to set up guidelines. Ask if you can speak for five minutes or so *without interruption*. You may have to trade for five minutes of their time, uninterrupted. And if you want to avoid the conversation slipping back into Lecture 101 (which you could almost recite by heart), make sure your words are not confrontational. Do not accuse them of this or that, like "Well, you are always out," or "You only want me to get good grades so I can go to Yale like you did." If you complain or accuse them of a particular sin they are forced to hit back to defend themselves, just as your friends would be. Try instead to explain how it feels—for instance, when they have no time to listen or when you find yourself alone night after night in the house—rather than criticize their behavior (even if they are constantly criticizing yours).

When you feel your parents have hurt you, the impulse is to hurt back. And even to sprinkle in some of those four letter words you know your parents hate to hear from you. Don't do it. It will only worsen tempers. That language is best left for use among your peers. Instead, continue to tell them how their behavior affects your life, not what you find wrong with them. That is usually a much more effective method of getting your message across. And put yourself in their shoes for a moment. How might you react if your child came to you with the problem or matter you are about to discuss? What might you say? Think about why you reacted as you did.

Be sure that conversation is issue-oriented, not judgmental. For example, "This is the problem; how can we solve it?" Remember, too, that they may be as fearful of what you are going to say as you are of what they are telling you. You represent a huge investment in ego, time, and money to them. They don't like to feel like failures any more than you do. So don't try to "stick it" to them. Understand that they have the same fears and insecurities that you have. Knowing they are operating from those feelings may help you make sense of some of the things they do say. They certainly have as many pressures and strains on their lives as you do. And sometimes it is those strains and pressures that make them so inattentive. Remember this especially if, on occasion, they seem not to hear what you are saying. Their minds may just be on overload. Or they may have had to face disaster at the office, even a put-down from the boss. Ask about those pressures. Your concern may open up a new kind of caring.

Another way to reach them might be to arrange some seminars, possibly through your school's parents' organization, that explore the concerns of your generation. A good way would be to use a panel of kids telling it like it appears to them. A title might be "Where is our generation headed?" or "What is it like to be a kid growing up in this neighborhood/community/school?" or even "How to talk to parents." Too often those meetings are devoted to other adults telling parents about kids, not kids telling parents about being kids.

Maybe you have tried one or all of these ideas or feel it is still futile. Hang in there. Closing down those lines of communication doesn't work either. It might be wiser in that case to find an adult intermediary—such as a coach, tutor, relative, or even a therapist—and ask for some suggestions or even ask that person to put in a word on your behalf.

I hope this helps a little, if only to trigger some ideas of your own.

Good luck!
Andrée Aelion Brooks

# Conclusions

A t the start of this book we pondered the question of why certain children from families of power and privilege seem to scoop up all those advantages and use them to live enriched lives—in the style in which they conduct themselves, in the excellence of their accomplishments, and the noble manner in which they deal with people. By contrast, others (often from the same or seemingly similar families) gravitate to the totally opposite extreme, becoming callous, selfish, arrogant, and exhibiting every sort of destructive behavior from alcoholism to an inability to settle down to any form of a meaningful existence.

I am convinced, after a year spent looking at these families, that the difficulty stems from two basic factors. First, it may emanate partially from the problem many high-achieving parents face in accepting the idea that one or more of their children may not naturally have the same capabilities, interests, or goals. That denial leads to inappropriate actions. And second, it may come from the misguided belief that their own power and wealth will automatically provide a wonderful life for their children—again resulting in inappropriate decisions.

There is no question that the child who is innately endowed with the necessary talents to make it in the intensely competitive, high-achieving world inhabited by his or her parents will thrive on all the enrichment. Meanwhile, a sibling or cousin who cannot keep pace with such a demanding drummer—or does not choose to do so—may develop a powerful loathing for that type of society and instead choose to identify with one where he or she will feel more comfortable. To the parents this may look like failure. And their silent reproach may lead to self-loathing which can foster even more self-destructive behavior.

On the second point—the satisfaction that comes from the notion "My children will never need to worry about money or have to face the hardships I had to endure"—the problem is one of perception. Many high-achieving parents have been so busy building wealth they have simply not had time to examine how it will affect their children. Further, it is difficult to accept the fact that the hard-won wealth you may be offering may actually do the child a disservice if not handled with the utmost finesse. The affluence may have also masked a basic truth: by removing one set of problems we open the door for others to take their place. And those problems (which I think deserve restating) include the following:

> by eliminating the pain the parent may set the child up for limited joy; by providing so much the parent may have limited the motivation and drive that make up the major ingredients of achievement—which in turn provide the individual with a sense of dignity and the comfort of self-sufficiency.

A key pattern that emerged among the families where most of the children turned out fine was a recognition that it was important to value those children's achievements without comparison to those of the parents—especially critical when that parent had indeed chalked up an impressive list of accolades. Thus rather than belittle that child's goals or accomplishments there was a conscious effort in these families to salute them. *That child's self-image and self-esteem had been painstakingly nurtured and enhanced every step of the way.* While we know it is important to do this in any family, it seemed especially so in fast-track households since everything about the setup conspired inadvertently to undermine the child's sense of self-worth.

Where the children turned out well there also seemed to be less of the oft-noted syndrome of the child becoming an extension of the parent; rather, those children were treated as separate human beings entitled to an independent set of achievements, failures, and direction. Nor had the parent felt a need to use the child to bolster his or her own self-worth. Instead of "child as product or accessory," it was "child as distinctive human being," even if those distinctions were not the kind that anyone would necessarily want to brag about.

## LIKELY CHARACTER TRAITS
## OF THESE CHILDREN AS ADULTS

What kind of adults will these children become? Clearly their behavior is likely to span the spectrum, but certain underlying characteristics may emerge. For example, having been taught to expect so much as children I think they will demand a great deal as adults—that "sense of entitlement" that Robert Coles talks about in his studies of the rich. Having grown up wearing Topsiders, Lacoste shirts, and taking ski vacations at Vail, they are not going to be satisfied to shop at the local discount store and take an RV on the road for a week. Having grown up as the chiefs, rather than the Indians, they are going to be equally demanding toward those around them, perhaps even a tad disdainful of anyone with a less gilded background. Time and again I heard these children say that they would be loath to give up the mountain lodge or the housekeeper. Habits formed early are not easily cast aside. There may therefore be a huge market for upscale goods and services (including, I might add, the sort of financial planner who can assume the role of surrogate parent). If hard times do hit I suspect these children will tap resources they never knew they had in order to fight for the diminished chance to enjoy those privileges.

I don't think these children are the sort who are going to be especially comfortable starting at the bottom, unless it is in the kind of temporary *play* job they take on as students or during the summer months. Susan Littwin's book *The Postponed Generation* is full of young adults who get quickly fed up with menial positions or jobs that carry obligations that seem tiresome or boring. This may be an outcome of the lack of "frustration tolerance" noted earlier in the book—a trait that apparently comes from a life where it does not matter if you smash a toy or a car or lose a job because these things can (and will) be replaced. We may therefore see a disturbing amount of job-hopping among these "Chiffies," as I have dubbed them (a modified acronym for children of fast-track parents).

With failure having carried such a stigma, the less able among them are likely to be risk-adverse, avoiding situations that could produce a major setback. Certain teachers I interviewed worried that the current parental obssession with success (as defined by large incomes and status occupations) may rob our society of divergent and creative thinkers—the sort of individuals who may not have ended up as chairman of the board but who are at the cutting edge of change. "Parents may be making the creative child feel awkward, out of step," warned Ann Gillinger, the director of Sierra Canyon School in the San Fernando Valley. "If so, it is a regrettable loss."

This same bred-from-the-cradle need to be a winner could create an obsessional winner, an adult who cannot weigh the possible trade-offs and who sees ethics as irrelevant. And without any moral or ethical restraints, history tells us that the human animal, if given a leadership position, is capable of great excesses of cruelty and insensitivity toward others.

Dr. David Elkind suspects that this kind of upbringing could result in severe stress which will show up in more phobias, more psychosomatic symptoms, more compulsions in every facet of their lives.

That same overdeveloped sense of competitiveness could undermine the very achievements that the child has been working so hard to obtain. John Rogers, the highly successful young black investment adviser, mentioned this to me. "You have to learn to work with others, to compromise, in order to succeed," he said. "If you have never been taught to cooperate, but only to compete, it's hard to change."

Psychologists told me they feared that the personal isolation bred of the same intense competitive atmosphere may make it difficult for some of these children to form good marriages or long-term relationships. Such relationships, as we all know, require a great deal of give and take. They also require sacrifice and occasionally placing another's need ahead of one's own. Thus they ask: are children who have been bred for competition, for winning, or with the idea that they are entitled to "have it all" been adequately prepared for the concept of taking second place or subordinating their own goals to that of another person? Further, if you add that background to a household where there was not much tolerance for failure or setback and not much consistent nurturing you may have an adult who could have a real problem with loving and compassion—traits that foster closeness. The dark side of a quest for perfection can also be a resistance to the sort of intimacy that allows a partner to be aware of any weakness or insecurity. Thus many of these children may be supremely successful. (I have no doubt about that.) They may become formidable opponents. *But they could also be lonely.*

This is not to suggest that being competitive is necessarily bad, only that, like any other type of behavior, it can be harmful if fostered without moderating influences.

## CHILDREN OF FAST-TRACK
## PARENTS AS PARENTS THEMSELVES

While doing my preliminary research, I walked into the home of a most accomplished young woman physician and her husband, also a doctor. It was a warm and sunny Sunday morning, and the slender woman and her husband were both keeping cool in bathing suits. On the wall were an impressive array of degrees from a number of Ivy League institutions. Running about the partially furnished house (they had had no time to complete it) were the couple's two lively toddlers, a girl and a boy. The woman had been recommended to me by her father, a highly successful lawyer, as an example of the new breed of "fast-track parent." But after just a few minutes the woman insisted she was actually "second-generation fast-track." I became intrigued. What did this mean to her life? It meant, I discovered, that she had indeed developed some of the traits about which we have just spoken. For instance, she wanted to stay home and nurture her children and to "have some fun" but somehow could not stop what she was doing, as though on a treadmill to keep on succeeding, "like it comes from so deeply within that I can't change," she said. "I'm perfectly aware of my problem but I find it hard to fight." It had become equally hard for her to relax, she said—"it was something I was never allowed to do as a child," she explained, her voice trailing off as if caught in an awkward memory.

As far as her children were concerned, she wanted none of the intense pressure for academic success that had characterized her own childhood. Like parents throughout time, she had chosen to give *her* children what she felt she herself had missed. In this case it was fun and a lid taken off the pressure. "I don't want them programmed to be a lawyer or doctor like we were," she said. "I have seen how it hurt my husband. He wanted to be an astronaut. He really suffered when his parents laughed and refused even to consider it. I don't want to do that to my kids. I wouldn't even let them take those ridiculous kindergarten achievement tests."

In California I came across a young psychologist who was equally eager to identify herself as second-generation fast-track. "You keep on feeling you have to run the fastest, jump the highest," said the woman as we chatted over lunch. "If I don't work one day I have to make up excuses for myself, like I am sick, to justify not doing anything. But I am learning to overcome it, just as if it were a disease. Now, when my son says, 'I have to *win*,' I tell him, 'It is more important to enjoy the race.' I tell both my children 'I love you for *no* reason.' It's not easy. I have to keep rehearsing these things as I drive along in the car. You see, I don't want them to lose respect for themselves like I used to do. But I acquired an incredible discipline. I can force myself to do almost anything."

## GENUINE MEMBERSHIP
## IN THE UPPER ECHELONS OF SOCIETY

Some results of this upbringing should be exceedingly positive. I see a group of young people who, having been bred for success, will be very comfortable with success, assuming the mantle of leadership as if it were a birthright. Those who do not make it may nevertheless retain delusions of power and privilege, as we see from history in the behavior of monarchs and their entourage following a palace coup. Such deposed aristocrats and leaders frequently continue to demand certain standards of living and continue to expect service from those around them as if they still held the same power and had as much wealth. And they seem so surprised when it is not there.

Much the same may happen to the children of fast-track parents who have been raised with certain assumptions about the level at which they will continue to live. In *Money and Class in America,* a book about attitudes toward wealth and upbringing in contemporary America, Lewis H. Lapham discovered this among some of his old prep school and Ivy League buddies. "[One of my school-mates] at Yale had assumed that the world would entertain him as its guest," writes Lapham. "He had little reason to think otherwise. Together with his grandmother's collection of Impressionist paintings and the houses in Southampton and Maine. . . . [But] things hadn't turned quite the way he had expected and in the bar of the Plaza he looked at me with a dazed expression." The school-mate clearly did not know how to behave like someone with only a modest income. There is an expression for it—"shabby genteel." It describes people who have retained upper-crust manners but not necessarily the means to continue the lifestyle.

These children will certainly not be fearful of competition, wherever they meet it. And that should be a great source of strength. Their high level of enrichment and education should also make them interesting, involved sorts of people, eager to be a part of a multitude of endeavors. If they can curb the arrogance it will make them entertaining to be around, too.

They will have an elegance and style that come very naturally, again because it was part of their world from the start—a poise that will stay with them no matter what. One characteristic of many fast-track parents described in this book was a social insecurity that required them to be bound by a checklist of lifestyle attainments to enable them to feel they qualified as bona fide members of the upper classes: the right address, belonging to the right private clubs, children at the right schools, the right kind of career, clothes, and so forth. It became a tyranny of sorts. By contrast, their children appear to be far more naturally assured about their privileged status—possibly because they were much closer to being "to the manor born" right from the start. So these children are likely to gain flexibility. In short: they may begin to exhibit "old money" rather than "new money" traits. And one of the hallmarks of old money is a genuine sense of belonging, irrespective of what you do, what you wear, and where you live. You can afford to skip one or two items on that list and not feel threatened.

Fast-track parents should therefore perhaps not be as worried about downward mobility as they seem at present. Nor should they panic if bad economic times do hit and it means taking the child temporarily out of a certain school or moving to a home that is not quite as fine. Indeed, the compensating value of such a change was beautifully articulated earlier, by families facing the economic panic that emanated from a divorce. It showed how having a little less did not haunt these children as much as it haunted the parents. It was sometimes welcomed since it may make the children feel more "normal" and useful. It even rekindled a sense of purpose.

I had an enlightening conversation on that point with a young woman in a rowhouse in a southern city. On the dining room table was a slightly tarnished set of ornate silver candlesticks. Fine antiques filled the living room. The woman had grown up, she explained, in a super-rich family in the South where she had lived on an estate in a household that included two maids, a cook, a laundress, and a gardener. She had married a young man from an equally prominent family who was now a government official. Wealth on both sides of the family had created, she admitted, "a flexibility in our lives that allowed us to chose what we wanted to do without worrying about how much we would be making."

However, in the inflation-prone late 1970s, a series of mishaps with their investments and lack of improvement in her husband's salary level caused their income to suffer to a point where they had to scale down their lifestyle substantially. They had moved to this smaller house. The woman felt compelled to go back to school to get an M.B.A.—

which ironically became not a hardship but a source of tremendous personal pride.

Does she feel cheated? "Oh, no," she said with a laugh and an impish grin. "I feel great. Living in a smaller house is cozier. I feel far less like Lady Bountiful, far less conspicuous than I did." In addition, she says she has a far easier time saying no to her own two children than many other parents in the neighborhood—the kind who seem to need to give their children a great deal as a measure of their own upward mobility. "I don't seem to need to have a lot of things to feel acceptable," she observed with a smile. "It's liberating."

However, several psychologists warned me that individuals who experience extreme downward mobility often become seriously depressed when they find they cannot afford to give their own children the educational and financial advantages they themselves received. Lewis Lapham found this, too. Continuing his anecdote about his schoolmate, Lapham wrote, "He couldn't do for his children what his parents had done for him, and his feeling of failure showed in his eyes. He had the look of a man who was being followed by the police."

Parents who have brought a child up with privilege may therefore have to remain vigilant for this and reinforce the fact—as Lapham notes—that in comparative terms that adult child and his or her children are still relatively prosperous. Moreover, if they stand back a moment they might see that they are using a ridiculous standard by which to judge themselves and their lives. Should this happen, the younger parents might also take solace in the idea that what goes around comes around. Perhaps their children, having received less and being born of parents who achieved less, will once again develop the intense drive and ambition that propelled their grandparents or great-grandparents to the top in the first place. Nor will those children start life haunted by the vast gaps between themselves and their parents' achievements.

## WOODSTOCK II?

If my conversations with teenagers were any indication of the future it is likely that a substantial number of the next generation may make a conscious effort to reclaim leisure time, the fun that appeared missing from their parents' lives. This could leave those children with a quest for a more balanced existence, especially if they can shake off the need to become as successful as their parents. Extreme ambition could actually fall into disrepute, and be looked upon as an aberration of the eighties. Some of them might just give us Woodstock II—some sort of grand statement that love and caring is as important, if not more so, than material possessions. It may also happen as a way for these children to gain the self-definition that they so desperately seek.

Others may quickly find that occupations geared strictly to bottom-line attainments might not be what they really want after all, especially since making more and more money can quickly lose its appeal if there are no further material mountains to climb, or the money is going to be there anyway. It is one of the fundamental differences of growing up "having had it all" that Burton Wixen noted in his book *Children of the Rich*. Once you have lived in the castle and reality has fractured the fantasy—you know for a fact that life is not that much better inside those oak-paneled halls—the quest to gain the money for an even grander castle of your own becomes less compelling.

Possibly this is why we see from the history of patrician families that a quest for power and public position so often follows a quest for money. The money is already made. It is time to turn to new challenges—politics, public service, philanthrophy, the arts. Certainly there will be more young people with the connections and backing to fill these roles than there ever were before. And that could be a tremendous resource for our society in the twenty-first century.

By contrast, those who have somehow been unable to shake off that feeling of being a failure when comparing themselves to their parents may become even more obsessed with matching the parental kind of success, creating a cadre of super workaholics. "No matter what you try to tell yourself," a young architect admitted to me as he talked about the many competitions he felt duty-bound to enter, "it still nags at you."

In sum, we may see three types of adults: the ones who become the mirror image of their parents; the ones who completely reject that lifestyle; and the ones who feel that in order to flourish as independent, autonomous adults they must flee the world of their parents for a while to be certain they can make it on their own merits—as many of the fourth-generation descendants of John D. Rockefeller have done.

## POLITICAL ATTITUDES

In discussions with psychologists and educators who constantly work with these families, it was suggested to me that it is logical to assume these children will be conservative and conformist in their political outlook, since they have too much to lose if there is a major upheaval.

Nor are they being raised during a period of activist liberal senti-ments—the sort that would encourage them to rush out to change society. If anything, they are likely to embrace global economic con-cerns since they have grown up far more globally oriented than their forebears—issues like economic interdependence, world trade, di-minishing natural resources.

It also seems to follow that they may be easy targets for an au-thoritarian regime. The logic is that many are products of strong, au-thoritarian parents; therefore, they will be comfortable in these types of settings. Many also learned along the way that it was often necessary to ignore the voice of conscience in order to get ahead. So they could be willing to accept and justify almost any action that furthers their interests. Winners among them may even co-opt the losers into what-ever enterprise is at hand to be sure of an obedient ally, especially since they are also known to be highly clannish—a natural outcome of a too-sheltered childhood.

Because these children may indeed face some difficulties dealing with the world as they grow older, or even while they are still growing up, it might be helpful to offer some personal recommendations.

## RECOMMENDATIONS FOR
## TEACHERS, COUNSELORS, AND PARENTS

High schools that primarily serve this segment of the student population might wish to think about creating a curriculum that could help the children understand how their socioeconomic background affects at-titude and outlook. Much like Black Studies or Women's Studies, the programs would allow these youngsters to see themselves and their situation through identification with others who have traveled the same road. Such insights could help them understand themselves without feeling as if they were abnormal or suffering from deviant emotions. Literature courses could analyze novels or biographies of Great Fam-ilies for such content; history or psychology courses could delve more deeply into Old Money behavorial patterns. These children also need more opportunities to mix with children and adults who are not social carbon copies of themselves, but who work and live with different values, standards, and levels of expectation. More co-op or exchange programs might help. It would certainly make them less insular and more in tune with the way the not-so-privileged live.

Parents, too, may benefit from such studies. Learning more about the handling of wealth from a psychological standpoint and the pitfalls of growing up amid too much affluence would be an ideal topic for at least one series of workshops. One unit might explore ways to talk about family money to help get that sensitive subject finally released from the closet. Certainly there is a need to redefine many problems discussed in this book in terms of how they emanate from the social pressures of the day and to understand more clearly how these attitudes affect the way a parent behaves. One myth that needs to be debunked is that a parent naturally acts in the best interests of the child. It is time to be more honest and realistic about the conflicting urge to act in one's own best interests. Community dialogue of the sort I witnessed at the start of this project—the kind that raises awareness that there are indeed problems in paradise and there is no stigma attached to such an admission—may be one place where such issues can be aired. For only through analysis, honesty, and issue definition can anyone begin to create solutions.

Another myth that needs debunking is the idea that money can protect these children from the vicissitudes of life. One way or another, life has a way of penetrating even the most carefully constructed barrier. Educational and financial advantages can certainly help, but it is like a general becoming too confident that he can win the war because his army to the north is so strong. He forgets that the enemy can sneak around and intrude upon his lines from the south or west with tactics he never knew existed. Similarly, money and influence can shield these children from one set of struggles. But they do not seem to lessen the pain that can come from a bad marriage, the loneliness from lack of friends, the malaise and sense of purposelessness emanating from too-great a reliance on that horn of plenty, the terror or anxiety that comes from a feeling of not being able to keep up. Nor should we forget how easily a privileged lifestyle can deny these young people small pleasures and pride in small victories, inadvertently setting them up instead for the agony of feeling like they have failed unless they have performed some truly outstanding deed.

Many of these children could end up with substantial power. Yet a key ingredient in good leadership—success in motivating and handling others—is a skill not high on the agenda in most fast-track households. These youngsters therefore need to be provided with greater opportunities for training in people-handling skills. More team projects at school might be one method. Lee Iacocca, the auto baron, noted in his autobiography how such interpersonal-skills training had become a major asset to his life and work. Good leadership also requires someone at the helm whom people admire, not simply fear. Are these children obtaining the values and moral fiber that are so often a prerequisite of that admiration?

We need to restore full-time motherhood to its rightful place as a dignified, worthwhile pursuit—irrespective of how the child turns out. It's time to stop heaping so much praise on Superwoman.

We need to be mindful of the special burden we are placing on the daughters of fast-track parents. We are asking them not only to succeed in the macho arena of their brothers. They must also be beautiful, slender, charming, and catch a young bachelor of appropriate standing, added attainments the menfolk do not have to match. And they must do so at a time when subtle prejudices and restraints still hamper their progress.

We need to consider the value of creating more self-help groups for these youngsters. The Women's Foundation in San Francisco could be an ideal model—with its regular workshops and retreats where all manner of personal and financial dilemmas are openly discussed without fear of ridicule or charges of elitism. High-achieving parents might wish to create their own support groups, or discuss issues that arise because of their status and achievement at special parent meetings at schools.

We need to redefine success, returning to a climate that gives nonfinancial achievement as much status as moneymaking. The idea that wealth equals worth is too limiting a vision—a trap of the 1980s.

We must continue to seek new ways to build these children's confidence in their own abilities—in settings that do not rely upon family wealth or connections. And parents need to be mindful that by "helping" them too long into adulthood a parent could be creating habits that could be self-defeating and hard to change. This may mean making a conscious effort to let go at some point. And we must take care that the parents' world does not appear to these children as a society with an entrance gate labeled "For Winners Only."

In sum: I think we can be optimistic. For in the final analysis the chances for these children to lead successful, meaningful lives is strong. The cycle of involvement and achievement is as likely to repeat itself as the cycle of poverty unfortunately does. Even so, we may need to accept the fact that though these youngsters may cherish the lifestyle every bit as much as their parents, they may need to gain it for themselves in a way that does not make them feel like an appendage of those parents. They have a terrible need to prove themselves in a setting not dependent upon family connections and influence. The story of the life of Edsel Ford, son of Henry Ford of automobile fame, is replete with examples of how Edsel was thwarted in this attempt, turning finally to the world of modern art (something his father knew little about) as a way of distinguishing his life from that of his famous father. The need was so strong that Edsel continued to spend a great deal of his energies fostering modern artists even though the elder Ford scoffed at his endeavors, maintaining that Edsel needed nothing more than the chance to follow in his father's automaking footsteps.

Finding one's niche, irrespective of familial ties, should therefore not be seen as an affront to the family but the fulfillment of a genuine psychological need. As Steven Rockefeller, the introspective son of Nelson Rockefeller, put it so well in the book *The Rockefellers,* "The issue is one of having something to offer that comes out of your own individual self, your own understanding, humanity and creativity, and not just out of your bank account."

# Acknowledgments

Dozens of witty, wise, and wonderful people gave a good deal of time and effort to help make this book possible. In particular I would like to thank my two grown children, Allyson and James, for their insights and comments. Special gratitude must also go to my research associate, Seymour Mund, for his valued suggestions and tireless labors; to Dr. Roy Nisenson for his professional input into my research as well as his comments on the manuscript. I am also deeply grateful for the encouragement and support of my two original editors, Patricia Hass and Cynthia Vartan, as well as my final editor, Mindy Werner, who saw the manuscript to completion with some truly exceptional editing.

I would also like to thank the following parents and professionals for allowing me to interview them at length: Dr. Marvin Schwarz, Dr. Sharon Press, Margaret Addis, Cornelius Bull, Dr. Peter Czuczka, Dr. David Elkind, Moreen Fielden, Dr. Samuel Klagsbrun, Dr. Martin Buccolo, Dennis Flavin, Tracy Gary, Howard Greene, Dr. Roy Grinker, Jr., Wanda Hill, Dr. Kenneth Howard, John Levy, Dr. Elena Lesser, Judith Stern Peck, Dr. Anne Petersen, William Clarkson IV, Sally Reed, Audrey Rosenman, the Reverend Mark Mullin, Dr. Sirgay Sanger, Ann Gillinger, Dr. Robert Goldman, Phyllis Steinbrecher, Dr. Sara Sparrow, Karen Manuel, Nicholas Thacher, Priscilla Vail, Dr. Charles William Wahl, Barbara-Jan Wilson, Bettie Youngs, Sheldon Zablow, Bret Easton Ellis, Francesca Harper, Nancy Caron, Jewel Lafontant, Stacy O'Donnell, Royal Kennedy Rodgers, John Rogers, Jr., Gloria Andujar, Doris Elliott, Dr. Harold Bloomfield, Judy Barber, Dr. Leland J. Axelson, Scott Bedrick, Barry Farber, Terry Carrilio Eisenberg, Selma Miller, Dr. Bernard Guerney, Cloe Madanes, Virginia Vogel, Esther Lee Yao, Sharlene Martin, John Couch and family, Marty Resnick, Suzanne Prescod, Dr. Carlotta

Miles, Elaine Mazlish, Earl Harrison Jr., Dr. Frank Pittman III, and Dr. Michael Stone.

Even though many of the young people I interviewed preferred to remain anonymous, I would not want to end without thanking them, too. They were wonderful, and without them there would have been no book. I wish all of them happiness and fulfillment.

# Appendix

## The Fast-Track Parents' Media Shelf

The following are reference sources for works and organizations mentioned in the book, as well as useful auxiliary readings. Sources are classified according to topic for easier reference.

CHILDHOOD AMONG THE RICH OR DISTINGUISHED

Aldrich, Nelson W. Jr. *Old Money*, Alfred A. Knopf, New York, 1988.

Coles, Robert. *Privileged Ones. Children of Crisis*, Vol. 5. Boston: Little, Brown and Company, 1977.

Collier, Peter, and David Horowitz. *The Rockefellers: An American Dynasty*. New York: Holt, Rinehart and Winston, 1976.

———. *The Kennedys: An American Drama*. New York: Summit Books, 1984.

———. *The Fords: An American Epic*. New York: Summit Books, 1987.

Crosby, Gary, and Ross Firestone. *Going My Own Way*. New York: Doubleday, 1983.

Ellis, Bret Easton. *Less Than Zero*. New York: Simon and Schuster, 1985.

Fisher, Carrie. *Postcards from the Edge*. New York: Simon and Schuster, 1987.

Fosdick, Raymond B. *John D. Rockefeller, Jr.: A Portrait*. New York: Harper and Brothers, 1956.

Goodwin, Doris Kearns. *The Fitzgeralds and the Kennedys: An American Saga*. New York: Simon and Schuster, 1987.

Grinker, Roy R. "The Poor Rich: The Children of the Super-Rich," paper presented at the 130th annual meeting of the American Psychiatric Association, 1977.

Heymann, David C. *Poor Little Rich Girl: The Life and Legend of Barbara Hutton*. New York: Pocket Books, 1983.

Klein, Patsy. *Growing Up Spoiled in Beverly Hills*. New York: Lyle Stuart, 1986.

Lapham, Lewis H. *Money and Class in America*. New York: Weidenfeld and Nicolson, 1987.

Pittman, Frank S., III. "Children of the Rich," *Family Process*, December 1985.

Reagan, Michael. *Michael Reagan: On the Outside Looking In*. New York: Zebra Books, 1988.

Rockwell, Norman. *My Adventures as an Illustrator*. Indianapolis, Ind.: Curtis Publishing Co., 1979.

Stone, Michael H. "The Child of a Famous Father or Mother," in *Basic Handbook of Child Psychiatry*, Vol. 1. New York: Basic Books, 1979.

———. "Upbringing in the Super-Rich," in *Modern Perspectives in the Psychiatry of Infancy*. New York: Brunner/Mazel, 1979.

———. "Special Problems in Borderline Adolescents from Wealthy Families," in *Adolescent Psychiatry*. Chicago: University of Chicago Press, 1969.

———, with Clarice J. Kestenbaum. "Maternal Deprivation in Children of the Wealthy." *History of Childhood Quarterly*, Vol. 1, no. 1 (Summer 1974).

Trump, Donald J., with Tony Schwartz. *Trump: The Art of the Deal*. New York: Random House, 1987.

Van Rensselaer, Philip. *Million Dollar Baby: An Intimate Portrait of Barbara Hutton*. New York: Putnam, 1979.

Weld, Jacqueline Bograd. *Peggy, the Wayward Guggenheim*. New York: E. P. Dutton, 1986.

Wixen, Burton N. *Children of the Rich*. New York: Crown, 1973.

## CAREGIVERS

Help!, 15 Bridge Street, Weston, CT 06883 (Live-in caregiver placement agency).

Helping Hands, P.O. Box 7068, Wilton, CT 06897 (Caregiver placement and research agency).

International Nanny Association, 976 West Foothill Blvd., Suite 596, Claremont, CA 91711. 714/622–6303. (Advocacy group and information on live-in caregivers)

Sweet, Robin O., and Mary-Ellen Siegel. *The Nanny Connection*. New York: Atheneum, 1987.

## ISSUES OF LEARNING AND LEARNING DISABILITIES

Armstrong, Thomas. *In Their Own Way*. Los Angeles: Jeremy P. Tarcher, Inc., 1987.

Coles, Gerald. *The Learning Mystique: A Critical Look at Learning Disabilities*. New York: Pantheon Books, 1987.

Doman, Glenn. *How to Multiply Your Baby's Intelligence*. New York: Doubleday, 1984.

———, with Janet Doman and Susan Aisen. *How to Give Your Baby Encyclopedic Knowledge*. Philadelphia: The Better Baby Press, 1984.

———. Instructional tapes: contact Institutes for the Achievement of Human Potential, 8801 Stenton Avenue, Philadelphia, PA 19118.

Elkind, David. *Miseducation: Preschoolers at Risk*. New York: Knopf, 1987.

Vail, Priscilla L. *Smart Kids with School Problems: Things to Know and Ways to Help*. New York: E. P. Dutton, 1987.

For further information on the U.S. Conference on Education and the Family held in Washington, D.C., in June 1988, contact:

Director of the Office of Research
Office of Educational Research and Improvement
U.S. Department of Education
555 New Jersey Avenue, N.W.
Washington, D.C. 20208

GENERAL CHILD-RAISING
ADVICE AND USEFUL OBSERVATIONS

Bell, Ruth, and Leni Zeiger Wildflower. *Talking with Your Teenager*. New York: Random House, 1983.

Bloomfield, Harold. *Making Peace with Your Parents*. New York: Ballantine, 1986.

Gardner, Janet, and Evelyn Kaye. *The Parents' Going-Away Planner*. New York: Dell, 1987.

Hersh, Stephen P. *The Executive Parent*. New York: Sovereign Books, 1979.

Hyatt, Carole, and Linda Gottleib. *When Smart People Fail*. New York: Simon and Schuster, 1987.

Kurshan, Neil. *Raising Your Child to Be a Mensch*. New York: Atheneum, 1987.

Oppenheim, Joanne. *Raising a Confident Child*. New York: Pantheon Books, 1984.

Quindlen, Anna. Quotes in this book taken from "Life in the 30's" column in *The New York Times*.

Sanger, Sirgay, and John Kelly. *The Woman Who Works, the Parent Who Cares*. Boston: Little, Brown and Company, 1987.

Segal, Julius. *Growing Up Smart and Happy*. New York: McGraw-Hill, 1985.

Youngs, Bettie B. *Helping Your Teenager Deal with Stress*. Los Angeles: Jeremy P. Tarcher, Inc., 1986.

————. *Stress in Children*. New York: Arbor House, 1985.

————. *Helping Your Teenager Deal with Stress*. Audiotape from Audio Renaissance Tapes, Inc., Los Angeles; distributed by St. Martin's Press, New York.

INDEPENDENT SCHOOL AND COLLEGE ADMISSIONS

*College Bound*, P.O. Box 6536, Evanston, IL 60204. (Newsletter serving college admissions advisers)

Dalton, Herbert F., Jr. "Admission Jitters," article in spring 1988 edition of *New York Times* supplement "Education Life."

Greene, Howard, and Robert Minton. *Scaling the Ivy Wall*. Boston: Little, Brown and Company, 1987.

Independent Educational Consultants Association, 38 Cove Road, P.O. Box 125, Forestdale, MA 02644. 617/477–2127.

Interim, the Center for Interim Programs, 233 Mt. Lucas Road, Princeton, NJ 08540. 609/924–0441.

National Association of College Admission Counselors, 9933 Lawler Avenue, Suite 500, Skokie, IL 60077. 312/676–0500.


YOUNG-ADULT BEHAVIOR

Brooks, Andrée. "Staying on at Home of Parents." *The New York Times*, November 4, 1985.

Littwin, Susan. *The Postponed Generation*. New York: William Morrow and Company, 1986.

Okimoto, Jean Davies, and Phyllis Jackson Stegall. *Boomerang Kids*. New York: Knopf, 1987.


INHERITED WEALTH AND HANDLING MONEY

Brooks, Andrée. "Teaching Children the Value of Money," *The New York Times*, November 9, 1987.

Kess, Sidney, and Bertil Westlin. *Finance and Estate Planning*, Vol. 1. New York: Commercial Clearing House Inc.

Kirkland, Richard I., Jr. "Should You Leave It All to the Children?" *Fortune*, September 29, 1986.

Levy, John L. "Coping with Inherited Wealth." Private study; contact C. G. Jung Institute, 2040 Gough Street, San Francisco, CA 94109.

*Robin Hood Was Right*. San Francisco: Vanguard Public Foundation, 1977.

Weinstein, Grace W. *Children and Money*. New York: Charterhouse, 1975.

The Women's Foundation, 3543 Eighteenth Street, San Francisco, CA 94110. 415/431–5677. (Support group on handling inherited wealth; chapters elsewhere.)


ANOREXIA AND BULIMIA

Bruch, Hilda. *The Golden Cage*. New York: Random House, 1979.

Brumberg, Joan Jacobs. *Fasting Girls*. Cambridge, MA: Harvard University Press, 1988.

Chernin, Kim. *The Hungry Self: Women, Eating, and Identity*. New York: Times Books, 1985.

*Family Therapy Today*. Special issue on anorexia and bulimia, Vol. 1, no. 4 (October 1986).

Levenkron, Steven. *Treating and Overcoming Anorexia Nervosa*. New York: Warner, 1982.

Orbach, Susie. *Hunger Strike: The Anorectic's Struggle as a Metaphor for Our Age*. New York: Norton, 1986.


DIVORCE AND REMARRIAGE

Einstein, Elizabeth. *The Stepfamily: Living, Loving, and Learning*. Boston: Shambala Publications, 1985.

Gardner, Richard A. *The Parents Book of Divorce*. New York: Doubleday, 1977.

Lofas, Jeanette, with Dawn B. Sova. *Step-parenting*. New York: Zebra Books, 1985.

Mayle, Peter. *Why Are We Getting a Divorce?* New York: Harmony Books, 1988. (For children.)

Rodgers, Joann Ellison, and Michael F. Cataldo. *Raising Sons: Practical Strategies for Single Mothers*. New York: New American Library, 1984.

Stepfamily Foundation, 333 West End Avenue, New York, New York 10023. 212/877-3244. (Support and counseling group for any adult entering remarriage or a marriage that will include stepchildren.)

Stepfamily Association of America, 602 East Joppa Road, Baltimore, MD 21204. 301/823-7570.


GENERAL ECONOMIC OUTLOOK

Batra, Ravi. *The Great Depression of 1990*. New York: Simon and Schuster, 1987.

Wattenberg, Ben J. *The Birth Dearth*. New York: Pharos Books, 1987.

# Index

Accountability, 24, 106
Achievement, pressure for: in middle years, 64, 65–66, 88–89; preschoolers and, 53–57
Addis, Margaret, 135
Adolescence, *see* Teenagers
Adopted children, 127
Adults, likely characteristics as, 235–242
Akers, John, 81
Alcohol, 100, 105, 121, 123, 126–27, 190, 199
Amateur Athletic Union, 86
American Academy of Pediatrics, 55
American Association of Marriage and Family Therapy, 180
Amniocentesis, 193
Andujar, Gloria, 45–46
Anorexia, 189–90, 198–99
Appearance, personal, 97, 100
Armstrong, Dr. Thomas, 194
Arrogance, 100–1, 118, 129
Asian families, 217–19
Associates in Adolescent Psychiatry, 124
Axelson, Leland J., 180

*Baby Boom*, 28
*Behavior Today*, 5
Bell, Ruth, 107
Better Baby Institute, 5
*Birth Dearth, The*, 157
Bloomfield, Dr. Harold, 70

*Boomerang Kids* (Okimoto and Stegall), 179, 185
Brazelton, Dr. T. Berry, 73
*Breakfast Club, The*, 123
Buccolo, Dr. Martin, 8, 9, 122, 123, 124, 126
Bulimia, 189–90, 198–99
Bull, Cornelius F., 142
"Buying" the child's way out of trouble, 24

*Careers*, 153
Careers of children, 149–60, 167–169; fears of overcrowded market, 152; of the future, 154–57; living well on less, 157–58; pleasing of parents, 151–52; redefining success, 153–54; self-sufficiency, 168–69; "trying out" a career, 158–60
Careers of parents, 14, 151; child-raising and career skills, 29–34; demands of, 7–8; mothers who take time out from, 190, 210–14
Caregivers, 21–23, 41–53; childcare industry, 155; impact of, on child's development, 46–49; jealousy of, 50; selecting live-in help, 42–46; training and guiding, 47–52, 77; treatment of, 49–50
Carrilio, Dr. Terry Eisenberg, 12–13
Cars, 115–16

Catalyst, 157
Celebrity youngsters, 24–27, 99; *see also names of individuals*
C. G. Jung Institute, 117, 164
Cheating, 101
Child care, *see* Caregivers
Child-raising skills, career skills and, 29–34
*Children and Money* (Weinstein), 114
*Children of the Rich* (Wixen), 25, 128, 167, 241
Chores, 23, 184; money linked to, 77–78, 114; *see also* Work
Clarkson, William, 87, 106
Clothing of children, 5, 47
Coaches, 71
Coles, Robert, 24, 90, 100, 102, 120, 194, 235
College, 13, 15, 174; admission to, 100, 101, 132–39, 144, 217
*College Bound*, 134, 137
Collier, Peter, 19, 31, 78, 119
Community obligation, 78–79, 118–120, 154, 166; public service careers, 156, 167
Competitiveness, 16, 130; of children, 54, 64–65, 101, 102–3, 236, 237–38; of parents, 12–13, 30–31; in sports, 86–87
Conclusions, 233–45
"Coping with Inherited Wealth," 164
Couch, John, 8
Craft skills, 156
Creative business, 167
Crosby, Gary, 26, 50–51
Czuczka, Dr. Peter, 54

Dalton, Herbert F., Jr., 142
Davis, Patti, 174
Daycare, 42
Discipline, 50–51, 77–78
Divorce, 7, 100, 181, 190; recent findings on, 207–9; single parents, 190, 200–9
Doman, Glenn, 5, 53, 55–56
Dornbusch, Sanford, 88
Down's syndrome, 192, 193
Down time, 79

Downward mobility, 239–40; fears of, 216–19
Drugs, 100, 103, 104–5, 121, 123, 126–27, 190, 193, 199
Dynamy, 141
Dyslexia, 194, 196–97

Early years, 41–60; bolstering self-esteem, 58–60; caregivers, 41–53; pressure to achieve, 53–57; toys, 57–58
Education, 6, 13, 15–16, 18, 53, 54, 55, 80–85, 88–89, 100, 101, 132–39, 144, 155, 174, 217
Educational Guidance Service, 137
Education for All Handicapped Children Act, 192–93
Elderly, career serving needs of, 154
Elkind, Dr. David, 16, 54, 55, 57, 91, 105, 218, 236
Elliott, Doris, 43–44
Ellis, Bret Easton, 101–2, 103, 129, 165
*Executive Parent, The* (Hersh), 30, 191–92
Extracurricular activities, 6, 71; excessive, 54, 65, 100

Failure, *see* Achievement, pressure for; Competitiveness; Perfection, expectations of
Family life: building, 67–79; of minority children, 219–20; stepfamily, 209
*Family Process*, 21, 30, 130
Family Therapy Institute, 122
Farber, Barry, 201
Fast-track parents: challenges to, 35–37; child-raising and career skills, 29–34; children of, as parents themselves, 237–38; description of, 3–8; the making of, 10–17; *see also specific issues confronting parents*
Federal Reserve Board, 162
Fielden, Moreen, 47, 48
*Finance and Estate Planning* (Kess and Westlin), 163
Financial planning, 166

Financial support, 172–74
Fisher, Carrie, 25–26
Fitness field, 156
Fitzgerald, F. Scott, 23, 78
*Fitzgeralds and the Kennedys, The* (Goodwin), 69, 70, 191
Flavin, Dennis, 153–54
Ford, Edsel, 31, 162, 244–45
*Fords, The* (Collier and Horowitz), 31, 162
Foreign country, living in a, 157
*Fortune*, 4, 169
Fosdick, Raymond B., 112
Four Winds, 121–27, 129
Friendships, 26, 64–65, 67–68, 100
Frustration tolerance, problems with, 57–58, 168, 235

Gary, Tracy, 164, 166, 168, 170
Gillinger, Ann, 88–89, 91, 235–36
Ginsburg, Judge Douglas H., 104–5
Glick, Dr. Paul C., 180
*Going My Own Way* (Crosby and Firestone), 26, 50–51
Goldman, Dr. Robert, 86, 87
Goodwin, Doris Kearns, 69–70, 191
Gottlieb, Linda, 86
Grandparents, 69–70, 209
*Great Gatsby, The* (Fitzgerald), 23, 78
Greene, Howard, 15, 82, 84–85, 136
Grinker, Dr. Roy, 22, 50, 128
Guerney, Dr. Bernard, 77
Guggenheim, Peggy, 22
Guilt, 172

Hahn, Kurt, 18
Help!, 43
Helping Hands, 44
Helping the less fortunate, 78–79, 118–20, 154, 166
*Helping Your Teenager Deal with Stress* (Youngs), 107
Hersh, Dr. Stephen, 30, 73, 191–92
Hill, Wanda, 219–20, 222
*History of Childhood Quarterly*, 21
Home-based businesses, 67
Horowitz, David, 19, 31, 78, 119
Howard, Kenneth, 68, 213

Hutton, Barbara, 161, 167
Hyatt, Carol, 86

Iacocca, Lee, 243
Incentive trust, 171
Independent Educational Consultants Association, 82
Influence, parental use of, 7, 24, 90–91, 138–39, 174
Inherited wealth, handling, 161–72
"Interim," 142
International Nanny Association, 43
Interpersonal skills, 243
*In Their Own Way* (Armstrong), 194
Investing, 117–18
Isolation and loneliness, 67, 68, 122, 236

*John D. Rockefeller Jr.: A Portrait* (Fosdick), 112–13
Journalism, 157–58
*Journal of Marriage and the Family*, 180
*Journal of Pediatrics, The*, 56

Kafka, Franz, 31
Kennedy family, 69, 70, 191, 195
Klagsbrun, Samuel C., 12, 31

Lafontant, Jewel, 220–21
Lapham, Lewis, 5, 151, 238, 240
Learning disabilities, 189, 191–97; one boy's tale, 195–97; prevention of, and coping mechanisms, 193–95; reasons for frequency of, 192–93
*Learning Mystique: A Critical Look at Learning Disabilities* (Coles), 194
Lesser, Dr. Elena, 48
*Less Than Zero* (Ellis), 101–2, 129
*Letter to My Father, A* (Kafka), 31
Levy, John, 117–18, 119, 164–65, 167, 168, 169
Life insurance trust, 163
Littwin, Susan, 147, 148, 173, 182, 235
Living trust, 163

Loneliness and isolation, 67, 68, 122, 236

MacArthur Foundation, 88
Madanes, Cloe, 122
*Making Peace with Your Parents* (Bloomfield), 70
Manuel, Karen, 47, 51
Manufacturing skills, 156
Martin, Sharlene, 44, 52
Mazlish, Elaine, 75
Meadow Wood Center, 127, 129
Middle years, 63–93; building family life, 67–79; motivation, 87–89; parental attitudes, 89–91; selection of schools, 81–85; sports in, 85–87; tutors, 92–93; values, 91–92
Miles, Dr. Carlotta, 46, 57, 217
Miller, Dr. Selma, 195
*Million Dollar Baby* (Van Rensselaer), 161
Milne, Dr. Ann M., 41
Minority fast-track parents, 190, 215–223; attitudes toward minorities, 219; benefits of strong family traditions, 219–20; fears about downward mobility, 216–19; ideas from parents and children, 220–23
*Miseducation: Preschoolers at Risk* (Elkind), 16, 91, 218
*Modern Perspectives in the Psychiatry of Infancy* (Stone), 21
*Money,* 114
*Money and Class in America* (Lapham), 5, 151, 238
Money issues: teenagers and, 112–120, 135; young adults and, 161–74
Mothers who stay home, executive, 190, 210–14
Motivation, 87–89, 167–68, 234
Mullin, Reverend Mark, 15, 81, 103
Mund, Seymour, 104, 106
*My Adventures as an Illustrator* (Rockwell), 83

*Nanny Connection, The* (Sweet and Siegel), 42–43
National Association of College Admission Counselors, 82
National Association of Home-Based Businesses, 67
National Association of Independent Schools, 141
National Collegiate Athletic Association, 139
National Institute of Child Health and Human Development, 68
National Outdoor Leadership Schools (NOLS), 141–42
National Restaurant Association, 74
*Newsweek,* 134, 157
*New York,* 7, 54, 173, 193
*New York Times, The,* 6, 16, 25–26, 119, 142, 214
Nisenson, Dr. Roy, 16–17, 49, 50, 91–92, 128, 130, 149
Nursery school, 16, 53, 54, 55

Okimoto, Jean Davies, 179, 185
*On the Outside Looking In* (Reagan), 90–91, 174
Open letter for children only, 227–230
Outward Bound, 141–42

Peck, Judith Stern, 158–59
Peer pressure, 104, 105, 115, 152
*Peggy, the Wayward Guggenheim* (Weld), 22
Perfection, expectations of, 5–6, 26, 55, 89, 123–24, 125–26, 236
Petersen, Dr. Anne, 5, 6
Pets, 71
Philanthropy, 78–79, 118–20, 154, 167
Physical ailments, pressure-related, 54, 55
Pilot trust, 171
Pittman, Dr. Frank S., III, 20–21, 23–24, 26, 30, 128, 130
Play groups, 46–47, 51–52
Political attitudes, 241–42
"Poor Rich, The," 128

*Postcards from the Edge* (Fisher), 26
Postgraduate (PG) year, 139–40
*Postponed Generation, The* (Littwin), 235
Praise, 59, 65
Pre-natal testing, 193
Prep school, 16
Preschoolers, *see* Early years
Prescod, Suzanne, 5
Press, Dr. Sharon, 127
Pressure, *see* Achievement, pressure for
"Private Lives," 15
Private teachers, 71; *see also* Tutors
*Privileged Ones* (Cole), 24, 90, 101, 120
Public service, careers in, 156, 167, 241; *see also* Community obligation

Quindlen, Anna, 6, 16, 214

*Reading Improvement*, 218
Reagan, Michael, 90–91, 99, 174
Rebellion, 13–14
Reciprocity with other parents, 71
Recommendations for teachers, counselors, and parents, 242–245
Reed, Sally, 134
Religion, 70–71
Remarriage, 209
Returning home: parent, after work, 73; young adults, 179–90
Rhodes, Frank H. T., 134–35
Rituals, family, 73–75, 107
*Robin Hood Was Right*, 167, 172
Rockefeller family, 19, 25, 71, 78, 112–13, 119, 174, 241, 245
*Rockefellers* (Collier and Horowitz), 19, 25, 78, 119, 165, 174, 245
Rockwell, Norman, 83
Rodgers, Royal Kennedy, 32
Rogers, John, Jr., 220–21, 223, 236
Rogers, John W., 220, 221
Roosevelt, Franklin, 106
Rosenman, Audrey, 6, 57, 58, 115

Sanger, Dr. Sirgay, 22–23, 49, 58, 78, 93, 192
*Scaling the Ivy Wall* (Greene), 136
Schwarz, Dr. Marvin, 122–23, 124, 126, 173–74
Sciences, careers in the, 157
Self-confidence, 23–24, 83, 183, 244
Self-esteem: child's, 22, 25, 31, 58–60, 69, 83, 116, 120, 167, 172–173, 183, 214, 234; parent's, 56, 85
Self-reliance, 168–69, 172–73, 174, 185
Servants, *see* Caregivers
Sex, 100, 181; promiscuity, 121, 123; single parent and, 208
Siblings, 70, 100; comparison of, 59, 65, 75–77; of learning disabled, 195
*Siblings Without Rivalry* (Mazlish), 75
Siegel, Mary-Ellen, 42
Single parents, 190, 200–9
*Smart Kids with School Problems: Things to Know and Ways to Help* (Vail), 216
Social organizers, 156
Sparrow, Dr. Sara, 56, 194–95
Sports, 85–87
Standards, setting of, 48–52, 77–78, 105–6, 125, 183–85
Stanford University Center for the Study of Families, Children, and Youth, 88
Stay-at-home executive mothers, 190, 210–14
Steinberg, Dr. Laurence, 88
Steinbrecher, Phyllis, 139, 140
Stepfamilies, 209
Stepfamily Association of America, 209
Stepfamily Foundation, 209
Stegall, Phyllis Jackson, 179, 185
Stereotyping of minorities, 217
Stepped-in trust, 171
Sterne, Dr. George, 55
Stone, Dr. Michael H., 21–22, 24, 26, 128–29

Success, redefining, 153–54, 244
Suicide threats, 121, 123–24, 127
Support groups, 244; see also specific groups
Sweet, O. Robin, 42

"Taking a year off," 140–42
Talking with Your Teenager (Bell and Wildflower), 107
Taylor, Zachary, 23, 40
Teaching career, 155
Teenagers, 97–107; college and alternative choices, 132–42, 144; emotional problems, 101–3; expectations of, 97; "losers," 143–144; money issues, 112–20; with serious problems, 121–31; view of parents, 99–100; ways to help, 103–7; words or actions by parents that helped or hurt, 108–11
Telephone contact, 72
Testing: for learning disabilities, 194–95; pre-natal, 193
Thacher, Nicholas S., 16, 46, 82, 105
Therapy, 121–31
Time, 42, 155
Toddler Time to Five, 47
Toys, 5, 57–58
Travel, 72–73
Trump, Donald, 75–76, 171
Trump: The Art of the Deal (Trump), 75–76
Trust officer, 170
Trusts, 163, 169–72, 195
Tutors, 92–93, 101, 139; see also Private teachers

U.S. News and World Report, 137
"Upbringing in the Super-Rich," 21, 129

Vail, Priscilla L., 216, 217
Values, 91–92
Vanderbilt, Gloria, 19
Van Rennsselaer, Philip, 161
Vogel, Virginia, 137, 138

Wahl, Dr. Charles William, 25
Weinstein, Grace W., 114
Weld, Jacqueline Bograd, 22
Werner, Emmy, 88
When Smart People Fail (Hyatt and Gottlieb), 86–87
Wildflower, Leni Zeiger, 107
Wilson, Barbara-Jan, 151–52, 158, 222
Wixen, Burton N., 25, 128, 167, 171, 241
Woman Who Works, the Parent Who Cares, The (Sanger), 21
Women as inheritors of wealth, 168, 170
Women's Foundation, The, 117, 164, 244
Women's movement, 15
Work, 115–16, 135; see also Careers of children; Careers of parents; Chores
Workaholism, 30, 168, 241

Yale Child Study Center, 56, 194
Yao, Esther Lee, 217, 218–19, 220
Young adults, 147–85; careers, 149–160; inherited wealth and financial support, 161–74; mother's and daughter's views of same situation, 175–78; returning home, 179–85
Youngs, Dr. Bettie, 8, 72, 103, 107, 213–14, 220

Zablow, Sheldon, 129